The Inner Life

II

C W Leadbeater

First published 2011

British Library Cataloguing in Publication Data

A catalogue record for this book is available from the British Library

ISBN-13: 978-1-908388-51-3

Printed and bound in Great Britain by Lightning Souce UK Ltd., 6 Precedent Drive, Rooksley, Milton Keynes MK13 8PR.

Cover Illustration:

FOREWORD TO THE INDIAN EDITION

Our evening "Talks" at the Theosophical Headquarters at Adyar have become quite an institution, and a very considerable amount of information, due to new research, often arising from some question put by a student, is given in this friendly and intimate circle. Our good Vice-President, Sir S. Subramania Iyer, found so much help and illumination from these talks, that he earnestly wished to share his pleasure with his brethren in the outer world, and gave a sum of money to help in their publication. I cordially endorse his view of their value, and commend this volume and those which will follow it to the earnest study of all our members. A second series is ready for the press, but the date of its issue will depend partly on the reception given tot he present.

Annie Besant

CONTENTS

INTRODUCTION 4
Author's Note 6

FIRST SECTION: THE AFTER-DEATH LIFE 7
The Theosophist After Death 7; The Relation Of The Dead To Earth 8; Conditions After Death 14; Animal Obsession 16; Individualised Animals 21; Localisation Of States 21; Heaven-Life Conditions 25; Karma In The Heaven Life 28

SECOND SECTION: ASTRAL WORK 34
Invisible Helpers 34; Remembering Astral Experience 41; The Higher Dimensions 46

THIRD SECTION: THE MENTAL BODY & THE POWER OF THOUGHT 49
The Mental Body 49; A Neglected Power 54; Intuition & Impulse 58; Thought-Centres 59; Thought And Elemental Essence 62;

FOURTH SECTION: PSYCHIC FACULTIES 64
Psychic Powers 64; Clairvoyance 69; The Mystic Chord 75; How Past Lives Are Seen 79; Foreseeing The Future 86;

FIFTH SECTION: DEVAS AND NATURE SPIRITS 89
The Aura Of The Deva 89; The Spirit Of A Tree 92;

SIXTH SECTION: THE WORLD & THE RACES OF MEN 93
The Building Of The System 93; The Planetary Chains 98; Successive Life-Waves 101; The Monads From The Moon 112; The Earth-Chain 118; Modes Of Individualisation 132; The Seven Types 139; Stray Notes On Races 140; Mars And Its Inhabitants 146;

SEVENTH SECTION: REINCARNATION 152
Three Laws Of Human Life 152; Personal Characteristics 160; Bringing Over Past Knowledge 161; The Intervals Between Lives 162.

EIGHTH SECTION: KARMA 168
The Law Of Equilibrium 168; The Method Of Karma 174; The Karma Of Death 177; Karma As An Educator 179; Varieties Of Karma 180; Animal Karma 183;

NINTH SECTION: THE THEOSOPHICAL SOCIETY & ITS FOUNDER 186
What is the theosophical society? 186; Theosophy And World-Leaders 190; Reminiscences 195; Faithful Unto Death 200; A Course Of Study In Theosophy 205;

INTRODUCTION

I wish that I could help my American readers to realise the conditions under which this book has been produced. The Theosophical Society as a whole does not by any means sufficiently understand or appreciate the work done at its Headquarters, and although for you in America it is away on the other side of the earth, I should like to help you to see it as it is. Readers of the "Messenger" must at least, have some general idea of the appearance of the place, and must know something of the life which is lived here - a long life, a strenuous life, and a life lived under very peculiar conditions. Nowhere else in the world at this present moment is there such a centre of influence - a centre constantly visited by the Great Ones, and therefore bathed in their wonderful magnetism. The vibrations here are marvellously stimulating, and all of us who live here are therefore constant strain of a very peculiar kind, a strain which brings out whatever is in us. Strong vibrations from other planes are playing all the while upon our various vehicles, and those parts of us which can in any sense respond to them are thereby raised, strengthened and purified. But it must be remembered that there is another side to this. There may well be in each of us some vibrations the character of which is too far removed from the level of these great influences to fall into harmony with them, and where that is the case intensification will still take place, but the result may well be evil rather than good. To live at Adyar is the most glorious of all opportunities for those who are able to take advantage of it, but its effect on those who are constitutionally unable to harmonize with its vibrations may be dangerous rather than helpful. If a student can bear it he may advance rapidly; if he cannot bear it he is better away.

The workers here live mostly in the great central building, within the immediate aura of the shrine room and the President. The students live chiefly half-a-mile away at various other houses, though all within the large estate which now belongs to the Society. Each during the day does his own work in his own way, but in the evening we all gather together upon the roof of the central building, in front of the President's rooms, formerly occupied by Madame Blavatsky herself, and there, under the marvellous night sky of India, so infinitely more brilliant than anything that we know in what are miscalled temperate climes, we sit and listen to her teaching. All through the summer of last year, so much of which she spent in a tour through the United States, it fell to my lot to take charge of the meetings of the students here. In the course of that time I delivered many informal little addresses and answered hundreds of questions. All that I said was taken down in shorthand, and this book is the result of those notes. In a number of cases it happened that what was said on the roof at the meetings was afterwards expanded into a little article for The Theosophist or The Adyar Bulletin; in all such cases I reprint the article instead of the stenographic report, as it has had the advantage of certain corrections and additions. Necessarily a book of this sort is fragmentary in its nature; necessarily also it contains a certain amount of repetition; though this latter has been excised wherever possible. Many of the subjects treated have also been dealt with in my earlier books, but what is written here represents in all cases the result of the latest discoveries in connection with those subjects. The subjects have been classified as far as possible, and this volume represents the first series, containing five sections. The second volume, containing the nine remaining sections, is now in the printer's hands. A list of the subjects of which it will treat will be found at the end of this volume.

C W Leadbeater

Adyar, July, 1910.

AUTHOR'S NOTE

While the President was absent from Adyar on a tour through England and America last year, it fell to my lot to take charge of the daily meetings of the students here. In the course of that time I delivered many informal little addresses and answered hundreds of questions. All that I said was taken down in shorthand, and this book is the result of those notes. In a number of cases it happened that what was said on the roof at the meetings was afterwards expanded into a little article for The Theosophist or The Adyar Bulletin; in all such cases I reprint the article instead of the stenographic report, as it has had the advantage of certain corrections and additions. Necessarily a book of this sort is fragmentary in its nature; necessarily also it contains a certain amount of repetition; though this latter has been excised wherever possible. Many of the subjects treated have also been dealt with in my earlier books, but what is written here represents in all cases the result of the latest discoveries in connection with those subjects The subjects have been classified as far as possible, and this volume is the second series, containing the nine remaining sections.

C. W. Leadbeater

Adyar, July, 1911.

First Section: The After-death Life

THE THEOSOPHIST AFTER DEATH

When a member of the Theosophical Society finds himself upon the astral plane after having permanently laid aside his physical body, it will be well for him to begin by taking stock, as it were - by seeing what is his position, what is the life before him, and how he can make the best use of it . He will do wisely to consult on these matters some friend who has had wider experience than himself, and in practice this is what dead members almost always do. Remember that when the member enters upon the astral plane after death he is not making his first appearance there. Usually he has already done much work there during the sleep of the physical body, and is therefore on familiar ground. As a general rule his first instinct is to make straight for our beloved President, which is probably quite the wisest thing for him to do, as there is no one better qualified to give him sound advice. So many possibilities open out in astral life that one cannot lay down any general rule, though a man cannot go far wrong who tries to make himself useful to those around him. There are plentiful opportunities for learning, as well as for work, and the new-comer will have to decide how he can best apportion his time between them.

The astral world will not be altered for the convenience of members of the Theosophical Society, any more than the physical world is, and they, like every one else, will have to encounter what happens to be there. If a drunken man is walking along a certain road, those who happen to pass along that road will meet him, whether they are members or not, and the astral plane does not, in this respect, differ from the physical. The members, being instructed in regard to the rules governing life on astral plane, ought to know better than the uninstructed how to deal with such unpleasant beings as happen to come in their way, but they are just as likely as any one else to meet them. They have, however, probably met such beings many times while functioning upon the astral plane during life, and there is no more reason to be afraid of them than before; indeed, meeting them then upon their own level, it will be far easier to come to an understanding with them and to give them such help as they are able to receive.

There is practically no difference between the condition of the ordinary person and the psychic after death, except that the psychic, being somewhat more familiar with astral matters, would feel more at home in his new environment. To be psychic means to be able to bring through into the physical consciousness something of the wider life; it is therefore in the condition of the physical vehicle that there is an inequality between the psychic and the ordinary person, but when the physical is dropped that inequality no longer exists.

THE RELATION OF THE DEAD TO EARTH

A dead man is often aware of the feelings of the family that he has left. If you try to think exactly what it is that can be manifested through the astral body, you may easily see how much he is likely to know. He does not necessarily follow in detail all the events of the physical life; he does not necessarily know what his friends are eating, or in what occupations they are engaged. But he knows whether they are glad or sorry, and he is at once aware of such feelings as love or hate, jealousy or envy.

When a drunkard hovers about a gin-shop it is only by partial materialisation (that is, by drawing round himself a veil of etheric matter) that he can draw in the odour of the alcohol. He does not smell it in at all the same sense as we do; and that is why he is always anxious to force others into the condition of drunkenness, so that he may be able partially to enter their physical bodies and obsess them, so that through those bodies he can once more directly experience the taste and the other sensations which he so ardently desires.

In the astral body there are exact counterparts of the eyes and the nose and the mouth, but we must not therefore think that the astral man sees with those eyes, hears with those ears, or can smell or taste through the nose or mouth. All the matter of the astral body is constantly in rapid motion from one part of it to another, so that it is quite impossible for any astral particles to be specialised in the same way as certain nerve-ends are specialised in the physical body. The senses of the astral body act not through special organs, but through every particle of the body, so that with astral sight a man can see equally well with any part of his body, and can see all around him simultaneously, instead of only in front of him. He could grasp at the astral counterpart of the hand of a living man, but as the two hands would pass through one another without any sense of contact, there would be no object in his doing so. It is, however, perfectly possible for him to materialise a hand which, though invisible, can be felt just as the ordinary physical hand can be, as may often be observed at séances.

There are three subdivisions of the astral plane from which it may be possible (though not desirable) for disembodied men to see and follow events taking place upon the physical plane. On the lowest sub-plane the man is usually occupied in other ways, and concerns himself little with what takes place in the physical world, except, as is explained in our literature, when he haunts vile resorts; but, in the next subdivision, he has very close touch with the physical plane, and may quite probably be conscious of a good many things in connection with it, though what he sees is never the physical matter itself, but always the astral counterpart of it. In rapidly diminishing degree this consciousness is also possible as he ascends through the next two sub-planes; but beyond that, it would be only by the special effort to communicate through a medium that contact with the physical plane could be gained, and from the highest sub-plane even that would be extremely difficult.

The extent of a man's power to see and follow physical events from the astral plane is determined by his character and disposition, as well as by the stage of development to which he has attained. Most of those whom we ordinarily call good people, living out their lives to their natural end, sweep through all these lower stages before awakening to astral consciousness, and they are therefore unlikely to be conscious of anything physical at all. Some few, however, even of these are drawn back into touch with this world by great anxiety about some one left behind.

Less developed persons have in their composition of the matter of these lower sub-planes, and are therefore much more likely to be able to follow to some extent what goes on upon earth. Most of all is this the case if they are people whose whole turn of thought is essentially of this world - who have in them little or nothing of spiritual aspiration or of high intellect. This downward tendency grows with the using, and a man who is at first happily unconscious of what lies below him may be so unfortunate as to have his attention attracted to it, frequently by selfish manifestations of the grief of the survivors. He then exerts his will to keep himself from rising out of touch with this life to which he no longer belongs; and in such a case his power of seeing earthly things increases for a time, and then he suffers mentally when he presently finds such power slipping from him. Such suffering is entirely due to the irregularity introduced into the astral life by his own action, for it is absolutely unknown in the ordinary and orderly evolution after death.

If it is complained that in this way the departed does not see the physical world exactly as it really is, we must answer that neither the departed nor we on this plane ever see the physical world as it really is at all, for we (or most of us) see only the solid and liquid portions thereof, and are altogether blind to the far vaster gaseous and etheric parts; while the departed does not see the physical matter at all, nor even the whole astral counterpart of it, but only that portion of the latter which belongs to the particular sub-plane upon which he is at the time. The only man who gets anything like a comprehensive view of affairs is he who has developed etheric and astral sight while still alive in the physical body.

Another difficulty in the way of the disembodied is that he by no means always recognises with any certainty the astral counterpart of the physical body even when he sees it. He usually requires considerable experience before he can clearly identify objects, and any attempt which he makes to deal with them is liable to be very vague and uncertain, as is often seen in haunted houses where stone-throwing, trampling, or vague movements of physical matter take place. This power of the identification of objects is thus largely a question of experience and knowledge, but it is little likely to be perfect unless he has known something of such matters before death.

A correspondent writes to ask whether a dead man can enjoy the astral counterpart of a play at a theatre, and whether there will be room for him there if the building is already full of people.

Certainly a theatre full of people has its astral counterpart, which is visible to dead people. The play, however, is not likely to afford them any enjoyment, since they cannot see the costumes and the expression of the actors at all as we see them, and the emotions of these actors, being only simulated and not real, make no impression upon the astral plane. Astral bodies can and constantly do interpenetrate one another fully, without in the least injuring one another. If you will think for a moment you will see that this must be so. When you sit next to any person in a railway carriage or in a tram-car your astral body and his must necessarily interpenetrate to a very large extent. There is not the slightest difficulty in such interpenetration, since the astral particles are enormously farther apart in proportion to their size even than physical particles are. At the same time they seriously affect one another as far as their rates of vibration are concerned, so that to sit in close proximity to a person of impure, jealous or angry thought is exceedingly prejudicial. A dead friend can, therefore, quite easily enter a theatre which is full of people - more especially as the people are seated upon the ground or the platforms, while the astral entity is far more probably floating about in the air.

The man who commits suicide runs away from school before the appointed lesson is learnt; he is guilty of the great presumption involved in taking into his own hands a decision which should be left to the working of the Great Law. The consequences of so great a rebellion against nature are always of a momentous character. They are certain to affect the next life, and quite probably more lives than one. The circumstances surrounding a suicide immediately after death are the same as they would be for the victim of an accident, since both of them arrive upon the astral plane with equal suddenness. But there is the enormous difference that the man who dies by accident, not expecting death, is thrown into a condition of unconsciousness and usually passes through the lowest sub-plane without knowing anything of its varied unpleasantness. The suicide, on the contrary, has acted deliberately, and is generally painfully aware of much that is horrible and repugnant to him. He cannot be saved from the sights and feelings which he has brought upon himself; but he may often be helped to understand them, and may be inspired with patience, perseverance and hope by the good offices of some kind friend.

While fully recognising that suicide is a mistake, and a most serious one, we are not called upon judge our brother who commits that mistake. There is a wide difference between different cases, and it is impossible for us to know the various factors which enter into each, although every one of them is duly taken into account in the working of the law of eternal justice.

In trying to estimate the conditions of a man's life on the astral plane after death, there are two prominent factors to be considered - the length of time which he stays upon any particular sub-plane and the amount of his consciousness upon it. The length of a man's stay upon any sub-plane depends, as has been said, upon the amount of matter belonging to that sub-plane he has built into himself during earth-life.

But the amount of consciousness that a person will have upon a given sub-plane does not invariably follow precisely the same law. Let us consider an extreme example of possible variation, in order that we may grasp its method. Suppose a man has brought over from his past incarnation tendencies requiring for their manifestation a large amount of the matter of the lowest sub-plane, and has in his present life been fortunate enough to learn in his earliest years the possibility and the necessity of controlling these tendencies. It is improbable that such a man's efforts at control would be uniformly and entirely successful; but if they were, the substitution of finer for grosser particles would progress steadily though slowly.

This process is at best a gradual one, and it might well happen that the man died before it was half completed. In that case there would undoubtedly be enough matter of the lowest sub-plane left in his astral body to ensure him no inconsiderable residence there; but it would be matter through which in this incarnation his consciousness had never been in the habit of functioning, and, as it could not suddenly acquire this habit, the result would be that the man would rest upon that sub-plane until his share of its matter was disintegrated, but would be all the while in a condition of unconsciousness - that is, he would practically sleep through the period of his sojourn there, and so would be entirely unaffected by its many disagreeables.

It will be seen that both these factors of post-mortem existence - the sub-plane to which the man is carried and the degree of his consciousness there - depend not in the least on the nature of his death, but upon the nature of his life, so that any accident, however sudden or terrible, can scarcely affect them. Nevertheless, there is reason behind the familiar old prayer of the Church: "From sudden death, good Lord, deliver us;" for though a sudden death does not necessarily affect the man's position upon the astral plane in any way for the worse, at least it does nothing to improve it, whereas the slow wasting away of the aged or the ravages of any kind of long-continued disease are almost invariably accompanied by a considerable loosening and breaking up of the astral particles, so that when the man recovers consciousness upon the astral plane, he finds some at any rate of his chief work there already done for him.

The great mental terror and disturbance which sometimes accompany accidental death are in themselves a very unfavourable preparation for the astral life; indeed, cases have been known in which such agitation and terror persisted after death, though that is happily rare. Still, the popular desire to have some time in which to prepare for death is not a mere superstition, but has a certain amount of reason at the back of it. Naturally, to anyone who is leading the Theosophical life it will make but little difference whether the transition from the physical plane to the astral comes slowly or quickly, since he is all the time doing his best to make as much progress as possible, and the object before him will remain the same in either case.

To sum up then: it seems clear that death by accident does not necessarily involve any lengthy residence on the lowest level of the astral plane, though it may in one sense be said slightly to prolong such residence, since it deprives the victim of the opportunity of burning out the particles belonging to that level during the sufferings of a lingering disease. In the case of young children it is exceedingly unlikely that in their short and comparatively blameless young lives they will have developed much affinity for the lowest subdivisions of astral life; indeed, as a matter of practical experience they are hardly ever to be found in connection with that sub-plane at all. In any case, whether they die by accident or disease, their life on the astral plane is a comparatively short one; the heaven-life, though much longer, is still in reasonable proportion to it, and their early reincarnation follows as soon as the forces which they have been able to set in motion during their short earth-lives work themselves out, precisely as we might expect from our observation of the action of the same great law in the case of adults.

Nothing that is likely to be done in ordinary life to his physical corpse need make any difference whatever to the man living on the astral plane. I am obliged to make these two reservations because, in the first case, outside of ordinary life there are certain horrible magical rites which would very seriously affect the condition of the man on the other plane, and in the second, although the state of the physical corpse need not make any difference to the real man, it nevertheless sometimes does, by reason of his ignorance or foolishness. Let me endeavour to explain.

The length of a man's astral life after he has put off his physical body depends mainly upon two factors - the nature of his past physical life, and his attitude of mind after what we call death. During his earth-life he is constantly influencing the building of matter into his astral body. He affects it directly by the passions, emotions and desires which he allows to hold sway over him; he affects it indirectly by the action upon it of his thoughts from above, and of all the details of his physical life (his continence or his debauchery, his cleanliness or his uncleanliness, his food and his drink) from below. If, by persistence in perversity along any of these lines, he is so stupid as to build for himself a coarse and gross astral vehicle, habituated to responding only to the lower vibrations of the plane, he will find himself after death bound to that plane during the long and slow process of that body's disintegration. On the other hand if, by decent and careful living, he gives himself a vehicle mainly composed of finer material, he will have very much less post-mortem trouble and discomfort, and his evolution will proceed much more rapidly and easily.

This much is generally understood, but the second great factor - his attitude of mind after death - seems often to be forgotten. The desirable thing is for him to realise his position on this little arc of his evolution - to learn that he is at this stage withdrawing steadily inward towards the plane of the true ego, and that consequently it is his business to disengage his thought as far as may be from things physical, and fix his attention more and more upon those spiritual matters which will occupy him during his life in the heaven-world. By doing this he will greatly facilitate the natural astral disintegration, and will avoid the sadly common mistake of unnecessarily delaying himself upon the lower levels of what should be so temporary a residence.

Many people, however, simply will not turn their thoughts upwards, but spend their time in struggling with all their might to keep in touch with the physical plane which they have left, thus causing great trouble to anyone who may be trying to help them. Earthly matters are the only ones in which they have ever had any living interest, and they cling to them with desperate tenacity even after death. Naturally, as time passes on, they find it increasingly difficult to keep hold of things down here, but instead of welcoming and encouraging this process of gradual refinement and spiritualisation they resist it vigorously by every means in their power. The mighty force of evolution is eventually too strong for them, and they are swept on in its beneficent current, yet they fight every step of the way, thereby not only causing themselves a vast amount of entirely unnecessary pain and sorrow, but also seriously delaying their upward progress.

Now, in this ignorant and disastrous opposition to the cosmic will a man is much assisted by the possession of his physical corpse as a kind of fulcrum on this plane. He is naturally in close rapport with it, and if he is so misguided as to wish to do so, he can use it as an anchor to hold him down firmly to the mud until its decomposition is far advanced. Cremation saves the man from himself in this matter, for, when the physical body has been thus properly disposed of, his boats are literally burned behind him, and his power of holding back is happily greatly diminished.

We see therefore that, while neither the burial nor the embalming of a corpse can in any way force the ego to whom it once belonged to prolong his stay upon the astral plane against his will, either of those causes is a distinct temptation to him to delay, and immensely facilitates his doing so if he should unfortunately wish it. No ego of any advancement would allow himself to be detained upon the astral plane, even by a proceeding so foolish as the embalming of his corpse. Whether his physical vehicle was burned or allowed to decay slowly in the usual loathsome manner, or indefinitely preserved as an Egyptian mummy, his astral body would pursue its own line of quick disintegration entirely unaffected.

Among the many advantages gained by cremation the principal are that it entirely prevents any attempt at partial and unnatural temporary reunion of the principles, or any endeavour to make use of the corpse for the purposes of the lower magic - to say nothing of the many dangers to the living which are avoided by its adoption.

CONDITIONS AFTER DEATH

Students often ask whether for the ordinary man a subconscious or an active existence is more desirable on the astral plane. This depends upon the nature of the active existence, and upon the stage of development of the ego concerned.

The ordinary man dies with a certain amount of unexhausted desire still in his composition, and this force must work itself out before it is possible for him to sink into a subconscious condition. If the only activity possible for him is that of the lower desires, it is obviously better for him that nothing should be allowed to interfere with his sinking into comparative unconsciousness as soon as possible, since any new karma that he makes is little likely to be of an advantageous kind.

If, on the other hand, he is sufficiently developed to be able to be of use to others on the astral plane, and especially if he has already been in the habit of working there during sleep, there is no reason why he should not usefully employ the time of his enforced sojourn there, though it would be inadvisable to set in motion new forces which would lengthen that sojourn. Those who are working under the direction of the pupils of the Masters of Wisdom will naturally avail themselves of their counsel, since they have had much experience along these lines, and can in turn consult others of still wider knowledge.

The astral life may be directed by the will, just as the physical life may be, always within the limits prescribed in each case by karma - that is to say, by our own previous action. The ordinary man has little will-power or initiative, and is very much the creature of the surroundings which he has made for himself, on the astral plane as on the physical; but a determined man can always make the best of his conditions and live his own life in spite of them. What has, after all, been caused by his will can gradually be changed by his will, if time permits.

A man does not rid himself of evil tendencies in the astral world any more than he would in this life, unless he definitely works to that end. Many of the desires which are so strong and persistent in him are such as need a physical body for their satisfaction, and since he has that no longer, they often cause him acute and prolonged suffering; but in process of time they wear themselves out, they become as it were atrophied, and die down because of this impossibility of fulfilment. In the same way the matter of the astral body slowly wears away and disintegrates as the consciousness is gradually withdrawn from it by the half-unconscious effort of the ego, and thus the man by degrees gets rid of what ever holds him back from the heaven-world.

But the worst of his trouble is that the man is generally not alive to the necessity of getting rid of the evil which detains him. It is obvious that if he realises the facts of the case and gives his mind to the work, he can greatly expedite both the processes referred to the above. If he knows that it is his business to kill out earthly desires, and to withdraw into himself as quickly as may be, he will earnestly set himself to do these things; instead of which he usually in his ignorance broods over the desires and so lengthens their life, and clings desperately to the grossest particles of astral matter as long as he possibly can, because the sensation connected with them seems nearest to that physical life for which he is so passionately longing. Thus we see why one of the most important parts of the work of the invisible helpers is to explain facts to the dead, and also why even a merely intellectual knowledge of Theosophical truths is of such inestimable value to a man.

The dead man when he first arrives upon the astral plane by no means always realises that he is dead, and even when that fact comes home to him it does not follow that he at once understands how the astral world differs from the physical. In the physical world man is the slave of a number of imperious necessities; he must have food and clothing and shelter; in order to procure these he must have money; and in most cases in order to obtain money he must do some kind of work. All this is so much a matter of course to us down here that the man who is set free from this slavery finds it difficult for a long time to believe that he is really free, and in many cases he continues unnecessarily to impose upon himself fetters which he has in reality cast aside.

So we sometimes see the newly dead trying to eat - sitting down to or preparing for themselves wholly imaginary meals, or building for themselves houses. I have actually seen a man in the summer-land building a house for himself stone by stone, and even though he made each of these stones for himself by an effort of his thought, he did not yet grasp the fact that he might just as well have made the whole house for himself, with the same amount of trouble, by a single effort of the same kind. He was gradually led to see that, by the discovery that the stones had no weight, which showed him that his present conditions differed from those to which he had been used on earth, and so led him to investigate further.

In the summer-land men surround themselves with landscapes of their own construction, though some avoid that trouble by accepting ready-made the landscapes which have already been constructed by others. Men living on the sixth sub-plane, upon the surface of the earth, find themselves surrounded by the astral counterparts of physically existing mountains, trees and lakes, and consequently are not under the necessity of manufacturing scenery for themselves; but men upon the higher subplanes, who float at some distance above the surface of the earth, usually provide themselves with whatever scenery they desire, by the method that I have described.

The commonest example of this is that they construct for themselves the weird scenes described in their various scriptures, and therefore in those regions we constantly find ourselves in presence of clumsy and unimaginative attempts to reproduce such ideas as jewels growing upon trees, and seas of glass mingled with fire, and creatures which are full of eyes within, and deities with a hundred heads and arms to correspond. In this way, as a consequence of ignorance and prejudice during their physical life, many men do a great deal of valueless work when they might be employing their time in the helping of their fellows.

To the man who has studied Theosophy and therefore understands these higher planes, one of their pleasantest characteristics is the utter restfulness and freedom which comes from the absence of all these imperious necessities which make a misery out of physical life. The dead man is the only absolutely free man, free to do whatever he wills and to spend his time as he chooses, free therefore to devote the whole of his energies to helping his fellows.

ANIMAL OBSESSION

We are familiar with the idea that an ego on its way down into reincarnation may sometimes be drawn aside from its course and indefinitely delayed at astral levels by the attraction of the group-soul of some kind of animal with whose characteristics it is in too close affinity. We know that the same affinity sometimes seizes upon a soul upon the astral plane after death, and detains it in very intimate association with an animal form, and also that as the result of gross cruelty it is possible to be karmically linked to an animal, and to suffer most horribly with it. All this was described by Mrs. Besant as follows, in a letter to an Indian paper, which was reproduced in The Theosophic Gleaner, vol. xv. page 231:

"The human ego does not reincarnate in an animal, for reincarnation means the entering into a physical vehicle which thereafter belongs to and is controlled by the ego. The penal connection of the human ego with an animal form is not reincarnation; for the animal soul, the proper owner of the vehicle, is not dispossessed, nor can the human ego control the body to which it is temporarily attached. Nor does the human ego become an animal, nor lose its human attributes, while undergoing its punishment. It does not have to evolve up again through the successive lower stages of humanity, but on being set free at once takes the grade of human form to which its previous evolution entitles it. (See the cases of Jada Bharata, and of the Rishi's wife set free by the touch of Rama's feet - cases which show that the popular idea that the man becomes a stone or an animal is erroneous.)

"The facts are these. When an ego, a human soul, by vicious appetite or otherwise, forms a very strong link of attachment to any type of animal, the astral body of such a person shows the corresponding animal characteristics, and in the astral world - where thoughts and passions are visible as forms - may take the animal shapes. Thus, after death, in Pretaloka the soul would be embodied in an astral vesture resembling, or approximating to, the animal whose qualities had been encouraged during earth-life. Either at this stage, or when the soul is returning towards reincarnation, and is again in the astral world, it may in extreme cases be linked by magnetic affinity to the astral body of the animal it has approached in character, and will then, through the animal's astral body, be chained as a prisoner to the animal's physical body. Thus chained, it cannot go onwards to Svarga if the tie be set up while it is a Preta; nor go onwards to human birth if it be descending towards physical life. It is truly undergoing penal servitude, chained to an animal; it is conscious in the astral world, has its human faculties, but it cannot control the brute body with which it is connected, nor express itself through that body on the physical plane. The animal organisation does not possess the mechanism needed by the human ego for self-expression; it can serve as a jailor, not as a vehicle. Further the animal soul is not ejected, but is the proper tenant and controller of its own body. Shri Shankaracharya hints very clearly at this difference between this penal imprisonment and becoming a stone, a tree or an animal. Such an imprisonment is not reincarnation, and to call it by that name is an inaccuracy; hence, while fully conversant with the above facts, I should always say that the human ego cannot reincarnate as an animal, cannot become an animal. This is not the only experience a degraded soul may have in the invisible world, of which hints may be found in the Hindu Shastras, for . . . the statements made are partial and very incomplete.

"In cases where the ego is not degraded enough for absolute imprisonment, but in which the astral body is strongly animalised, it may pass on normally to human re-birth, but the animal characteristics will be largely reproduced in the physical body - as witness the ` monsters' who in fact are sometimes repulsively animal, pig-faced, dog-faced, etc. Men, by yielding to the most bestial vices, entail on themselves penalties more terrible than they for the most part realise, for nature's laws work on unbrokenly and bring to every man the harvest of the seeds he sows. The suffering entailed on the conscious human entity thus cut off for the time from progress and from self-expression is very great, and is of course reformatory in its action; it is somewhat similar to that endured by other egos, who are linked to bodies human in form, but without healthy brains - those we call idiots, lunatics, etc. Idiocy and lunacy are the results of vices other in kind from those that bring about the animal servitude above explained, but the ego in these cases also is attached to a form through which he cannot express himself."

These instances are the explanation (or at least a part of the explanation) of the widely-spread belief that a man may under certain circumstances reincarnate in an animal body. In Oriental books, what we should call three stages of one life are quite commonly spoken of as separate lives. It is said that when a man dies to the physical plane he is reborn at once on the astral plane - meaning simply that his specially and wholly astral life begins then; and in the same way what we should describe as the passing into the heaven-life is called a death on the astral plane and a rebirth at the higher level. This being so, it is easy to understand that one of the abnormal cases above mentioned might be described as ` rebirth as an animal,' although it is not at all what we should mean by such a term if we employed it in Theosophical literature.

In recent investigations our attention has been drawn to a type of case differing somewhat from either of the above in that the link with the animal is intentionally made by the human being, in order to escape from something which he feels to be far worse. No doubt this type also was known to the ancients, and forms one of the classes referred to in the tradition of animal incarnations. Let me endeavour to explain it.

When a man dies, the etheric part of his physical body is withdrawn from the denser part, and shortly afterwards (usually within a few hours) the astral breaks away from the etheric, and the man's life on the astral plane is begun. Normally the man is unconscious until he has freed himself from the etheric, and so when he awakens to a new life it is that of the astral plane. But there are some people who cling so desperately to material existence that their astral vehicles cannot altogether separate from the etheric, and they awaken still surrounded by etheric matter.

The etheric body is only a part of the physical, and is not in itself a vehicle of consciousness - not a body in which a man can live and function. So these poor people are in a very unpleasant condition, suspended as it were between two planes. They are shut out from the astral world by the shell of etheric matter which surrounds them, and at the same time they have lost the physical sense-organs by which alone they can come fully into touch with the world of ordinary earth-life.

The result is that they drift about, lonely, dumb and terrified, in a thick and gloomy fog, unable to hold intercourse with the denizens of either plane, glimpsing sometimes other drifting souls in their own unfortunate positions, yet powerless to communicate even with them, incapable of joining them or of arresting their aimless wandering as they are swept on and engulfed in the rayless night. Now and again the etheric veil may part sufficiently to permit one glance into lower astral scenes, but that is rarely encouraging, and indeed is often mistaken for a glimpse into hell; sometimes for a moment some familiar earthly object may be half-seen - usually from passing contact with a strong thought-image; but such rare and tantalising liftings of the fog only make its darkness the more soul-shaking and hopeless when it shuts down again.

All the while the poor soul cannot realise that if he would but let go his frenzied grasp on matter he would slip at once (through a few moments of unconsciousness) into the ordinary life of the astral plane. But it is just that feeling that he cannot bear - the feeling of losing even the miserable half-consciousness that he has; he clings even to the horrors of this grey world of all-embracing fog rather than let himself sink into what seems to him a sea of nothingness and complete extinction. Occasionally, as the result of wicked and blasphemous teaching on earth, he fears to let himself go lest he should fall into hell. In either case, his suffering, his hopelessness and utter dreariness are usually extreme.

Out of this unpleasant but self-imposed predicament there are several ways. There are members of our band of invisible helpers who devote themselves specially to seeking out souls who are in this painful condition, and trying to persuade them to let themselves sink out of it; and there are also many kindly people among the dead who take this up as a sort of branch of astral slum work. Sometimes such efforts are successful, but on the whole few of the victims have faith and courage enough to let go their hold on what to them is life, poor apology though it be. In process of time the etheric shell wears out, and the ordinary course of nature reasserts itself in spite of their struggles; and sometimes in sheer despair they anticipate this result, deciding that annihilation is preferable to such a life, and so recklessly letting themselves go - the result being an overwhelming but pleasant surprise to them.

In their earlier struggles, however, there are some who are so unfortunate as to discover unnatural methods of reviving to some extent their touch with the physical plane instead of sinking into the astral. They can do this readily through a medium, but usually the medium's 'spirit-guide'sternly forbids them access. He is quite right to do so, for in their terror and their great need they are often utterly unscrupulous, and they would obsess and even madden the medium, fighting as a drowning man fights for life; and all absolutely uselessly, since the eventual result could only be to prolong their sufferings by strengthening that material part of which most of all they should get rid.

Occasionally they contrive to seize upon some one who is unconsciously a medium - some sensitive young girl, usually; but they can be successful in such an attempt only when the ego of the young girl has weakened his hold on his vehicles by allowing the indulgence of undesirable thoughts or passions. When the ego's relations with his vehicles are normal and healthy he cannot be dispossessed by the frantic efforts of such poor souls as we have been describing.

An animal, however, has no ego behind him, though he has a fragment of a group-soul which may be said to stand for him in the place of an ego. The hold of this fragment upon his vehicles is by no means what that of an ego would be, and so it comes to pass that what for the moment we may call the 'soul' of the animal can be dispossessed much more easily than that of a man. Sometimes, as I have said, the human soul wandering in the grey world is unfortunate enough to discover this, and so in his madness he obsesses the body of an animal, or if he cannot quite drive out the animal soul he contrives to gain partial control, so as to share the tenement to some extent with the rightful owner. In such a case he is once more in touch with the physical plane through the animal, he sees through the animal's eyes (often a very remarkable experience) and he feels any pain inflicted upon the animal; in fact, so far as his own consciousness is concerned, he is the animal for the time being.

An old and respected member of one of our English Branches related that he had received a visit from a man who came to ask for advice under peculiar circumstances. The visitor was a man who gave the impression of having seen better days, but he had fallen into such abject poverty that he was compelled to take any work that offered, and thus it happened that he had become a slaughter-man at a huge abattoir. He declared that he was absolutely unable to execute his loathsome task, because when he prepared to slaughter the creatures he was constantly checked by cries of heart-rending anguish, and by voices which said: "Have mercy upon us! Do not strike, for we are human beings entangled with these animals, and we suffer their pain." So, since he had heard that the

Theosophical Society occupied itself with unusual and uncanny matters, he came to it to ask for advice. No doubt this man was somewhat clairaudient, or perhaps simply sensitive enough to catch the thoughts of these poor creatures who had associated themselves with the animals, and these thoughts naturally symbolised themselves to him as audible cries for mercy. No wonder he was unable to continue his occupation.

This may well give pause to the devourer of flesh, to the man who calls the murder of animals 'sport,' and most of all to the vivisector; the man who kills or tortures an animal may be inflicting unspeakable suffering upon a human being.

I have little doubt that the possibility for a material-minded man of this uncanny blunder is at least part of the rationale of the belief of various tribes that certain creatures must never be killed "lest one should unawares be dispossessing the spirit of an ancestor." For the man who thus entangles himself with an animal cannot abandon that animal's body at will; even if he learnt enough to make him desire to withdraw, he could do so only gradually and by considerable effort, extending probably over many days. It is usually only at the death of the animal that he is set free, and even then there remains an astral entanglement to shake off. After the death of the animal such a soul sometimes struggles to obsess another member of the same herd, or indeed any other creature whom he can seize in his desperation.

I have noticed that animals obsessed or semi-obsessed by human beings are often shunned or feared by the rest of the herd, and indeed they are themselves often half-maddened by anger and terror at the strangeness of the thing and at their own helplessness. The animals most commonly seized upon seem to be the less developed ones - cattle, sheep and swine. More intelligent creatures, such as dogs, cats and horses, would presumably not be so easily dispossessed - though my attention was once drawn to a peculiarly horrible instance in which a Catholic priest had in this way attached himself to a cat. Then there is the well-known case of the monkey of Pandharpur, who betrayed so curious a knowledge of Brahmana ceremonies. But in most cases the obsessing soul has to be satisfied with what he can get, for the effort to overpower even the more stupid beasts usually taxes his powers to the utmost.

This obsession of an animal seems to be the modern substitute for the awful life of the vampire. In the time of the fourth root-race, men who had a mad clinging to material life sometimes contrived to maintain a low and unspeakably horrible form of it in their own physical bodies by absorbing living blood from others. In the fifth race that happily seems no longer to be possible, but people of the same type occasionally fall into this snare of animal obsession - bad enough, indubitably, but still not so utterly gruesome and disgusting as vampirism. So even in its very worst and lowest aspects the world is improving!

I have known of isolated cases of two other types of animal connection; one in which a wicked dead person was in the habit of temporarily seizing the body of a certain animal for specific evil purposes, and another in which an Oriental magician had, as an act of revenge for an insult to his religious faith, mesmerically linked his unhappy victim to an animal form after death. This could be done only if there existed in the victim some weakness through which such a magician could seize upon him, and if he had intentionally done something which gave him a karmic hold upon him. Normally neither of these cases would be at all possible.

All obsessions, whether of a human or an animal body, are an evil and a hindrance to the obsessing soul, for they temporarily strengthen his hold upon the material, and so delay his natural progress into the astral life, besides of course making all sorts of undesirable karmic links. This grey life, like almost all other unpleasant possibilities connected with the life after death, can come only as the result of ignorance of the real conditions of that life. The more we learn of life and death, the more emphatic appears the duty of making every effort to spread the knowledge of Theosophy, for it becomes ever clearer and clearer that in that knowledge is life and happiness and progress for all.

INDIVIDUALISED ANIMALS

When an individualised animal dies he has a happy astral life of considerable length, during which he usually remains in the immediate neighbourhood of his earthly home and in the closest touch with his especial friend and protector - able to see and enjoy the society of his friend as fully as ever, though himself invisible to the latter, his memory of the past being of course just as perfect as it was on earth. This will be followed by a still happier period of what has sometimes been called dozing consciousness, which will last until in some future world the human form is assumed. During all this time he is in a state analogous to that of a human being in the heaven-world, though at a somewhat lower level. He creates his own surroundings, even though he may be but drowsily conscious of them, and they will undoubtedly include the presence of his earth-friend in his very best and most sympathetic mood. For every entity which comes into connection with it, whether only just entering upon human evolution or preparing to pass beyond it, the heaven-world means the highest bliss of which that entity is, at his level, capable.

LOCALISATION OF STATES

The idea of location applies to the sub-planes of the astral, but only to a limited extent. Matter of all the stages undoubtedly surrounds us here on the surface of the earth, and the living man, employing his astral body during the sleep of the physical, comes into touch with them all simultaneously, and is able to receive impressions from them all. That is, if I, using my astral body during sleep, look at another living man's astral body, I see the whole of it, including of course matter of every sub-plane. But in the case of the average dead man, there has been a rearrangement of the matter of his astral body, consequent upon the proceedings of what is commonly called the desire-elemental, and broadly speaking only one type of astral matter is available to receive impressions.

What we usually call 'sight' on the astral plane is not really sight at all, for that word implies the use of an organ specialised to receive certain vibrations. Astral cognition is arranged on an entirely different scheme. It has often been said that a man can 'see' with any part of his astral body - that is, every particle of that body is capable of receiving impressions from without and transmitting them to the consciousness within. But every particle is not capable of receiving every possible impression.

For example, I became cognizant of the lowest kind of astral matter only by means of matter of the same subdivision existing in my own astral body; and I receive its vibrations through the particles of that lowest type of matter which happen to be at the moment on the surface of my astral body. Since during life all the particles of the astral body are constantly in motion among themselves, much as are the particles of a boiling liquid, it inevitably happens that all the subdivisions of matter are represented upon the surface of the astral body, and that is why I am able to see all the stages simultaneously. The ordinary man after death has for practical purposes only one type of matter outside, because of the concentric shell arrangement; therefore his view of the astral world around him is a very imperfect one.

If he, immured in a shell of matter of the lowest stage, looks at a living man's astral body, he can see only that part of it which consists of that lowest type of matter; but as he has no means of realising the limitation of his faculties, he inevitably assumes that he sees the whole of the other man's astral body, and therefore that the other man is a person possessing no characteristics but those eminently unsatisfactory ones which alone express themselves through matter of that particular subdivision.

He is living in the midst of all sorts of high influences and beautiful thought-forms, but is almost entirely unconscious of their existence, because those particles of his astral body which could respond to their vibrations are carefully shut in where they cannot be reached. That lowest type of astral matter corresponds to the solid subdivision of physical matter, and the astral counterpart of any solid physical object is composed of that lowest subdivision of astral matter - the seventh class of astral matter, if we number the sub-planes from above downwards. The astral counterparts of the floor, walls and furniture of a room are all of the lowest type of astral matter, and consequently the man newly dead usually sees these counterparts vividly, and is almost entirely unconscious of the vast sea of thought-forms which encompasses him, because nearly all those forms are built out of combinations of the finer types of astral matter.

In process of time, as the consciousness steadily withdraws inward; the shell of this coarsest type of matter atrophies and begins to disintegrate, and matter of a somewhat higher type is as it were uncovered, and becomes the surface through which impressions can be received. Since this usually happens gradually, it means that the man finds the counterparts of physical objects growing dimmer and dimmer, while the thought-forms become more and more vivid to him, so that without necessarily moving at all in space, he finds himself living in a different world. If while this process is going on he should encounter you at intervals he will be sensible of what will appear to him as a great improvement in your character - not that you have necessarily changed, but that he is becoming able to appreciate the higher vibrations of that character, and is losing the power to receive the lower ones. Your disposition may remain just what it was, but the dead man having commenced by seeing only its worst features, will pass it all slowly in review until presently he reaches a condition in which only the best and highest side of it is within his consciousness.

This then is what is meant by passing from one sub-plane to another - that the man loses sight of one part of the wonderful complexity which is the astral world, and that another part of it comes into his view. It is after all only a repetition on a smaller scale of what happens to each one of us as we pass from plane to plane. The whole astral world and the whole mental world are both of them around us here and now, yet so long as our consciousness is focussed in the physical brain we are blankly unconscious of them. At death the consciousness is transferred to the astral body, and at once we find ourselves seeing the astral part of our world, having lost sight of the physical. When later on we lose the astral body in turn, and live in the mental body, we are then conscious (though only partially) of the mental part of our world, and have altogether lost for the time both the astral and the physical. Just as it is possible for the man living on the astral plane to defy the desire-elemental and insist upon keeping the particles of his astral body in constant motion, just as they were during his physical life, so it is possible for the man still in physical life to train himself to have at his command the physical and astral and mental consciousness practically simultaneously; but this means considerable advancement.

To sum up the foregoing, then: 'rising higher' in the ordinary spiritualistic sense is simply raising the consciousness from one stage of the astral to another, the matter of the astral body having in the first place been arranged after death by the desire-elemental. In such a case the consciousness can act only through the shell of matter which lies outermost, and consequently at first the dead man is confined to the perception of the lowest subplane, and can only become conscious of a higher sub-plane when that outer coating of denser matter is in great part worn away. Consequently such a man in the earlier part of his post-mortem existence is naturally shut off from all the best and pleasantest part of astral life; and when he escapes from that condition he may in one sense be said to have risen higher.

A Theosophist, who comprehends the conditions of the astral plane, altogether declines to permit the rearrangement of his astral body by the desire-elemental in the first place; or if that should happen during the momentary unconsciousness which immediately succeeds death, those of us who are trying to help the man immediately break up the elemental's arrangement and restore the astral body to exactly the condition in which it was during life, with all its varieties of matter mingled in the natural way, so that the dead man can perceive the whole of the astral plane, instead of only one subdivision of it. In this way his astral life is perfect from the first, and he can be a much more useful person than if he were confined to the consciousness of one subdivision only.

Still, as explained in *The Inner Life*, Vol. I, in the chapter on spheres, there is just this much of truth behind the idea of location as connected with the sub-planes. Here on the surface of the earth we are in presence of matter in the solid, liquid, gaseous and etheric conditions. But it is undoubtedly true that, broadly speaking, the solid matter forms the basic, that the liquid matter is usually resting upon it, and that the gaseous matter rests upon both of these lower forms. There is a certain amount of solid matter and a great deal of liquid matter floating in the air above us, but still it remains broadly true that the zone of solid matter is limited by the surface of the earth, and the zone of liquid matter by the upper surface of the clouds, while the zone of gaseous matter extends a great many miles above that, and the zone of specialised etheric matter a great deal farther still. So that although all classes of matter exist around us here, we might yet say that in one sense each has a zone of its own, and that in each case the zone of a finer type of matter extends somewhat farther from the centre of the earth than the zone of the denser type of matter next below it.

A similar condition exists with regard to astral matter. All possible kinds of it exist here close about us, and the great majority of the denizens of the astral world spend most of their lives comparatively near to the surface of the physical earth; but as they withdraw into themselves, and their consciousness touches the higher types of matter, they find it easier and more natural than before to soar away from that surface into regions where there are fewer disturbing currents. I was once brought into touch with the case of a dead man who informed a friend of mine, during a series of spiritualistic séances, that he frequently found himself about five hundred miles above the surface of the earth. In this case the questioner was one who was well versed in occultism, and who would therefore know well how to conduct his enquiries and the investigations of his friend on the other side intelligently and scientifically; so that there might well be some truth in his friend's assertions.

The finer types of astral matter extend almost to the orbit of the moon, whence the name that the Greeks gave to the astral plane - the sublunar world. In fact, so nearly does the limit of astral matter coincide with that orbit, that the astral envelopes of the moon and the earth usually touch one another at perigee, but not at apogee. I knew, likewise, of a case in which a dead man reached the moon, but could not then return. That was because the continuity of astral matter failed him - the tide of space had flowed in between, as it were, and he had to wait until communication was re-established the approach of the satellite to its primary.

HEAVEN-LIFE CONDITIONS

The principal difficulty in understanding the conditions of the heaven-world comes from our inveterate habit of thinking of the personality as the man. If two friends are bound by ties of affection, we must try to remember that the bond is between the souls and not the bodies - that they are friends now on earth because in quite different bodies they have known and loved each other perhaps for thousands of years. That fact draws their physical bodies together on this plane, but it does not enable them to understand more of one another than their physical capabilities permit; and further, each wears three heavy veils, in the shape of the mental, astral and physical bodies, to conceal his real self from the other.

When one of them dies he passes on to the astral plane, and there he meets his living friend face to face during the sleep of the latter. Even already he can see somewhat more of his friend than before, because for each of them, during those hours of sleep, the heaviest of the three veils has been withdrawn. The dead man is still dealing with the personality of his friend only, and therefore if some great sorrow should fall upon the waking life of that friend, it would inevitably be reflected in his astral life, and the dead man would perceive it. For our sleeping and walking lives are in reality but one, and during our sleep we are aware of that fact, and have the continuous memory of both open before us. You will see, therefore, that the astral body of his living friend (with which the dead man is dealing) is the astral body of the personality, and he is therefore fully conscious of what is happening to that personality.

When the heaven-world is reached all this is changed. The dead man is then functioning in his mental body - the same mental body which he has used during his past earth-life; but he does not meet there the mental body which his friend is using during life. On the contrary, the dead man himself by his thought builds for his friend an entirely separate mental body, and it is the ego of his friend which ensouls it, working from its own level and from the causal body. This is an additional opportunity for mental-plane activity for the friend, and is entirely separate in every way from the personality of his physical life.

It is not possible for one man to ensoul more than one physical body at one time, but it is quite possible for him to ensoul simultaneously any number of the thought-forms which other people may make of him on the mental plane in the course of their heaven-life. I think it is a misunderstanding of this fact which had led some to think that several physical bodies may be incarnations of one man.

You will see, therefore, that any sorrow or trouble which may fall upon the personality of the living man, and may conceivably influence his mental body, will not in the least affect his other thought-form which his ego is using as an additional mental body. If in that manifestation he knows at all of such sorrow or trouble, he will regard it as he would from the causal body - that is to say, it will not be to him a sorrow or trouble at all, but only a lesson, or the working out of some karma. There is no delusion at all in this view of his, because he is seeing the matter as it really is, from the point of view of the ego on his own plane. It is our lower personal view that is the delusion, because we see sorrow and trouble where in reality there are only the steps on our upward way.

The two friends may know far more of each other at that level, because each has now only one veil, that of the mental body, cast over his individuality; but there is still that veil. If the dead man has known only one side of his friend during life, it will be only through that side that the friend can express himself in the heaven-world. He can express that side of himself much more fully and satisfactorily than ever before; but he is largely confined to that side. Still, it is a fuller expression than the dead man has ever been able to see upon the lower planes. He by no means forgets that there is such a thing as suffering, because he remembers clearly his past life; but he understands now many things that were not clear when he was on the physical plane, and the delight of the present is for him so great that sorrow seems to him almost like a dream.

It is asked how we who still live on earth converse with our friends in heaven; if by we you mean our personality, that does not converse with friends in heaven. The real ego does do so, as has been said, but in the veil of this personality we know nothing of that.

Suppose that a good Catholic mother died, who dearly loved her daughter, and that after the mother had reached the heaven-world, her daughter embraced Theosophy. The mother would go on imagining her daughter as merely orthodox; would she not in this be under a delusion? Yes, she would, for this is an instance of one of the possible limitations to which I have previously referred. If the mother could see only such of her daughter's thought as could be expressed by orthodox ideas, there would naturally be points in the new revelation which had come to the daughter which the mother would be little able to grasp. But in so far as the ego of the daughter profited by what the personality had learnt, there would be a tendency on her part gradually to widen out and perfect the conception of the mother, but always along the lines to which the mother was accustomed. There would be no sense of difference of opinion, and no avoidance of subjects of religion.

You will understand that I am speaking here of the ordinary person; in the case of a more advanced man who was already fully conscious in the causal body, he would put himself down consciously into the thought-form provided for him by a friend in the heaven-world, as into an additional mental body, and work through it with definite intention; so that if such a man should acquire additional knowledge he could directly and intentionally communicate it to that friend. In this way the Masters work on such of their pupils as take the heaven-life, and alter their characters immensely.

A man's condition in the heaven-life depends upon the amount of spiritual force in him. Of two people of the same class or type the more spiritual would naturally remain a longer time; but it must be borne in mind that the force may be used up quickly or slowly according to the necessities of each man's evolution.

Those who have devoted themselves especially to the work of serving the Great Ones, and through them humanity, are likely in this respect to have experiences differing somewhat from the ordinary. It is evident that our Masters have already, many millennia ago, formed a special band of servers and helpers from those who have offered themselves for such work, and They use this body of men as a kind of regiment of pioneers to be sent wherever special work of that kind is needed.

Those who have read the lives of Alcyone, as published in The Theosophist, will realise that the hero of that remarkable story is a member of that band - or perhaps we should rather say of one of those bands; and for that reason it will be found that over and over again the same set of people come together in all sorts of different places, in their successive incarnations. It is obvious that in a group of a hundred people there must be many divergences; some of them will assuredly generate more spiritual force than others, and their karma would naturally be such as to take them into differing surroundings, yet the one great fact that they are devoted to service overpowers all these considerations, and they are brought together in order that they may be utilised as a whole.

Be sure that in this there is no injustice, and that no one of them, for this or any other reason, escapes one jot of the karma which is legitimately due to him. Indeed, those who offer themselves for service not infrequently suffer considerably in the course of that service - sometimes because it is necessary that their past karma should be cleared up quickly, in order that they may be free to do higher work without any hindrance from it, and in other cases because their work may have made it impossible for them to reap life after life the karma that would otherwise have come to them, and so a considerable accumulation may descend upon them at once in some gigantic catastrophe. Instances of the working of both these methods may be found in the lives of Alcyone.

In the case of the great bulk of humanity there is no special interference from without, and the heaven-life of each works itself out at whatever may be its ordinary rate. Naturally this difference in the time of working out involves also a difference of intensity which is shown by a greater or less brilliancy in the light of the mental body. The more developed man, especially if he has before him the idea of service, usually generates karma during his heaven-life, and thus he may modify it even while it is in progress.

It is true that Madame Blavatsky states in The Key To Theosophy that it is impossible for a materialist to have any heaven-life, as he had not while on earth believed in any such condition; but it seems probable that she was employing the word materialist in a more restricted sense than that in which it is generally used, for in the same volume she also asserts that for them no conscious life after death is possible at all, whereas it is a matter of common knowledge among those whose nightly work lies upon the astral plane that many of those whom we usually call materialists are to be met with there, and are certainly not unconscious.

For example, a prominent materialist intimately known to one of our members was not long ago discovered by his friend in the highest subdivision of the astral world, where he had surrounded himself with his books and was continuing his studies almost as he might have done on earth. On being questioned by his friend he readily admitted that the theories which he had held while on earth were confuted by the irresistible logic of facts, but his own agnostic tendencies were still strong enough to make him unwilling to accept what his friend told him as to the existence of the still higher spiritual state of the heaven-world. Yet there was certainly much in this man's character which could find its full result only in the heaven-world, and since his entire disbelief in any life after death has not prevented his astral experience, there seems no reason to suppose that it can check the due working out of the higher forces in him upon the mental plane.

We constantly find down here that nature makes no allowance for our ignorance of her laws; if, under an impression that fire does not burn, a man puts his hand into a flame, he is speedily convinced of his error. In the same way a man's disbelief in a future existence does not affect the facts of nature, and in some cases at least he simply finds out after death that he was under a mistake. The kind of materialism referred to by Madame Blavatsky was probably something much coarser and more aggressive than ordinary agnosticism - something which would render it exceedingly unlikely that a man who held it would have any qualities requiring a heaven-life in which to work themselves out; but no such case as that has yet come under our observation.

KARMA IN THE HEAVEN LIFE

In the earlier days of our study of Theosophy we were led to look upon all other worlds but the physical as almost exclusively the theatre of results and not of causes. It was supposed that man spent his physical life to a large extent in generating karma, and his existence on the astral and mental planes in working it out, and the suggestion that a man could by any means make any more karma, even on the astral plane, was regarded as almost heretical.

As the years rolled on and some of us became able to study astral conditions at first-hand, it became obvious that this idea had been an error, since it was manifestly possible for us in working on that plane to performs actions of various sorts which produced far-reaching results, We soon saw also that not only the man still attached to a physical body could produce these results, but that they were equally within the power of one who had cast off that vehicle. We found that any developed man is in every way quite as active during his astral life after physical death as during his physical life before it; that he can unquestionably help or hinder not only his own progress but that of others quite as much after death as before, and consequently that he is all the time generating karma of the greatest importance.

This modified view of after-death conditions gradually found its way into our literature, and may be considered now as universally accepted by all

Theosophists. But for many years after we had corrected our misconceptions upon this important point, we still held to the idea that in the heaven-world at least man could do practically nothing but enjoy the conditions which he had made for himself during the previous stages of his existence. Broadly speaking, this is true for the ordinary man, though we do not always realize that even in the course of that enjoyment the inhabitant of the heaven-world is affecting others, and therefore producing results.

One who has succeeded in raising his consciousness to the level of the causal body has already unified the higher and lower selves (to use the older terminology), and to him the statements made as to average humanity naturally do not apply. Such an one has the consciousness of the ego at his disposal during the whole of his physical life, and that is not at all affected by the death of the physical body, nor even by the second and third deaths in which he leaves behind him the astral and the mental bodies respectively. For him the whole of that series of incarnations is only one long life, and what we call an incarnation is to him a day in that life. All through his human evolution his consciousness is fully active, and it naturally follows that he is making karma just as much at one period of it as at another; and while his condition at any one moment is the result of the causes which he has set in motion in the past, there is no instant at which he is not modifying his conditions by the exercise of thought and will.

Men who have reached that level are at present rare; but there are others who possess a similar power in a minor degree. Every human being, after he has passed through his life on the astral and lower mental planes, has a momentary flash of the consciousness of the ego, in which he sees his last life as a whole, and gathers from it the impression of success or failure in the work which it was meant to do; and along with this he has also a forecast of the life before him, with the knowledge of the general lesson which that is to teach, or the specific progress which he is intended to make in it. Only very slowly does the ego awaken to the value of these glimpses, but when he comes to understand them he naturally begins to make use of them.

Thus by imperceptible degrees he arrives at a stage in his evolution when this glimpse is no longer momentary - when he is able to consider the question much more fully, and to devote some time to his plans for the life which lies before him. His consciousness gradually increases, and he comes to have an appreciable life on the higher levels of the mental plane each time that he touches them. When he arrives at this stage he soon finds that he is one among a vast number of other egos, and that he can do something else with his life among them besides making plans for his own future. He may and does live a conscious life among his peers, in the course of which he influences them in many ways, and is himself influenced in turn. Here therefore is a possibility of making karma, and of making it on a scale which is entirely out of his reach on these lower planes, for every thought on those higher mental levels has a force quite out of proportion to that of our limited thought during physical life.

This of which I am speaking is quite distinct from the consciousness which comes with the unifying of the higher and lower selves. When that feat has been performed the man's consciousness resides in the ego all the time, and from that ego it plays through whatever vehicle he may happen to be using. But in the case of a man who has not yet achieved that union the consciousness of the ego on his own plane comes into activity only when he is no longer hampered by any lower vehicles, and exists only until he puts himself down again into incarnation; for as soon as he takes up a lower body his consciousness can manifest for the time only through that body.

Short of that perfect consciousness of the ego, there are stages of development which it is necessary to note. The ordinary ` man in the street' has usually no definite and reliable consciousness outside of the physical plane. His astral body may be fully developed and quite capable of being used as a vehicle in any and every way; yet he is probably not in the habit of so using it, and therefore his experiences of the astral world are of a vague and uncertain character. He may sometimes remember one of them vividly, but on the whole the time of the sleep of the physical body is for him a blank.

The next stage beyond this is that of the gradual development of the habit of using the astral body, accompanied as time goes on by some recollection of what is done in it. The end of this is the opening of the astral consciousness, though usually that comes only as the result of definite efforts along the line of meditation. When this opening is attained the man's consciousness is continuous through night and day, and up to the end of the astral life, so that he avoids the usual temporary suspension of consciousness at the death of the physical body.

The next stage beyond this - a long stage usually - is the development of the consciousness of the mental body, and when that is achieved, each personality remains conscious from physical birth until the end of its life in the heaven-world. But even then it is only the consciousness of the personality, and not yet of the ego, and still another step must be taken before complete unification is attained.

It is clear that men who have reached any of these stages are making karma as far as their consciousness reaches; but what as to the ordinary man, who has not yet quite succeeded in linking even the astral consciousness to the physical? In so far as he has any activities on the astral plane during sleep, he must be producing results. If he feels, even blindly, love and affection towards certain persons, and goes out towards them during sleep with vague thoughts of good-will, he must inevitably affect them to a certain extent, and the effect must be a good one. Therefore there is no possibility of avoiding a reaction upon himself which will also be good. The same is true if the feeling unfortunately be one of dislike or of active hatred, and the result for him in that case cannot but be painful.

When, after death, he lives entirely in the astral world, his consciousness is usually much more definite than it has been during the sleep of his physical body, and he is correspondingly better able to think and act with determination in regard to other men, and so his opportunities of making good or bad karma are the greater. But when such a man ends his astral life and passes into the heaven-world he reaches a condition where activity is no longer possible for him. He has encouraged activities in his mental body, during life, in certain directions only, and now that he comes to live entirely in that mental body he finds himself enclosed within it as in a tower, shut off from the world around him and able to look out upon it only through the windows in it which he has opened by means of those activities.

Through those windows the mighty forces of the plane play upon him; he responds to them and leads a life of vivid joy - which is, however, confined to those particular lines. But, though he is thus shut away from the full enjoyment of the possibilities of the mental world, it must not be supposed that he is in the slightest degree conscious of any curtailment of his activities or his feelings. He is, on the contrary, filled with bliss to the very utmost of which he is capable, and it is to him incredible that there can be any greater joy than that which he is himself experiencing. True, he has shut himself in within certain limits; but he is quite unconscious of those limits, and he has all that he can possibly desire or think of within them. He has surrounded himself with images of his friends, so that through these images he is actually in closer connection with them than he has ever been on any other plane.

Let us see then what are his possibilities for making karma in this curiously limited life - limited, we must remember, from the point of view of the mental world only, for along the lines of its special directions its possibilities are far greater than those of physical life. A man under such conditions cannot originate a fresh line of affection or devotion, but his affection and devotion along the lines which he has already decided will be distinctly much more powerful than they ever could have been while he was labouring under the heavy limitations of the physical body.

An ordinary man such as we have described is, quite unintentionally and unconsciously to himself, producing three separate results, during the whole of his heaven-life. Let us take as an example the emotion of affection. He feels this strongly for certain friends, and it is probable that even after his death those friends still think of him with kindly remembrance, and thus his memory is not without its effect even upon their personalities. But entirely apart from this is the effect to which I have above referred - that he makes an image of each friend and, in so doing, draws forth a strong response from the ego of that friend. The affection which he pours upon that ego (manifesting through the thought-form which he has made for it) is a mighty power for good, which bears no inconsiderable part in the evolution of that ego. It evokes from him an amount of affection which would not otherwise be stirred up in him; and the steady intensification of that most admirable quality throughout the centuries of the heaven-life raises the friend considerably in the scale of evolution. To do this for another ego is unquestionably an act which generates karma, even though the man who has set all this machinery in motion has done so uncomprehendingly.

Occasionally the action of such a force upon the ego of a surviving friend may manifest itself even in the personality of that friend upon the physical plane. The action is upon the ego through the special thought-form; but the personality of the surviving friend in this world is a manifestation of the same ego, and if the ego be considerably modified it is at least possible that that modification may show itself in the physical manifestation on this lower plane. It may be asked why the thought of the man in the heaven-world should not act upon his friend precisely as does the thought of a living man - why the vibrations sent forth from his mental body cannot strike directly upon the mental body of his friend, and why it should not generate a thought-form which would travel through space and attach itself to his friend in the ordinary way. If he were moving freely and consciously about the mental plane that is precisely what would happen, but the reason that it does not lies in the peculiar condition of the man in the heaven-world.

The man in the heaven-life has shut himself out absolutely from the rest of the world - from the mental plane as much as from the lower levels, and he is living inside the shell of his own thoughts. If his thoughts could reach us in the ordinary way, ours could reach him in precisely the same way, but we know that that is not so. The thought-form which he makes of his friend is within his own shell, and therefore he can act upon it; and, since the ego of the friend has poured himself down into that thought-form, the force reaches the ego of the friend in that way, and from that ego it may, as we have said, to some extent manifest itself even in the personality of the friend down here. The shell is as regards the mental plane much like the shell of an egg on the physical plane. The only way to get anything into the shell of an egg, without breaking it, would be to pour it in from the fourth dimension, or to find a force whose vibrations are sufficiently fine to penetrate between the particles of the shell without disturbing them. This is true also of this mental shell; it cannot be penetrated by any vibrations of matter of its own level, but the finer vibrations which belong to the ego can pass through it without disturbing it in the least; so that it can be acted upon freely from above, but not from below.

The thought-form made by the dead man may be considered as a kind of additional artificial mental body, made for and presented to the friend upon whom the love is being poured forth. The personality down here knows nothing of this, but the ego is fully conscious of it and plunges down into it with delight and avidity, realising incidentally that this affords him an additional opportunity of manifestation, and therefore of evolution. From this it follows that the man who has made himself generally beloved - the man who has many real friends - will evolve with far greater rapidity than a more ordinary man; and this again is obviously the karma of his development within himself of the qualities which make him so lovable.

So much for the direct result of his action upon individuals; but there are also two aspects of its general action which must not be ignored. A man who thus pours out a great flood of affection, and evokes in response other floods from his friends, is distinctly improving the mental atmosphere in his neighborhood. It is good for the world and for the humanity evolving in it that its mental atmosphere should thus be charged with such feelings, for they play upon all its inhabitants - devas, men, animals, plants - and on every one of these widely different forms of life they have their influence, and always an influence for good.

The second and more important of the results produced for the world at large will be readily comprehensible to those who have studied the book on Thought-forms, as an attempt is there made to indicate the outpouring which flows down from the LOGOS in response to a thought of unselfish devotion. It has often been explained that such response comes not only to the individual who originated the thought, but that it also helps to fill the reservoir of spiritual force, which is held by the Nirmanakaya at the disposal of the Masters of Wisdom and their pupils, to be used for the helping of mankind. What is true of devotion is true also of unselfish affection, and if every outrush of such affection or devotion during the comparatively limited physical life produces so magnificent a result, it is easy to see that a far stronger outrush, sustained through a period of perhaps a thousand years, will make to that reservoir a really considerable contribution, and this will bring to the world a benefit which is not calculable in any terms that we can use upon the physical plane.

So it is clear that while a man's power for good augments as his consciousness in these higher worlds increases, even the quite ordinary man, who has as yet no special development of consciousness, is nevertheless capable of doing an enormous amount of good during his sojourn upon the higher planes. During his long stay in the heaven-world he may benefit his fellow-men, and so make a large amount of good karma for himself; but, in order to do that, he must be a man of unselfish love or unselfish devotion. It is this quality of unselfishness, of self-forgetfulness, which puts the power into his hands; and that, therefore, is the virtue which every man must cultivate now in full consciousness, in order that after death he may use to the best advantage those far longer periods whose conditions it is now so impossible for him to realize.

Second Section: Astral Work

INVISIBLE HELPERS

People often write to us, applying to be admitted to the band of invisible helpers, and asking what preparation is necessary. Those who desire to take up this work should familiarise themselves thoroughly with the book written under that title, and should especially take care to develope within themselves the qualifications which are there described. I have little to add to what I have there written, except that I should advise every one who wishes to take up work on the astral plane to learn as much as he can beforehand of the conditions of life on that plane.

In the astral life we are absolutely the same persons as we are down here, but with certain limitations removed. Our interests and activities on that plane resemble those on the physical; a student is still studious; an idle person is still idle; an active helper on the physical plane is still a helper there. Some people still gossip there just as venomously as ever, and are still continuing to make just the same bad karma by doing so. Most dead people haunt for a long time the places to which they have been accustomed in life. Many a man hovers round his ancestral home, and continues daily to visit the astral counterpart of the temple which he used to support. Others drift round and make pilgrimages, without trouble or expense, to all the great shrines which during life they have in vain wished to visit.

There is perfect continuity in the astral life. That life is in many ways much more real than this, or at least much nearer to reality, and this physical existence is only a series of breaks in it during which our activity is greatly limited and our consciousness but partially operative. To most of us in this lower life the night seems a blank, and in the morning we remember nothing of what we have done; but we must not therefore suppose that we are equally dense on the astral plane. That wider consciousness fully includes this, and every night we remember vividly not only what we did on all previous nights, but also all that we have done on the intermediate days. It is the physical brain which is dull and clogged, and it is upon return to it that we lose our memory of all except that with which it has been directly concerned. The astral life is much more vivid and its emotions are far stronger than any that we know down here. What we ordinarily call an emotion is only the comparatively small fragment of one which remains after the greater part of it has been exhausted in setting in motion the clumsy physical particles, so it is not difficult to see how far more intense and real that other life must be.

And yet, although this is quite true, and true of everybody, ordinary people usually do very little in the way of real work on the astral plane. They do not know, in fact, that they can work, and even if they did know they would probably see no particular reason why they should. A man may spend a very enjoyable time in the astral world, just drifting about and experiencing various pleasurable emotions. That seems to most people the only thing to do, and it needs a powerful motive to rouse them out of that, and make them take the trouble of devoting their time to the helping of others. We must admit that for the ordinary man this motive does not exist; but when we have begun to study Theosophy, and in that way learn the course of evolution and the purpose of things, there arises within us an earnest desire to help forward that evolution, to accomplish that purpose, and to put our fellow-men in the way of understanding it also, in order that thereby their troubles may be lightened and the path of their progress made easier.

Now, when a man thus awakens to his duty, how is he to set about it? We are all of us capable of such work, to a greater or less extent, though probably not in the habit of doing it. All people of ordinary culture and development have their astral bodies in working order, just as all reasonably healthy people possess the necessary muscles and the necessary strength in them to enable them to swim; but if they have not learnt how to use them they will need a certain amount of instruction before they can usefully or even safely take to the water. The difficulty with the ordinary person is not that the astral body cannot act, but that for thousands of years that body has been accustomed to being set in motion only by impressions received from below through the physical vehicle, so that men do not realise that the astral body can work on its own plane and on its own account, and that the will can act upon it directly. People remain ` unawake' astrally because they get into the habit of waiting for the familiar physical vibrations to call out their astral activity.

There are several ways in which a man may begin to help. Suppose, for example, that a relation or friend dies. In order to reach and to help him during sleep, all that is necessary is to think of him before retiring to rest, with the resolve to give him whatever assistance he most needs. We do not need any help in order to find him, or to communicate with him. We must try to understand that as soon as we leave the physical body at night we stand side by side with a departed friend, exactly as we did when he was with us on the physical plane. One great thing to remember is the necessity of curbing all sorrow for the so-called dead, because it cannot but react upon him.

If a man allows himself to despair about the dead, the feeling of despair will affect them very strongly, for emotions play through the astral body, and consequently those who are living in their astral vehicles are much more readily and deeply influenced by them than people who have a physical body to deaden their perceptions. The dead can see us, but it is our astral body that they see; consequently they are at once aware of our emotions, but not necessarily of the details of our physical condition. They know whether we are happy or miserable, but not what book we are reading, for example. The emotion is obvious to them, but not necessarily the thought which causes it. The dead man carries on with him his affections and hatreds; he knows his old friends when he meets them, and he also often forms new friendships among new companions whom he meets for the first time on the astral plane.

Not only must we avoid sorrow, but also excitement of any kind. The invisible helper must above all things keep perfectly calm. I have known a worthy lady who was full of the most earnest desire to help, and in her eagerness to do so keyed herself up into a tremendous state of excitement. Now, excitement shows itself in the astral body in great increased of size, violent vibration and the flashing forth of fiery colours. So the newly-dead person, who was quite unused to astral surroundings, and consequently in a state of timidity and nervousness, was horrified to see a huge flaming, flashing sphere come rushing at him with evident intention. Naturally he took this for the theological devil in propria persona , and fled shrieking before it to the ends of the earth, though for a long time it increases his terror by persistently following him.

One case in which it is often possible for even a beginner to make himself useful is that of some friend of neighbour who is known to be about to die. If one has access to him physically, and if his illness is of a nature which makes it possible to discuss with him the conditions of death and of its after-states, a little rational explanation of these will often very greatly relieve his mind and lighten his burdens. Indeed, the mere meeting with a person who speaks confidently and cheerfully about the life beyond the grave is frequently the greatest consolation to one who finds himself approaching it.

If, however, for any reason, this physical communication is impossible, much may be done during sleep by acting upon the dying man from the astral plane. An untrained person seeking to give such help should follow the rules laid down in our books; he should fix the intention of aiding that particular person in his mind before going to sleep, and he should even decide as far as possible upon the arguments which should be presented and even the very words which should be used, for the more precise and definite the resolution is made while awake, the more certain it is to be faithfully and accurately carried out in the astral body during sleep.

The explanation to be given to the sick man is necessarily the same in both cases. The main object of the helper is to calm and encourage the sufferer, to induce him to realise that death is a perfectly natural and usually an easy process, and in no case a formidable or terrible leap into an unknown abyss. The natural of the astral world, the way in which a man ought to order his life in it if he wishes to make the best of it, and the preparation necessary for progress toward the heaven-world which lies beyond; all these should be gradually explained by the helper to the dying man. The helper should always remember that his own attitude and state of mind produces even more effect than his argument or his advice, and consequently he must be exceedingly careful to approach his task with the greatest calmness and confidence. If the helper himself is in a condition of nervous excitement he is quite likely to do more harm than good, as did the poor lady whom I have just mentioned.

The assistance offered should be continued after death. There will be a certain period of unconsciousness then, but it may last only for a moment, though often the moment expands into a few minutes, or several hours, and sometimes even into many days or weeks. A trained pupil naturally observes for himself the condition of the ` dead' man's consciousness and regulates his assistance accordingly; the untrained man will do well to offer such assistance immediately after death, and also to hold himself in readiness to give it for several succeeding nights, in order that he may not fail to be at hand when his services are needed. So many diverse circumstances affect the duration of this period of unconsciousness that it is scarcely possible to lay down any general rule in the matter.

We should at least determine each night to comfort someone who is in trouble, and if we know the exact nature of the trouble we must do our best to adapt our measures to the needs of the case. If the sufferer be weak and exhausted, the helper should use his will to pour into him physical strength. If, on the other hand, he is excited or hysterical, the helper should endeavour to enfold him in a special aura of calm and gentleness - wrap him up, as it were in a strong thought-form of peace and harmony, just as one would wrap up a person in a blanket.

It is often difficult for one who tries to help to believe that he can have been successful, when he wakes in the morning and remembers nothing whatever of what has taken place. As a matter of fact some measure of success is absolutely certain, and as the helper goes on with his work he will often receive cheering little indications that he is producing definite results in spite of his lack of memory.

Many a member has set himself to try this, and for a long time has known nothing as to results, until one day it has happened to him to meet physically the person whom he has been trying to assist, and to be much comforted to see the improvement in him. Sometimes it happens that the friend dates the commencement of his recovery from a particular night on which he had a pleasant or a remarkable dream; and the helper is startled when he remembers that it was on that very night that he made a specially determined effort to help that man. The first time that this happens, the helper probably persuades himself that it is a mere accident; but when a sufficient number of coincidences have accumulated he begins to see that there is something more in it than that. The beginner therefore should do his best, and be content to wait as far as result are concerned.

There is another simple experiment which has greatly helped some beginners in gaining confidence. Let a man resolve to visit astrally some room which is well known to him - one, let us say, in a friend's house; and let him note carefully the arrangement of the furniture and books. Or if, without previously intending it, the experimenter finds himself during sleep in a spot which he recognises (that is, in ordinary parlance, if he dreams of a certain place) he should set himself to observe it with great care. If when he remembers this in the morning it seems to him that everything in that room was exactly as when he last saw it physically, there is nothing to prove that it was not really a mere dream or memory; but if he recollects some decided change in the arrangements, or if there is something new and unexpected, it is distinctly worth his while to go physically in the morning to visit that room, in order to test whether his nocturnal vision has been correct.

All those of us who are definitely engaged in astral work have necessarily at one time or another taken in hand a number of cases which needed help. Such help may occasionally be of the nature of a surgical operation - something which can be done once for all, and then put aside; but far more often what is needed is comfort, reassurance and strengthening which must be repeated day after day in order that it may gradually sink into the texture of some wounded nature and transmute it into something braver and nobler. Or sometimes it is knowledge which must be given little by little as the mind opens to it and is able to bear it. Thus it comes that each worker has a number of chronic cases, clients, patients - call them what you will - whom he visits every night, just as a doctor upon earth makes a regular round among his patients.

It often happens also that those who have been thus helped are filled with gratitude towards the worker, and attach themselves to him in order to second his efforts, and to pass on to others the benefits which they have thus received. So it comes that each worker is usually the centre of a small group, the leader of a little band of helpers for whom he is always able to find constant employment. For example, a large number of people who die are much in the position of children afraid of the dark. One may reason with them, and argue patiently and convincingly that there is nothing whatever to fear; but a hand that the child can hold is of more practical use to him than a whole chapter of arguments.

The astral worker, with a score of other cases needing immediate attention, cannot possibly spend the whole night in standing by and comforting one nervous or doubting patient; but he can detach for that purpose one of his earnest followers who is not so busily occupied, and is therefore able to devote himself to that charitable work. For to comfort the child in the dark no brilliant scientific knowledge is needed; what he wants is a kindly hand and the sense of companionship. So that work can be found in the astral world for any number of workers, and everyone who wishes, man, woman or child, may be one of them. For the larger and more comprehensive varieties of work, and for the direction of the work, much knowledge is of course required; but a heart full of love and the earnest desire to help is equipment enough to enable any one to become one of the minor comforters, and even that humble effort brings in its train a blessing beyond all calculation.

When the astral worker finally lays aside the physical body for this incarnation, he finds himself among an army of grateful friends who rejoice unreservedly that he is now able to spend the whole of his life with them instead of only a third of it. For such a worker there will be no sense of strangeness or newness in the condition of the life after death. The change for him means only that he will then be able to devote the whole of his time to what is even now by far the happiest and most effective part of his work - a part which he takes up every night with joy and lays aside every morning with regret - the real life, in which our days of physical existence are but dull and featureless interludes.

There are one or two other points with regard to the astral life which it is desirable for the worker to try to understand. One of these is the method of what I suppose we must call speech - the communication of ideas on the astral plane.

It is not always easy to understand down here the substitute for language which is used in the astral world. Sound in the ordinary sense of the word is not possible there - indeed it is not possible even in the higher part of the purely physical plane. As soon as one rises above the air into the etheric regions, there is no more possibility of sound as we understand the word. Yet the symbol of sound is used very much higher, for we constantly find references to the spoken word of the LOGOS, which calls the worlds into manifestation.

If in the morning we remember an experience of the previous night, such as the meeting with a friend or the attendance at a lecture, it will always seem to us that we heard a voice in the usual terrestrial way, and that we ourselves replied to it, also audibly. In reality this is not so; it is merely that when we bring through a recollection to the physical brain we instinctively express it in terms of the ordinary senses. Yet it would not be correct to say that the language of the astral world is thought-transference; the most that could be said is that it is the transference of a thought formulated in a particular way.

In the mental world one formulates a thought and it is instantly transmitted to the mind of another without any expression in the form of words. Therefore on that plane language does not matter in the least; but helpers working in the astral world, who have not yet the power to use the mental vehicle, must depend on the facilities offered by the astral plane itself. These lie as it were half way between the thought-transference of the mental world and the concrete speech of the physical, but it is still necessary to formulate the thought in words. It is as though one showed such formulation to the other party in the dialogue, and he replied (almost simultaneously, but not quite) by showing in the same way his formulated reply. For this exchange it is necessary that the two parties should have a language in common; therefore the more languages an astral-plane helper knows, the more useful he is.

The pupils of the Masters, however, have been taught to form a special kind of temporary vehicle, in order to meet these difficulties. They habitually leave their astral bodies with the physical; they travel about in their mental bodies, and they materialise a temporary astral body from surrounding matter when they need it for astral work. All who have been taught to do this have the advantage of the mental-plane method of thought-transference so far as understanding another man is concerned, though their power to convey a thought in that way is limited by the degree of development of that other man's astral body.

Apart from definitely trained pupils, there are very few people who consciously work in the mental body - for to do so means years of practice in meditation and special effort. We know that a man in the heaven-world shuts himself up within a shell of his own thoughts, and that these thoughts then act as channels through which the life of the mental world can affect him. But we cannot call this functioning on the mental plane, for that involves the free moving about on that plane, and the observation of what exists there.

Fortunately, the mental elemental does not rearrange the mental body after death, so that we have not the same kind of trouble with it as with the desire-elemental on the astral plane. Indeed, the elemental essence of the mental plane differs greatly from that of the astral. It is a whole chain behind the other, and therefore it has not the same force. It is trying to deal with, for it is largely responsible for our wandering thoughts, as it darts constantly from one thing to another; but at least it does not make a shell of any sort, although certain portions of the mental body may become hardened, as I have explained when dealing with that subject.

When a man function in the mental vehicle he leaves the astral body behind him in a condition of suspended animation, along with the physical. If he finds it necessary he can easily surround that torpid astral body with a shell, or he can set up in it vibrations which render it impervious to all evil influences. It is unquestionably possible for any man in process of time, by meditation upon the LOGOS or the Master, to raise himself first to the astral and then to the mental levels; but none can say how long it will take, as that depends entirely upon the past of the student.

It is quite possible for any person when upon the astral plane after death to set himself to study, and to acquire entirely new ideas. I have known people who learnt Theosophy for the first time in the astral world. I have even heard of a case in which a lady learnt music there, but that is unusual. Probably some dead person gave her lessons, or it may be that the teacher was a living musician who was on the astral plane at the same time as the lady. In astral life people often think that they are playing on astral instruments, but in reality they are only making vibrations by their thought, which produce the effect of sound. There is a special class of devas who respond to music and express themselves through it, and sometimes they are willing to teach people to whom music is the first and only thing in life.

Most dead people shut themselves out from many of the possibilities of the plane, by accepting the rearrangement of the body at death, which prevents them from seeing anything belonging to the higher levels. The Theosophist will not allow this rearrangement, because he intends to work, and therefore he must be free to move through all the sub-planes. We cannot get rid of elemental essence, but we can subdue the desire-elemental, draw in the finer types of matter, and make the ego strong to keep the upper hand. The essence wants violent emotion, so as to evolve downwards - which, it must be remembered, is its proper and legitimate course of evolution. If it knew of our existence, we should appear to it to be evil beings and tempters, trying to prevent the evolution which it knows to be right for it. If we steadfastly refuse to allow our astral body to vibrate at the rate peculiar to the coarser matter, that coarser matter will gradually be discharged from the body, which will become finer in texture, and the desire-elemental will be of a less active kind.

The rearrangement which the desire-elemental produces after death is over the surface of the counterpart of the physical body, not over the surface of the egg which surrounds it. The elemental tries to inspire a feeling of terror in the man who is jolting him out of this arrangement, in order to deter him from doing so. This is one reason why it is so useful to have knowledge of these matters before death.

There is no such thing as sleep in the astral world. The need of sleep on the physical plane is that it calms the physical centres and allows them time to rebuild themselves chemically, so that the astral body can work more freely, through a better vehicle; but on the astral plane there is no fatigue, unless we may call by that name the gradual slackening down of all the energies when the end of the astral life is approaching.

It is possible to forget upon the astral plane, just as it is upon the physical. I mean in this case not the loss of memory between two planes, which is so common, but the actually being unable to remember on the astral plane to-night some of the details of what one did last night or last year. Indeed, perhaps it is even easier to forget on the astral plane than on the physical , because that world is so busy and so populous.

Knowledge of a person in the astral world does not necessarily mean knowledge of the physical life of that person. For example, many of us know Madame Blavatsky in her new body exceedingly well on the astral plane, yet none of us have yet seen that body physically. She often uses her old form, though generally the new astral body now.

REMEMBERING ASTRAL EXPERIENCE

When you leave your body to-night, you will remember all that you did last night and during the day - in fact, you will have the whole of your present waking memory, plus that of your nightly astral life. The astral memory includes the physical, but your physical brain does not remember the astral experience, for the simple reason that it had no share in it.

A special link must be made, or rather an obstacle must be removed, in order to bring the memory through into the physical brain. In the slow course of evolution the power of perfect memory will come to every one, so that there will no longer be any veil between the two planes. Apart from this full development sometimes something occurs which the man feels that he ought to remember on the physical plane, and in that case he makes a special effort to impress it upon the brain, in order that it may be remembered in the morning. There are some events, too, which make such a vivid impression upon the astral body that they become impressed upon the physical brain by a kind of repercussion.

It is comparatively rarely, however, that such an impression is perfect, and there may be many stages of imperfection. This is one source of what we call dreams, and we know how confused and incomplete and even ridiculous they may often be. One form of distortion which frequently occurs in the case of the unpractised helper is that he confuses himself with the person to whom he has been giving assistance.

I remember a case of a member of our band who was deputed to assist the victim of an explosion. He was warned a few minutes beforehand, and had time enough to make an effort to calm and steady the man's mind, and then immediately after the outburst had taken place he was still on hand to continue the same process; but in the morning, when he described the event to me, he declared that it seemed exactly as though he himself had been the victim of the explosion. He had identified himself so closely with his patient that he felt the shock and the sensation of flying upwards exactly as, we must presume, the victim felt them. In another case the same member was called upon to assist a soldier who was driving an ammunition waggon down an execrable mountain road, and was thrown off and killed by the wheels passing over his body. In this case also our member entirely identified himself with the soldier, and his memory of the event was that he had dreamed of driving such a waggon and being thrown from it and killed, just as the real driver had been.

In other cases what is remembered is not at all what really happened, but rather a sort of symbolic description of it, sometimes quite elaborate and poetical. This comes evidently from the image-making characteristic of the ego - his faculty of instantaneous dramatisation - and it sometimes happens that the symbol is recollected without its key; it comes through untranslated, as it were, so that unless the helper has a more experienced friend at hand to explain matters, he may have only a vague idea of what he has really done. A good instance of this came before my notice many years ago - so many that, as I made no record of it at the time; I am not now quite certain of one or two of its points, and am therefore obliged to omit some of it, and make it a little less interesting than I think it really was.

The helper came to me one morning to relate an exceedingly vivid dream which he felt sure was in reality something more than a dream. He remembered having seen a certain young lady drowning in the sea. I believe that he had the impression that she had been intentionally thrown in, though I do not think that he had any vision of the person who was supposed to have done this. He himself could not directly assist her, as he was present only in the astral body, and did not know how to materialise himself; but his keen sense of the imminence of the peril gave him strength to impress the idea of danger upon the young lady's lover, and to bring him to the scene, when he at once plunged in and brought her ashore, delivering her into the arms of her father. The helper remembered the faces of all these three characters quite clearly, and was able so to describe them that they were afterwards readily recognisable. The helper begged me to look into this case, so that he might know how far his clear remembrance was reliable.

On doing so, I found to my surprise that the whole story was symbolic, and that the facts which had really occurred were of a different nature. The young lady was motherless, and lived practically alone with her father. She seems to have been rich as well as beautiful, and no doubt there were various aspirants to her hand. Our story, however, has to do only with two of these; one, a most estimable but bashful young fellow of the neighbourhood, who had adored her since childhood, had grown up in friendly relations with her, and had in fact the usual half-understood, half-implied engagement which belongs to a boy-and-girl love affair. The other was a person distinctly of the adventurer type, handsome and dashing and captivating on the surface, but in reality a fortune-hunter of false and unreliable type. She was dazzled by his superficial brilliancy, and easily persuaded herself that her attraction for him was real affection, and that her previous feelings of comradeship for her boy friend amounted to nothing.

Her father, however, was much more clear-sighted than she, and when the adventurer was presented to him he seems to have received him with marked coolness, and declined altogether, though kindly enough, to sanction his daughter's marriage with a gentleman of whom he knew nothing. This was a great blow to the young lady, and the adventurer, meeting her in secret, easily persuaded her that she was a terribly ill-used and misunderstood person, that her father was quite unbearably tyrannical and ridiculously old-fashioned, that the only thing left for her to do as a girl of spirit was to show that she meant what she said by eloping with him (the aforesaid adventurer) after which of course the father would come round to a more sensible view of life, and the future would take on the rosiest of hues.

The foolish girl believed him, and he gradually worked upon her feelings until she consented; and the particular night upon which our friend the helper came upon the scene was that which had been chosen for the elopement. In true melodramatic style the adventurer was waiting round the corner with a carriage, and the girl was in her room hurriedly preparing herself to slip out and join him.

Not unnaturally, when it came actually to the point her mind was much disturbed, and she found it very difficult to take the final step. It was this fluttering of the mind, this earnest desire for aid in decision, which attracted the notice of the helper as he was drifting casually by. Reading her thoughts, he quickly grasped the situation, and at once began to try to influence her against the rash step which she contemplated. Her mind, however, was in such a condition that he was unable to impress himself upon her as he wished, and he looked round in great anxiety for someone who should prove more amenable to his influence. He tried to seize upon the father, but he was engaged in his library in some literary work of so engrossing a character that it proved impossible to attract his attention.

Fortunately, however, the half-forgotten lover of her youth happened to be within reach, wandering about in the starlight and looking up at her window in the approved style of young lovers all the world over. The helper pounced upon him, seeing the condition of his sentiments, and to his great delight found him more receptive. His deep love made him anxious, and it was easy enough to influence him to walk far enough to see the carriage and the adventurer in waiting around the corner. His affection quickened his wits, and he instantly grasped the situation, and was filled with horror and dismay. To do him justice, at that supreme moment it was not of himself that he thought, not that he was on the eve of losing her, but that she was on the eve of throwing herself away and ruining the whole of her future life. In his excitement he forgot all about convention; he made his way into the house (for he had known the place since childhood), rushed up the stairs and met her at the door of her room.

The words which he said to her neither he nor she can remember now, but in wild and earnest pleading he besought her to think before doing this terrible thing, to realise clearly into what an abyss she was about to throw herself, to bethink herself well before entering upon the path of destruction, and at least, before doing anything more, to consult openly with the loving father whom she was requiting so ill for his ceaseless care of her.

The shock of his sudden appearance and the fervour of his objurgations awakened her as from a sort of trance; and she offered scarcely any resistance when he dragged her off then and there to her father as he sat working in his library. The astonishment of the father may be imagined, when the story was unfolded before him. He had had not the slightest conception of his daughter's attitude, and she herself, now that the spell was shaken off, could not imagine how she had ever been able really to contemplate such a step. Both she and her father overflowed with gratitude to the loyal young lover, and before he left her that night she had ratified the old childish engagement, and promised to be his wife at no remote date.

This was what had really happened, and one can see that the symbolism chosen by the ego of the helper was by no means inapt, however misleading it may have been as to the actual facts.

Sometimes nothing comes through that can be called an actual memory, but only the effect of something that has been seen or that has happened. A man may wake in the morning with a strong feeling of elation and success, without in the least being able to recall in what he has succeeded. This generally means some good piece of work well done, but it is often impossible for the man to recover the details. At other times he may bring back with him a feeling of reverence, a sense of great holiness. This usually means that he has been in the presence of some one much greater than himself, or has seen some direct evidence of the greater power. Sometimes, on the other hand, a person may wake with a feeling of terrible fear. That is sometimes due only to the alarm of the physical body at some unaccustomed sensation; but it is sometimes also due to having encountered something horrible in the astral world. Or again it may arise merely from sympathy with some astral entity who is in a state of terror, for it is a frequent thing on the astral plane that one person should be strongly influenced by sympathy with another's condition.

Few people, however, when in the astral body, care whether the physical brain remembers or not, and nine out of ten much dislike returning to the body. But if you specially wish to get into the habit remembering, the procedure which I should recommend is the following:

To make the link, first remember, when you are out of the body, that you wish to do so. Then you must determine to come back into the body slowly, instead of with a rush and a little jerk, as is usually the case. It is this jerk that prevents one from remembering Stop yourself and say, just before you awake: "There is my body; I am just about to enter it. As soon as I am in it I will make it sit up and write down all it can remember." Then enter it calmly, sit up instantly and write down all you are able to remember at once. If you wait a few minutes, all will usually be lost. But each fact that you bring through will serve as a link for other memories. The notes may seem a little incoherent when you read them over afterwards, but never mind that; it is because you are trying to give an account in physical words of the experiences of another plane. In this way you will gradually recover the memory though it may take a long time; great patience is necessary.

You should try to remember when out of the body that you are in the astral world, and that it would be a comfort to the physical consciousness if some memory could be carried through. Be systematic in your efforts. Every time that you succeed in bringing something through, it will make it easier to remember next time, and will bring nearer the period when there will be habitual automatic recollection. At present there is a moment of unconsciousness between sleeping and waking, and this acts as a veil. It is caused by the closely-woven web of atomic matter through which the vibrations have to pass.

In coming back to the physical body from the astral world there is a feeling of great constraint, as though one were being enveloped in a thick, heavy cloak. The joy of life on the astral plane is so great that physical life in comparison with it seems no life at all. Many men who can function in the astral world during the sleep of the physical body regard the daily return to the physical world as men often do their daily journey to the office. They do not positively dislike it, but they would not do it unless they were compelled.

When the man is free in the mental world, the astral life similarly seems a state of bondage, and so on, until we reach the buddhic world, which is in its essence bliss. After once reaching that level, although the man on the physical plane is still cramped and unable to express the bliss, he nevertheless has it all the time, and he knows that all others who are unable to feel it now will feel and know it at some future time. Even if only for a moment you could feel the reality of the higher planes, your life would never again be the same.

Astral pleasures are much greater than those of the physical world, and there is danger of people being turned aside by them from the path of progress. It is quite impossible to realise while one is confined in the physical body the great attractiveness of these pleasures. But even the delights of the astral life do not present a serious danger to those who have realised a little of something higher. After death one should try to pass through the astral levels as speedily as possible, consistently with usefulness, and not yield to its refined pleasures any more than to the physical. One must not only overcome physical desire by knowledge of the astral or the heaven-life, but also go beyond even them, and this not merely not for the sake of the joy of the spiritual life, but in order to replace the fleeting by the everlasting.

THE HIGHER DIMENSIONS

If there are seven dimensions at all, there are seven dimensions always and everywhere, and it makes no difference to that fundamental fact in nature whether the consciousness of any individual happens to be acting through his physical body; his astral body or his nirvanic vehicle. In the last case he has the power to see and understand the whole thing. In any of the other cases his capacities are limited. There is therefore no such thing as a three-dimensional or four-dimensional object or being. If space has seven dimensions, every object must exist within that space, and the difference between us is merely in our power of perception.

Physically we see only three dimensions, and therefore we see all objects and beings very partially. One who has the power to see four dimensions still sees objects only partially, although he sees more of them than the other man. We find ourselves in the midst of a vast universe built of matter of varying degrees of tenuity, which exists in a space of (let us suppose) seven dimensions. But we find ourselves in possession of a consciousness which is capable of appreciating only three of those dimensions, and only matter of certain degrees of tenuity. All matter of other and higher degrees is for us as if it did not exist. All dimensions beyond the three are also to us as though they did not exist.

But our lack of perceptive power does not in any way affect the objects themselves. A man picks up (let us say) a piece of stone. He can see only the physical particles of that stone, but that in no way affects the undoubted fact that that stone at the same time possesses within it particles of matter of the astral and mental and other higher planes. In just the same way, that stone must theoretically possess some sort of extension, however small, in all the seven dimensions; but that fact is in no way affected by the other fact that the man's consciousness can appreciate only three of those dimensions.

To examine that object the man is using a physical organ (the eye) which is capable of appreciating only certain rates of undulation radiated by certain types of matter. If he should develope what we call astral consciousness he would then be employing an organ which is capable of responding only to the vibrations radiated by another and finer part of that piece of stone. If in developing the astral consciousness he had lost the physical - that is, if he had left his physical body - he would be able to see only the astral and not the physical. But of course the object itself is not affected in any way, and the physical part of it has not ceased to exist because the man has for the time lost the power to see it. If he developed his astral consciousness so that he could use it simultaneously with the physical, he would then be able to see both the physical and astral parts of the object at the same time, though probably not both with equal clearness at absolutely the same moment.

Now, just as all the higher forms of matter exist in every object, although untrained people cannot see them, so all the dimensions of space must appertain to every object, although the number of those dimensions that we can observe depends upon the condition of our consciousness. In physical life we can normally conceive only three, though by careful special training the brain may be educated into grasping some of the simpler fourth-dimensional forms. The astral consciousness has the power of grasping four of these dimensions, but it by no means follows that a man who opens his astral consciousness immediately perceives the extension of every object in four dimensions; on the contrary, it is quite certain that the average man does not perceive this at all when he enters the astral plane. He realises it only as a certain blurring - a kind of incomprehensible difference in the things that he used to see; and most men go through their astral lives without discovering more than that of the qualities of the matter which surrounds them.

We should say, then, not that the possession of astral vision at once causes the man to appreciate the fourth dimension, but rather that it gives him the power to develop that faculty by long, careful and patient practice, if he knows anything about the matter and cares to take the trouble. Entities belonging to the astral plane, and presumably ignorant of any other (such as nature-spirits, for example) have by nature the faculty of seeing the fourth-dimensional aspect of all objects. But we must not therefore suppose that they see them perfectly, since they perceive only the astral matter in them and not the physical, just as we with our different kind of limitation perceive only the physical and not the astral.

It has never been taught, so far as I am aware, that the entities of the astral plane are conscious of us upon the physical plane. They quite clearly and definitely are not conscious of physical matter of any kind. But they are conscious of the astral counterpart of that physical matter, which for all practical purposes comes to very nearly the same thing, though not quite.

I should not expect the higher dimensions to manifest themselves as qualities of matter to our physical consciousness, though it is conceivable that some of them might do so in certain special cases. The density of a gas, for example, might de a measure of its extent in the fourth dimension.

If an object passes through a wall, the question of the fourth dimension is not raised, nor are the properties connected with it employed at all. But in order that the object may so pass through, either it or a portion of the wall corresponding in size to it must be disintegrated - that is, reduced either to the atomic or to one of the etheric conditions, so that the particles may pass freely among one another without hindrance. That is entirely a three-dimensional method. Another and quite different feat is not to disintegrate at all either the object or the wall, but to bring the entire object in by another direction altogether, where there is no wall. But that direction is unknown to us in our physical consciousness.

If one had a cup made of porous earthenware, one could not doubt fill it with water by the process of reducing the water to steam and forcing it through the sides of the cup; that would be equivalent to the ordinary process of disintegration and reintegration, for the water, reduced to a higher state for the purpose of being forced through the pores of the cup, would resume its natural condition when it had passed through. But it would also be possible to fill the cup by the simpler process of taking off the lid and pouring in the water from above, and in this case the water need not be change in any way, because it is introduced into the cup from a direction in which there is no wall to penetrate. These are simply two ways of producing the same result, and they do not mutually exclude each other.

Third Section: The Mental Body and The Power of Thought

THE MENTAL BODY

After reading *Man Visible and Invisible* students have sometimes remarked that the list of qualities there given seems incomplete, and that nothing is said as to some others which are at least equally common - such for example as courage, dignity, cheerfulness, truthfulness, loyalty. The reason that these were not included in that first account is that they have not, as have those other qualities, readily distinguishable colours; but it must not therefore be supposed that their presence or absence would be indistinguishable by clairvoyant vision. Such qualities are indicated by differences in the structure of the mental body, or by changes in its surface; but it might be said, broadly speaking, that they are represented rather by form than by colour.

It will be remembered that, in the drawings of the mental body given in the book above mentioned, the colours which indicate some of the principal qualities are shown, and something is said as to their general arrangement in the vehicle. In a general way, all the colours denoting good qualities are to be found in the upper half, and those denoting unpleasant qualities are mostly in the lower half. The violet of high aspiration, the blue of devotion, the rose-colour of affection, the yellow which indicates intellect, and even the orange of pride or ambition - all these belong to the upper part, while thoughts prompted by anger, selfishness or jealousy gravitate towards the bottom of the ovoid. While the illustrations there given fairly indicate what would be the appearance of the mental body if it ever were really at rest, there is considerable variation from those types when the man is in the act of thinking strongly or definitely.

The mental unit may be regarded as the heart and centre of the mental body, and upon the relative activity of the different part of that unit the appearance of the body as a whole to a great extent depends. The various activities of the mind fall naturally into certain classes or divisions, and these divisions are expressed through different parts of the mental unit. Mental units are by no means all the same. They differ greatly according to the type and the development of their owners. If such a mental unit lay at rest the force radiating from it would make a number of funnels in the mental body, just as the light shining through the slide in a magic lantern makes a large radiating funnel of light in the air between the lantern and the sheet.

In this case the surface of the mental body may be likened to the sheet, because it is only at the surface that the effect becomes visible to one who is looking at the mental body from the outside; so that, if the mental unit were at rest, we should see on the surface of the mental body a number of pictures in colour, representing the various types of thought common to the person, with presumably dark spaces between them. But the mental unit, like all other chemical combinations, is rotating rapidly on its axis and the effect of this is that in the mental body we have a series of bands, not always quite clearly defined, nor always of the same width, but still readily distinguishable, and usually in about the same relative position.

Where aspirational thought exists, it invariably shows itself in a beautiful little violet circle at the top of the ovoid of the mental body. As the aspirant draws near to the gateway of the Path this circle increases in size and radiancy, and in the initiate it is a splendid glowing cap of the most lovely colour imaginable. Below it comes often the blue ring of devotional thought, usually rather a narrow one, except in the case of the few whose religion is really deep and genuine. Next to that we may have the much broader zone of affectionate thought, which may be of any shade of crimson or rose-colour, according to the type of affection which it indicates. Near the zone of affection, and frequently closely connected with it, we have the orange band which expresses proud and ambitious thought; and again in intimate relation with pride comes the yellow belt of intellect, commonly divided into two bands, denoting respectively the philosophical and the scientific types of thought. The place of this yellow colour varies much in different men; sometimes it fills the whole of the upper part of the egg, rising above devotion and affection, and in such a case pride is generally excessive.

Below the group already described, and occupying the middle section of the ovoid, is the broad belt devoted to concrete shapes - the part of the mental body from which all ordinary thought-forms issue. The principal colours here is green, shaded often with brown or yellow according to the disposition of the person.

There is no part of the mental body which varies more widely than this. Some people have their mental bodies crowded with a vast number of concrete images, whereas others have only few. In some they are clear and well-outlined, in others they are vague and hazy to the last degree; in some they are classified and labelled and arranged in the most orderly fashion, in others they are not arranged at all, but are left in hopeless confusion.

In the lower part of the ovoid come the belts expressing all kinds of undesirable thoughts. A kind of muddy precipitate of selfishness too often fills the lower third or even the half of the mental body, and above this is sometimes a ring portraying hatred, cunning or fear. Naturally, as men develop, this lower part vanishes, and the upper gradually expands until it fills the whole body, as shown in the illustrations in Man Visible and Invisible.

Degrees in the feeling which prompts thought are expressed by brilliance of colour. In devotional feeling, for example, we may have the three stages of respect, reverence and worship; in affection we may have the stages of good-will, friendship and love. The stronger the thought the larger is the vibration; the more spiritual and unselfish the thought the higher is the vibration. The first produces brilliancy, the second delicacy of colour.

Within these different rings or zones we usually see more or less clearly marked striations, and many qualities of the man can be judged by an examination of these striations. The possession of a strong will, for example, brings the whole mental body into far more level definite lines. All the striations and radiations are steady, firm and clearly distinguishable, whereas in the case of a weak and vacillating person this firmness and strength of line would be conspicuously absent; the lines separating the different qualities would be indeterminate, and the striations and radiations would be small, weak and wavy. Courage is shown by firm and very strongly-marked lines, especially in the orange band connected with pride. Dignity also expresses itself principally in the same part of the mental body, but by a calm steadiness and assuredness which is quite different from the lines of courage.

Truthfulness and accuracy are portrayed very clearly by regularity in the striations of the part of the mental body devoted to concrete forms, and by the clearness and correctness of the images which appear there. Loyalty shows itself by an intensification both of affection and of devotion, and by the constant formation, in that part of the ovoid, of figures of the person to whom the loyalty is felt. In many cases of loyalty, affection and devotion, a very strong permanent image is made of the objects of these feelings, and that remains floating in the aura of the thinker, so that, when his thought turns towards the loved or adored one, the force which he pours out strengthens that already existing image, instead of forming a new one as it would normally do.

Joy shows itself in a general brightening and radiancy of both the mental and the astral bodies, as also in a peculiar rippling of the surface of the body. General cheerfulness shows itself in a modified bubbling form of this, and also in a steady serenity which is pleasant to see. Surprise, on the other hand, is shown by a sharp constriction of the mental body, accompanied by an increased glow in the bands of affection if the surprise is a pleasant one, and by a change of colour usually involving the display of a good deal of brown and grey in the lower part of the ovoid when the surprise is an unpleasant one. This constriction is usually communicated to both the astral and the physical bodies, and often causes singularly unpleasant feelings, which affect sometimes the solar plexus (resulting in sinking and sickness) and sometimes the heart-centre, in which case it brings palpitation or even death; so that a sudden surprise may occasionally kill one who has a weak heart. Awe is the same as wonder, except that it accompanied by a profound change in the devotional part of the mental body, which usually swells out under this influence, and has its striations more strongly marked.

At the moment when a person's thought is strongly directed into one or another of these channels, the part of the mental body which corresponds to that thought usually bulges outwards in form in addition to brightening in colour, and so disturbs for the time the symmetry of the ovoid. In many people such bulging is permanent, and that always means that the amount of thought of that type is steadily increasing. If, for example, a person takes up some scientific study, and therefore suddenly turns his thoughts in that direction much more than before, the first effect will be such protuberance as I have described; but if he keeps the amount of his thought on scientific subjects steadily at the same level which he has now adopted, the protruding portion will gradually sink back into the general outline of the ovoid, but the band of its colour will have become wider than before.

If however the man's interest in scientific subjects steadily increases in force, the protrusion will still remain in evidence even though the band has widened. The general effect of this is that in the undeveloped man the lower portion of the ovoid tends always to be larger than the upper, so that the mental and astral bodies have the appearance of an egg with the small end uppermost; while in the more developed man the qualities expressing themselves in the higher part are always tending to increase, and consequently we have for the time the effect of an egg with its smaller end pointing downwards. But the tendency always is for the symmetry of the ovoid to re-assert itself by degrees, so that such appearances are only temporary.

Reference has frequently been made to the ceaseless motion of the matter in both the mental and astral bodies. When the astral body, for example, is disturbed by any sudden emotion, all its matter is swept about as if by a violent hurricane, so that for the time being the colours become very much mixed. Presently, however, by the specific gravity of the different types of matter which reflect or emit these various colours, the whole arrangement will sort itself once more into its usual zones. Even then the matter is by no means at rest, as the particles are all the time rushing round these zones, though comparatively rarely leaving their own belt and intruding on another. But this movement within its own zone is entirely a healthy one; one in whom there is no such circulation is a mental crustacean, incapable of growth until he bursts his shell. The activity of the matter in any particular zone increases in proportion to the amount of thought devoted to the subject of which it is an expression.

If the man should permit his thought upon any given subject to stagnate, that stagnation will be faithfully reproduced in the matter appropriate to the subject. If a prejudice should grow up in man, thought on that particular subject ceases altogether, and a small eddy forms in which the mental matter runs round and round until it coagulates and becomes a kind of wart. Unless and until this wart is worn away or forcibly rooted out, the man cannot use that particular part of his mental body, and is incapable of rational thought on that subject. This foul thickened mass blocks all free movement either outward or inward; it prevents him on the one hand from seeing accurately, or from receiving any reliable new impressions on the matter in question, and on the other from sending out any clear thought with regard to it.

These diseased spots in the mental body are unfortunately also centres of infection; the inability to see clearly increases and spreads. If part of the man's mental body is already stagnant, the other parts are likely to be affected; if a man allows himself to have a prejudice on one subject he will probably soon develope prejudices on others, because the healthy flow of mental matter has been checked and the habit of untruth has been formed. Religious prejudice is the commonest and the most serious of all, and it completely prevents any approach to rational thought with regard to the subject. Unfortunately a very large number of people have the whole of that part of their mental bodies which should be occupied with religious matters inactive, ossified and covered with warts, so that even the most rudimentary conception of what religion really is remains utterly impossible for them until a catastrophic change has taken place.

It may be remembered that in Man Visible and Invisible drawings were given of the astral bodies of men of the devotional and scientific types. Variants of these with which we frequently meet are the intuitional person and the matter-of-fact person. The latter has generally much of yellow in his mental body, and his various bands of colour are usually regular and in order. He has far less emotion and less imagination than the intuitional man, and therefore often in certain ways less power and enthusiasm; but on the other hand he is far less likely to make mistakes, and what he does will generally be well and carefully done. In the vehicle of the intuitional man we find much more of blue, but the colours are generally vague and the whole body ill-regulated. He suffers much more than the steadier type, but sometimes through that suffering he is able to make rapid progress. Of course, both the glow and enthusiasm and the steadiness and regularity have their place in the perfect man; it is only a question of which is acquired first.

Mystical thought and the presence of psychic faculties are indicated by colours of which we have no equivalents on the physical plane. When a man begins to develope along occult lines, the whole of his mental body must be rapidly purified and brought into thorough working order, for every part of it will be needed, and every part must be absolutely at its best if he is to make any real progress. It is eminently necessary that he should be able to make strong and clear thought-forms, and in addition to this it is a great help and comfort to him if he is able to visualise them clearly. The two acts must not be confused; one man may be able to make a stronger and clearer thought-form than another, and yet not be able to visualise it so well. The formation of a thought is a direct act of the will, working through the mental body; the visualisation is simply the power to see clairvoyantly the thought-form which he has made. Let him think strongly of any object, and the image of it is there in the mental body - just as much there whether he can visualise it or not.

It must be remembered that all mental work done on the physical plane must be done through the physical brain, so that in order to succeed it is necessary not only to develope the mental body, but to get the physical brain into order, so that the mental body may readily work through it. It is well known that certain parts of the brain are connected with certain qualities in the man and with his power to think along certain lines, and all these must be brought into order and duly correlated with the zones in the mental body.

Another point, the greatest of all, is that there is another connection to be made and kept active - the connection between the ego and his mental body; for he is the force behind, which makes use of all these qualities and powers. In order that we may think of anything we must first remember it; in order that we may remember it we must have paid attention to it; and the paying of attention is the descent of the ego into his vehicles in order to look out through them. Many a man with a fine mental body and a good brain makes little use of them because he pays little attention to life - that is to say, because the ego is putting but little of himself down into these lower planes, and so the vehicles are left to run riot at their own will. I have written elsewhere of the cure for this state of affairs; put very briefly it comes to this: Give the ego the conditions which he desires, and he will promptly put himself down more fully, to take advantage of them. If he desires to develope affection, give him the opportunity by cultivating affection to the fullest extent on these lower planes, and at once the ego will respond. If he desires principally wisdom, then endeavour by study to make yourself wise upon the physical plane, and once more the ego will appreciate your effort and be delighted to co-operate. Find out what he wants and give it to him, and you will have no reason to complain of his response.

A NEGLECTED POWER

People who have not made a special study of the matter never understand what a tremendous power there is in thought. Steam-power, water-power, these are real to them, because they can see them at work; but thought-power is vague and shadowy and intangible to them. Yet those who have taken the trouble to look into the subject know very well that one is just as real as the other.

This is true in two senses - directly and indirectly. Everybody, when it occurs to him, recognises the indirect action of thought, for it is obvious that a man must think before he can do anything, and the thought is the motive power of his act just as the water is the motive power of the mill. But people do not generally know that thought has also a direct action on matter - that whether or not a man translates his thought into a deed, the thought itself has already produced an effect.

Our readers are already aware that there are many kinds of matter finer than those which are visible to physical sight, and that the force of man's thought acts directly upon some of these and sets them in motion. A thought shows itself as a vibration in the mental body of man; that vibration is communicated to external matter, and an effect is produced. Thought therefore is itself a real and definite power; and the point of vivid interest about it is that everyone of us possesses this power. A comparatively small number of rich men have concentrated in their hands the steam-power and the electric power of the world; money is needed to buy its use, and therefore for many it is unattainable. But here is a power which is already in the hands of everyone, poor and rich, young and old alike; all we have to do is to learn to use it. Indeed, we are all of us using it to some extent even now, but because we do not understand it we often unconsciously do harm with it instead of good, both to ourselves and to others.

Those who have read the book called Thought-Forms will remember how it is there explained that a thought produces two principal external effects - a radiating vibration and a floating form. Let us see how these affect the thinker himself, and how they affect others.

The first point to remember is the force of habit. If we accustom our mental bodies to a certain type of vibration they learn to reproduce it easily and readily. If we let ourselves think a certain kind of thought to-day, it will be appreciably easier to think that same thought to-morrow. If a man allows himself to begin to think evil of others, it soon becomes easy to think more evil of them and difficult to think any good of them. Hence arises a ridiculous prejudice which absolutely blinds the man to the good points in his neighbours, and enormously magnifies the evil in them.

Then his thoughts begin to stir up his emotions; because he sees only the evil in others he begins to hate them. The vibrations of mental matter excite those of the denser matter called astral, just as the wind disturbs the surface of the sea. We all know that by thinking over what he considers his wrongs a man can easily make himself angry, though we often seem to forget the inevitable corollary that by thinking calmly and reasonably a man can prevent or dismiss anger.

Still another reaction upon the thinker is produced by the thought-form which he generates. If the thought be aimed at someone else, the form flies like a missile towards that person, but if the thought be (as is so often the case) connected chiefly with the thinker himself, the form remains floating near him, ever ready to react upon him and reproduce itself - that is to say, to stir up in his mind the same thought once more. The man will feel as though it were put into his mind from without, and if it happens to be an evil thought he will probably think that the devil is tempting him, whereas the experience is nothing but the mechanical result of his own previous thought.

Now see how this fragment of knowledge can be utilised. Obviously every thought or emotion produces a permanent effect, for it strengthens or weakens a tendency; furthermore, it is constantly reacting upon the thinker. It is clear therefore that we must exercise the greatest care as to what thought or emotion we permit to arise within ourselves. We must not excuse ourselves, as so many do, by saying that undesirable feelings are natural under certain conditions; we must assert our prerogative as rulers of this kingdom of our mind and emotions. If we can get into the habit of evil thought, it must be equally possible to get into the habit of good thought. We can accustom ourselves to look for the desirable rather than the undesirable qualities in the people whom we meet; and it will surprise us to find how numerous and how important those desirable qualities are. Thus we shall come to like these people instead of disliking them, and there will be at least a possibility that we may do them something approaching to justice in our estimate of them.

We may set ourselves definitely as a useful exercise to think good and kindly thoughts, and if we do we shall very soon begin to perceive the result this practice. Our minds will begin to work more easily along the grooves of admiration and appreciation instead of along those of suspicion and disparagement; and when for the moment our brains are unoccupied, the thoughts which present themselves will be good instead of bad, because they will be the reaction of the gracious forms with which we have laboured to surround ourselves. "As a man thinketh in his heart, so is he;" and it is obvious that the systematic use of thought-power will make life much easier and pleasanter for us.

Now let us see how our thought affects others. The radiating undulation, like many other vibrations in nature, tends to reproduce itself. Put an object in front of a fire, and presently that object becomes hot; why? Because the radiations of rapid vibration coming from the incandescent matter in the grate have stirred the molecules of the object into more rapid oscillation also. Just in the same way if we persistently pour the undulation of kindly thought upon another, it must in time awaken a similar vibration of kindly thought in him Thought forms directed towards him will hover about him and act upon him for good when opportunity offers. Just as a bad thought may be a tempting demon either to the thinker or to another, so a good thought may be a veritable guardian angel, encouraging virtue and repelling vice.

A grumbling and fault-finding attitude towards others is unfortunately sadly common at the present day, and those who adopt it never seem to realise the harm that they are doing. If we study its result scientifically we shall see that the prevalent habit of malicious gossip is nothing short of wicked. It does not matter whether there is or is not any foundation for scandal; in either case it cannot but cause harm. Here we have a number of people fixing their minds upon some supposed evil quality in another, and drawing to it the attention of scores of others to whom such an idea would never otherwise have occurred.

Suppose they accuse their victim of jealousy. Some hundreds of people at once begin to pour upon this unhappy sufferer streams of thought suggesting the idea of jealousy. Is it not obvious that if the poor man has any tendency towards that unpleasant quality, it cannot but be greatly intensified by such a cataract? And if, as is commonly the case, there is no reason whatever for the spiteful rumour, those who so eagerly spread it are at any rate doing their best to create in the man the very vice over the imagined presence of which they gloat so savagely.

Think of your friends by all means, but think of their good points, not only because that is a much healthier occupation for you, but because by doing so you strengthen them. When you are reluctantly compelled to recognise the presence of some evil quality in a friend, take especial care not to think of it, but think instead of the opposite virtue which you wish him to develope. If he happen to be parsimonious or lacking in affection, carefully avoid gossiping about this defect or even fixing your thought upon it, because if you do, the vibration which you will send him will simply make matters worse. Instead of that, think with all your strength of the quality which be needs, flood him with the undulations of generosity and love, for in that way you will really help your brother.

Use your thought-power in ways such as these, and you will become a veritable centre of blessing in your corner of the world. But remember that you have only a limited amount of this force, and if you want to have enough to be useful you must not waste it.

The average man is simply a centre of agitated vibration; he is constantly in a condition of worry, of trouble about something, or in a condition of deep depression, or else he is unduly excited in the endeavour to grasp something. For one reason or another he is always in a state of unnecessary agitation, usually about the merest trifle. This means that he is all the time wasting force, frittering away vainly that for the profitable use of which he is definitely responsible - that which might make him healthier and happier.

Another way in which he wastes a vast amount of energy is by unnecessary argument; he is always trying to make somebody else agree with his opinions. He forgets that there are always several sides to any question, whether it be of religion, of politics, or of expediency, that the other man has a perfect right to his own point of view, and that anyhow it does not matter, since the facts of the case will remain the same, whatever either of them may think. The great majority of the subjects about which men argue are not in the least worth the trouble of discussion, and those who talk most loudly and most confidently about them are usually precisely those who know least.

The man who wishes to do useful work, either for himself or for others, by means of thought-power, must conserve his energies; he must be calm and philosophic; he must consider carefully before he speaks or acts. But let no one doubt that the power is a mighty one, that any one who will take the trouble may learn how to use it, and that by its use each one of us may make much progress and may do much good to the world around him.

You should understand this power of thought, and the duty of repressing evil, unkind or selfish thoughts. Thoughts will produce their effect, whether we wish it or not. Each time you control them it makes control easier. Sending out of thoughts to others is as real as giving money; and it is a form of charity which is possible for the poorest of men. A wise man produces his results intentionally. To radiate depression is wrong, and it prevents higher thoughts from coming in.

It causes much suffering to sensitive people, and is responsible for much of the terror of children at night. It is not right to cloud a young life, as so many do, by allowing bad and miserable thoughts to fall upon it. Forget your depression, and send strengthening thoughts to sick people instead.

Your thoughts are not (as you might suppose) exclusively your own business, for your vibrations affect others. Evil thoughts reach much farther than evil words, but they cannot affect a man who is entirely free from the quality which they carry. The thought of the desire for drink could not enter the body of a purely temperate man, for example. It would strike upon his astral body, but it could not penetrate, and it would then return to the sender.

The will can be trained to act directly upon physical matter. The example of this which is most likely to be within your own experience is that a picture which is much used for purposes of meditation may often be observed to change in expression; the actual physical particles are unquestionably affected by the power of the strong sustained thought. Madame Blavatsky used to make her pupils practise this, telling them to suspend a needle by a silk thread, and then learn to move it by the force of the will. A sculptor also uses this power of thought in an entirely different way. When he sees a block of marble he makes a strong thought-form of the statue which he can carve out of it. Then he plants this thought-form inside the block of marble, and proceeds to chip away the marble which lies outside the thought-form, until only that portion of it which is interpenetrated by it remains.

Make it a practice to set apart a little time each day which shall be devoted to formulating good thoughts about other people, and sending them to them. It is capital practice for you, and it will unquestionably do good to your patients also.

INTUITION AND IMPULSE

You ask how you are to distinguish impulse from intuition. I fully appreciate your dilemma. At first it is difficult for the student to do this, but take comfort from the thought that the difficulty of decision is only a temporary matter. As you grow you will reach a stage at which you will be absolutely certain with regard to intuition, for the distinction between that and impulse will be so clear that mistake will be impossible.

But since both come to the brain from within, they seem at first exactly alike, and therefore great care is necessary, and it is hard to arrive at a decision. One or two considerations may perhaps help you. I have heard Mrs. Besant say that it is well always to wait awhile whenever the circumstances permit such a course, because if we wait a little an impulse usually grows weaker, while an intuition is unaffected by the passage of time. Then an impulse is almost always accompanied by excitement; there is always something personal about it, so that if it is not at once obeyed - if anything crosses - it there arises a feeling of resentment; whereas a true intuition, though decided, is surrounded by a sense of calm strength. The impulse is a surging of the astral body; the intuition is a scrap of knowledge from the ego impressed upon the personality.

Sometimes the sudden impression is not really from within at all, but from without; a message or suggestion from some one on a higher plane - most commonly some passing dead person, or perhaps a departed relation. It is well to treat such advice precisely as though it were given on the physical plane - to take it if it commends itself to our reason, and ignore it if it does not; for a person is not necessarily wiser than we merely because he happens to be dead. In this matter as in all others we must regulate our actions by strong, sturdy common-sense, and not rush off wildly after imaginations and dreams.

At this stage I should advise you always to follow reason when you are certain of the premises from which you reason. You will learn in time and by experience whether your intuitions can invariably be trusted. The mere impulse has its birth in the astral body, while the true intuition comes directly from the higher mental plane, or sometimes even from the buddhic. Of course the latter, if you could only be sure of it, might be followed without the slightest hesitation, but in this transition stage through which you are passing one is compelled to take a certain amount of risk - either that of sometimes missing a gleam of higher truth through clinging too closely to the reason, or that of being occasionally misled by mistaking an impulse from an intuition. Myself, I have so deep-rooted a horror of this last possibility that I have again and again followed reason as against intuition, and it was only after repeatedly finding that a certain type of intuition was always correct that I allowed myself to depend fully upon it. You too will no doubt pass through these successive stages, and you need not be in the least troubled about it.

THOUGHT-CENTRES

In the higher levels of the mental plane our thoughts act with greater force because we have the field almost to ourselves. We have not many other thoughts to contend with in that region. All people when thinking of the same thing tend to come to some extent into rapport with one another. Any strong thought anywhere in the world may be attracted to you, and you may be influenced by the thinker of it. Strong thought acts fairly constantly, and is more likely to act in connection with those subjects about which comparatively few are thinking, because in those cases the vibrations are more distinctive, and have freer play. Any sudden idea or vision which comes to you may be simply the thought-form of some person who is keenly interested in the subject in hand. The person may be at any distance from you, though it is true that physical proximity makes such transference easier.

There is such a thing as a kind of psychometrisation of a thought-form. Masses of thought on a given subject are very definite things, which have a place in space. Thoughts on the same subject and of the same character tend to aggregate. For many subjects there is a thought-centre, a definite space in the atmosphere; and thoughts on one of these subjects tend to gravitate to its centre, which absorbs any amount of ideas, coherent and incoherent, right and wrong. In this definite centre you would find all the thought about a given subject drawn to a focus, and might then psychometrise the different thought forms, follow them to their thinkers, and acquire other information from them.

It is easy to see that when one thinks of something a little difficult, one may attract the thought of another person who has studied the same subject, and even the person himself if he be on the astral plane. In the latter case the person may be either conscious or unconscious. Plenty of people, either dead or asleep, do try to help others along their particular lines; any one of such, seeing another struggling with some kind of conception, would be likely to go and try to suggest the way in which he thinks that other man ought to think of it. It does not follow, of course, that his ideas would be correct.

If you think you will see that this is perfectly natural. You would help people on this physical plane simply from pure good-nature. So also after death. You feel the same sympathies without a physical body; and though your idea may be wrong or right, you give it. I do not know of any method that is open to the ordinary student for ascertaining the exact source of an idea which strikes him. One has to develope the astral and mental sight in order to see the thought-form, and trace from whom it conies. It is connected by vibration with its creator.

Sometimes such an idea may come in symbolic form; the serpent and elephant, for example, are often used to signify wisdom. There are many sets of symbolisms. Each ego has his own system, though some forms seem general in dreams. It is said that to dream of water signifies trouble of some sort, though I do not see any connection. But even though there be no real connection, an ego (or for that matter some other entity who desires to communicate) may use the symbol if he knows that it is understood by the personality. Water has no necessary relation to trouble, but an ego who could not convey a clear message to his personality, and knew that it held that peculiar belief about water, might very likely impress such a dream on its brain when he wished to warn it of some impending misfortune. When a passing thought crosses the mind, it is usually caused by suggestion. The power or thought and the multiplicity of thought-forms are tremendously great, and yet they are but little understood and taken into account.

In the ease of a particular idea coming into the mind, any one of half-a-dozen things may have happened. It is only speculation to offer suggestions in any particular case without actual knowledge of what took place. One is quite likely to be affected by one's own thought-forms. You may make thought-forms about a subject which will hover about you and persist proportionately to the energy you put into them; and these often react upon you just as though they were new suggestions from outside. In a place like Adyar any new-comer will find a mass of thought-forms already floating about, and probably he may accept some of these ready-made rather than set to work to produce new ones for himself. One should take up thought-forms with caution. I have seen a man take up thought-forms and be converted by them when they were quite wrong, and he himself had before been perfectly accurate in his opinion. Sometimes, however, it is advantageous to try to put oneself in touch with a thought-form at the beginning of study.

There are upon the astral plane vast numbers of thought-forms of a comparatively permanent nature, often the result of the accumulative work of many generations of people . Many such thought-forms refer to alleged religious history, and the seeing of them by sensitive people is responsible for a great many quite genuine accounts given by untrained seers and seeresses - such for example as Anne Catherine Emmerich. She had visions in the most perfect detail of the events of the passion of Jesus exactly as it is recorded in the Gospels, including many events which we know never really occurred. Yet I have no doubt that the statements of that seeress were perfectly genuine; she was not labouring under an hallucination, but only under a mistake as to the nature of what she saw.

To read the records clearly and correctly needs special training; it is not a matter of faith or of goodness, but of a special kind of knowledge. There is nothing whatever to show that the saint in question had this particular form of knowledge; on the contrary, she probably never heard of such records at all. She would therefore most likely be quite incapable of reading a record clearly, and certainly, if she did happen to see one, she would be unable to distinguish it from any other kind of vision.

In all probability what she saw was a set of such collective thought-forms as we have described. It is well-known to all investigators that any great historical event upon which much is supposed to depend has been constantly thought of and vividly imaged to themselves by successive generations of people. Such scenes would be, for the English, the signing of Magna Charta by King John, and for the Americans the signing of the Declaration of Independence.

Now these vivid images which people make are real things, and are clearly to be seen by anyone who possesses a little psychic development. They are definite forms existing in the first place upon the mental plane, and wherever there is any strong emotion connected with them they are brought down to the astral plane and materialised there in astral matter. They are also perpetually strengthened by all the new thoughts which are ever being turned upon them. Naturally, different people imagine these scenes differently, and the eventual result is often something like a composite photograph; but the form in which such an imagination was originally cast largely influences the thought of all sensitives upon subject, and tends to make them image it as others have done.

This product of thought (often, be it observed, of quite ignorant thought) is much easier to see than the true record, for while, as we have said, the latter feat requires training, the former needs nothing but a glimpse of the mental plane, such as frequently comes to almost all pure and high-minded ecstatics. Indeed in many cases it does not need even this, because the thought-forms exist upon the astral levels as well.

Another point to be borne in mind is that it is not in the least necessary for the creation of such a thought-form that the scenes should ever have had any real existence. Few scenes from real history have been so strongly depicted by popular fancy in England as have some of the situations from Shakespeare's plays, from Bunyan's *Pilgrim's Progress,* and from various fairy stories, such as Cinderella or Aladdin's Lamp. A clairvoyant obtaining a glimpse of one of these collective thought-forms might very easily suppose that he had come across the real foundation of the story; but since he knows these tales to be fictions he would be more likely to think that he had simply dreamt of them.

Now, ever since the Christian religion materialised the glorious conceptions originally committed to its charge, and tried to represent them as a series of events in a human life, devout souls in all countries under its sway have been striving as a pious exercise to picture the supposed events as vividly as possible. Consequently we are here provided with a set of thought-forms of quite exceptional strength and prominence - a set which can hardly fail to attract the attention of any ecstatic the bent of whose mind is at all in their direction. No doubt they were seen by Anne Catherine Emmerich, and by many another. But when such clairvoyants come, in the course of their progress, to deal with the realities of life, they will be taught, as are those who have the inestimable privilege of the guidance of the Masters of Wisdom, how to distinguish between the result of devout but ignorant thought and the imperishable record which is the true memory of nature; and then they will find that these scenes, to which they have devoted so much attention, were but symbols of truths higher and wider and grander far than they had ever dreamt, even in the highest flights which were made possible for them by their splendid purity and piety.

THOUGHT AND ELEMENTAL ESSENCE

Elemental essence when moulded by thought adopts a certain colour - a colour which is expressive of the nature of the thought or feeling. Of course all that this really means is that the essence composing the thought-form is for the time compelled to vibrate at a certain definite rate by the thought which is ensouling it. The evolution of the elemental essence is to learn to respond to all possible rates of undulation; when therefore a thought holds it for a time vibrating at a certain rate, it is helped to this extent, that it has now become habituated to that particular rate of oscillation, so that next time it comes within reach of a similar one, it will respond to it much more readily than before.

Presently those atoms of essence, having passed back again into the general mass, will be caught up again by some other thought, and will then have to swing at some totally different rate, and so will evolve a little further by acquiring the capacity to respond to the second type of undulation. So by slow degrees the thoughts, not only of man, but also of nature-spirits and devas, and even of animals so far as they do think, are evolving the elemental essence which surrounds them - slowly teaching here a few atoms, and there a few atoms, to respond to this or that different rate of oscillation, until at last a stage will be reached when all the particles of the essence shall be ready to answer at any moment to any possible rate of vibration, and that will be the completion of their evolution.

It is for this reason that the occultist avoids when possible the destruction of an artificial elemental, even when it is of evil character, preferring rather to defend himself or others against it by using the protection of a shell. It is possible to dissipate an artificial elemental instantly by an exertion of will-power, just as it is possible on the physical plane to kill a poisonous snake in order that it may do no further harm; but neither course of action would commend itself to an occultist, except in very unusual circumstances.

Whether the thought ensouling it is evil or good makes no difference whatever to the essence; all that is required for its development is to be used by thought of some kind. The difference between the good and the evil would be shown by the quality of essence which it affected, the evil thought or desire needing for its appropriate expression the coarser or denser matter, while the higher thought would require correspondingly finer and more rapidly vibrating matter for its covering. There are plenty of undeveloped people always thinking the coarser lower thoughts, and their very ignorance and grossness are made use of by the great Law as evolutionary forces to help on a certain stage of the work that is to be done. It is for us, who have learnt a little more than they, to strive ever to think the high and holy thoughts which cause the evolution of a finer kind of elemental matter, and so to work in a field where at present the labourers are far too few.

Fourth Section: Psychic Faculties

PSYCHIC POWERS

The possession of psychic powers does not necessarily involve high moral character, any more than does the possession of great physical strength. It is quite true that the man who enters the Path of Holiness will presently find such powers developing in him, but it is quite possible to gain many of the powers without the holiness. Powers can be developed by any one who will take the trouble, and a man may learn clairvoyance or mesmerism just as he may learn to play the piano, if he is willing to go through the necessary hard work. It is far better and safer for the vast majority of people to work at the development of character, to try to fit themselves for the Path, and to leave the powers to unfold in due course, as they certainly will. Some people are in too much of a hurry to do this, and set themselves to force the powers sooner. Well, if they are quite certain that they desire them only for the sake of helping others, and that they are wise enough to use them rightly, it may be that no harm will come of it; but it is not easy to be quite certain on these points, and the slightest deflection from the right line will mean disaster.

If a man must try to obtain the powers, there are two ways open to him; of course there are many more than two methods, but I mean that they all fall under two heads - the temporary and the permanent. The temporary method is to deaden the physical sense in some way - actively by drugs, by self-hypnotisation, or by inducing giddiness, for example, or passively by being mesmerised - so that the astral senses may come to the surface. The permanent way is to work at the development of the ego, so that he may be able to control the lower vehicles and use them as he wishes.

It is somewhat like controlling a troublesome horse. A man who knows nothing of riding may so stupefy a horse with drugs that he can somehow keep on his back, but that will not in the least enable him to control any other horse. So a man who stupefies his physical body may use his astral senses to some extent, but that will in no way help him to manage another physical body in his next birth. The man who will take the far greater trouble of learning to ride properly can then manage any horse, and the man who developes his ego until it can manage one set of vehicles will be able to control any others that are given to him in future lives. This latter course means real evolution; the other does not necessarily involve anything of the sort. It does not follow that everyone who is on the Path must have psychic powers; they are not absolutely necessary until a certain stage of it is reached.

Short of the real psychic powers there are various other methods by which men endeavour to obtain some of the same results. One of these, for example, is the repetition of invocations. Charms and ceremonies may sometimes produce an effect; it depends upon the way in which they are performed. I have seen a man who was able to answer questions in rather a curious way; he first entranced himself by repeating charms over and over again, and his invocations not only influenced himself, but also attracted nature-spirits who went for the desired information, obtained it and put it into his mind.

Lord Tennyson, by repeating his own name over and over again and drawing his consciousness further and further within himself, raised himself into touch with the ego, and then all this life seemed to him child's play, and death nothing but the entrance into a greater life.

The result of many repetitions may often be to throw oneself into the trance condition; but this is not a training of the ego. Its effects last at most only for one life, whereas the powers which result from real spiritual development reappear in subsequent bodies. The man who entrances himself by the repetition of words or charms may probably return as a medium or at least a mediumistic person in his next life, and it must be remembered that mediumship is not a power, but a condition.

Such repetitions may easily lead on to the coarser physical mediumship (by which I mean the sitting for materialisation and sensational phenomena of all sorts) which is frequently injurious to health. I do not know that mere trance-speaking injures the body quite so much, though considering the feebleness of the platitudes which are usually the staple of the communications it might certainly be thought likely to weaken the mind!

Let us consider what it is that is required from a physical medium. When an entity on the astral plane, whether it be a dead man or a nature-spirit, wants to produce any result on dense physical matter - to play on a piano for example, to cause raps, or to hold a pencil in order to write - he needs an etheric body through which to work, because astral matter cannot act directly on the lower forms of physical matter, but requires the etheric matter as an intermediary to convey the vibrations from the one to the other - much in the same way as a fire cannot be lighted with paper and coals alone; the wood is needed as an intermediary, otherwise the paper will all burn away without affecting the coal.

That which constitutes a man a physical medium is a want of cohesion between the etheric and the dense parts of the physical vehicle, so that an astral entity can easily withdraw a good deal of the man's etheric body and use it for his own purposes. Of course he returns it - in fact its constant tendency is to flow back to the medium, as may be seen from the action of the materialised form - but still the frequent withdrawal of part of the man's body in this way cannot but cause great disturbance and danger to his health.

The etheric double is the vehicle of vitality, the life-principle, which is perpetually circulating through our bodies; and when any part of our etheric double is withdrawn that life-circulation is checked and its current broken. A terrible drain on vitality is then set up, and that is why the medium is so often in a state of collapse after a séance, and also why so many mediums in the long run become drunkards, having first taken to stimulants in order to satisfy the dreadful craving for support which is caused by this sudden loss of strength.

It can never under any circumstances be a good thing for the health to be constantly subjected to such a drain as this, even though in some cases the more intelligent and careful "spirits" try to pour strength into their medium after a séance, in order to make up for the loss, and thus support him without absolute breakdown for a much longer period than would otherwise be possible.

In cases of materialisation, dense physical matter, probably chiefly in the form of gases or liquids, is frequently borrowed from the body of the medium, who actually decreases temporarily in size and weight; and when it takes place, naturally that is a further source of serious disturbance to all the functions.

Of the mediums with whom I used to have sittings thirty years ago one is now blind, another died a confirmed drunkard, and a third, finding himself menaced apoplexy and paralysis, escaped with his life only by giving up séances altogether.

Another form of materialisation is that in which the astral body is temporarily solidified. The ordinary materialising "spirit" takes his material from the medium, because that, being already specialised, is more easily arranged into human form, and more readily condensed and moulded than free ether would be. No one connected with any school of white magic would think it right to interfere with the etheric double of any man in order to produce a materialisation, nor would he disturb his own if he wished to make himself visible at a distance. He would simply condense, and build into and around his astral body a sufficient quantity of the surrounding ether to materialise it, and hold it in that form by an effort of will as long as he needed it.

When part of the etheric double is removed from the physical, as in the case of materialisation of the ordinary kind, a connecting current is visible to any one capable of seeing matter in the etheric condition; but the method of connection with the astral body is entirely different, for nothing in the nature of a cord or current of astral matter joins the two forms. Yet it is difficult to express in terms of this plane the exact nature of the exceeding closeness of the sympathy between them; perhaps the nearest approximation we can get to the idea is that of two instruments tuned to exactly the same pitch, so that whatever note is struck upon one of them instantly evokes a precisely corresponding sound from the other.

There is no harm in using will-power to cure diseases, so long as no money or other consideration is taken for what is done. There are several methods; the simplest is the pouring in of vitality. Nature will cure most diseases if the man can be strengthened and supported while she is left to do her work. This is especially true of the various nervous diseases which are so painfully common at the present day. The rest-cure, which is often advised for them, is quite the best thing that can be suggested, but recovery might often be greatly hastened if vitality were poured into the patient in addition. Any man who has surplus vitality may direct it by his will to a particular person; when he is not doing that, it simply radiates from him in all directions, flowing out principally through the hands. If a man is depleted of strength so that his spleen does not do its work properly, the pouring in of specialised vitality is often of the greatest help to him in keeping the machinery of the body going until he is able to manufacture it for himself.

Many minor diseases can be cured merely by increasing the circulation of the vitality. A headache, for example, is generally due either to a slight congestion of blood, or to a similar congestion of the vital fluid; in either case a clairvoyant who can see the obstruction may deal with it by sending a strong current through the head, and washing away the congested matter. A man who cannot see can also produce this result, but since he does not know exactly where to direct this force he generally wastes a great deal of it.

Sometimes people perform cures by imposing their own magnetic conditions upon others. This is based on the theory (which is quite correct) that all disease is in harmony of some sort, and that if perfect harmony can be restored the disease will disappear. So in this case the person who wishes to effect a cure first raises his own vibrations to the highest degree which is possible for him, fills himself with thoughts of love and health and harmony, and then proceeds to enfold the patient within his aura, the idea being that his own powerful vibrations will overbear these of the patient, and gradually bring him into the same harmonious and healthy condition. This method is often effective, but we must remember that it involves imposing the whole of the personality of the magnetiser upon the patient, which may not always be desirable for either of the persons concerned.

One should take care not to be caught or entangled on the astral plane, as a man easily may be, and that through his virtues as well as his vices, if he be not exceedingly cautious. For example, it is possible to affect others by thought, and thus obtain whatever is wanted from them, and the temptation of this power to an ordinary man would be overwhelming. Again, you could easily force those whom you love out of a wrong path into a right one if you wished, but this you must not do; you may only persuade and argue. Here again is a temptation. You may by force prevent your friend from doing wrong, but often the weakening effect of the compulsion on his mind will do him more harm than the wrong-doing from which you save him. Drunkenness can be cured by mesmerising the man, but it is far better to persuade him gradually to conquer the weakness for himself, since this is a thing which he will have to do in some life. It is said that in some cases the man has yielded himself to this awful habit for so long that his will power is entirely in abeyance, and he actually has not the strength to refrain; and it is claimed that for such a man mesmerism is necessary, for it is the only method of giving him an opportunity to reassert himself as a human being, and to regain some sort of control of his vehicles. This may be so, and I can well understand the desire to save by any lawful means the soul which has come to so dire a pass;

yet even then I would counsel the greatest care in the use of mesmerism, and in the choice of the mesmerist.

A man can use the faculties of his astral body without moving away from his physical vehicle. That is called the possession of astral powers in the waking state, and is a definite stage in development. But it is more usual for the astral body to leave the physical when it is intended to operate or observe at a distance from the physical body.

The Indian term "sky-walker" generally refers only to one who is able thus to travel in his astral body. But sometimes also it means levitation, in which the physical body is lifted and floats in the air. In India this happens to some ascetics, and some of the greatest of Christian saints have in deep meditation been thus raised from the ground. It involves, however, the expenditure of a good deal of force. When a disciple is commissioned to undertake some special work for humanity, the adepts may give to him for the purpose some extra force, but though he is left free to use it as he pleases, he must not fritter it away uselessly. So it happens that even those who can produce these strange effects at will do not do so to amuse themselves or others, but only for real work. It would be quite possible for some disciple to use this force for the purpose of carrying his physical body through the air to a distant place; but as that would mean a tremendous expenditure of force, it is not likely that he would so use it unless definitely directed to do so.

On the other hand there have been cases in which such powers were used - for example, to save a man from undeserved suffering. There was once a case in which a young man was accused of the forgery of an important document. He was to a certain extent technically guilty, although quite innocent of any evil intention. He had very foolishly imitated a certain signature upon a blank sheet of paper, and then some one who was unfriendly to him had obtained possession of the sheet of paper, written in certain instructions above the signature, and then cleverly cut the paper so as to make it appear to be a letter conveying orders. The accused had to admit that the signature was in his writing, but his account of the circumstances under which it was written was not unnaturally disbelieved, and it seemed impossible for him to escape the most terrible consequences. But it happened that one of our Masters was called as a witness to testify to the handwriting of the prisoner. The sheet was handed to Him with the question:

"Do you recognise that handwriting as that of the prisoner?"

The Master just glanced at it, and instantly returned it, saying:

"Is this the sheet which you intended to give me?"

In that instant the sheet had become an absolute blank! The counsel for the prosecution of course supposed that in some utterly incomprehensible way he had mislaid the paper; but for want of it the prosecution fell through, and so the young man was saved.

CLAIRVOYANCE

The possession of clairvoyant power is a very great privilege and a very great advantage, and if properly and sensibly used it may be a blessing and a help to its fortunate holder, just as surely as, if it is misused, it may often be a hindrance and a curse. The principal dangers attendant upon it arise from pride, ignorance, and impurity, and if these be avoided, as they easily may be, nothing but good can come from it.

Pride is the first great danger. The possession of a faculty which, though it is the heritage of the whole human race, is as yet manifested only very occasionally, often causes the ignorant clairvoyant to feel himself (or still more frequently herself) exalted above his fellows, chosen by the Almighty for some mission of world-wide importance, dowered with a discernment that can never err, selected under angelic guidance to be the founder of a new dispensation, and so on. It should be remembered that there are always plenty of sportive and mischievous entities on the other side of the veil who are ready and even anxious to foster all such delusions, to reflect and embody all such thoughts, and to fill whatever role of archangel or spirit-guide may happen to be suggested to them. Unfortunately it is so fatally easy to persuade the average man that he really is a very fine fellow at bottom, and quite worthy to be the recipient of a special revelation, even though his friends have through blindness or prejudice somehow failed hitherto to appreciate him.

Another danger, perhaps the greatest of all because it is the mother of all others, is ignorance. If the clairvoyant knows anything of the history of his subject, if he at all understands the conditions of those other planes into which his vision is penetrating, he cannot of course suppose himself the only person who was ever so highly favoured, nor can he feel with self-complacent certainty that it is impossible for him to mistake. But when he is, as so many are, in the densest ignorance as to history, conditions and everything else, he is liable in the first place to make all kinds of mistakes as to what he sees, and secondly to be the easy prey of all sorts of designing and deceptive entities from the astral plane. He has no criterion by which to judge what he sees, or thinks he sees, no test to apply to his visions or communications, and so he has no sense of relative proportion or the fitness of things, and he magnifies a copy-book maxim into a fragment of divine wisdom, a platitude of the most ordinary type into an angelic message. Then again, for want of common knowledge on scientific subjects he will often utterly misunderstand what his faculties enable him to perceive, and he will in consequence gravely promulgate the grossest absurdities.

The third danger is that of impurity. The man who is pure in thought and life, pure in intention and free from the taint of selfishness, is by that very fact guarded from the influence of undesirable entities from other planes. There is in him nothing upon which they can play; he is no fit medium for them. On the other hand all good influences naturally surround such a man, and hasten to use him as a channel through which they may act, and thus a still further barrier is erected about him against all which is mean and low and evil. The man of impure life or motive, on the contrary, inevitably attracts to himself all that is worst in the invisible world which so closely surrounds us; he responds readily to it, while it will be hardly possible for the forces of good to make any impression upon him.

But a clairvoyant who will bear in mind all these dangers, and strive to avoid them, who will take the trouble to study the history and the rationale of clairvoyance, who will see to it that his heart is humble and his motives are pure - such a man may assuredly learn very much from these powers of which he finds himself in possession, and may make them of the greatest use to him in the work which he has to do.

Having first taken good heed to the training of his character, let him observe and note down carefully any visions which come to him; let him patiently endeavour to disentangle the core of truth in them from the various accretions and exaggerations which are sure at first to be almost inextricably confused with them; let him in every possible way test and check them and endeavour to ascertain which of them are reliable, and in what way these reliable ones differ from others which have proved less trustworthy - and he will very soon find himself evolving order out of chaos, and learning to distinguish what he can trust and what he must for the present put aside as incomprehensible.

He will probably find in course of time that he gets impressions, whether by direct sight or only by feeling, in reference to the various people with whom he comes into contact. Once more the careful noting down of every such impression as soon as it occurs, and the impartial testing and checking of it as opportunity offers, will soon show our friend how far these feelings or visions are to be relied on; and as soon as he finds that they are correct and dependable he has made a very great advance, for he is in possession of a power which enables him to be of far more use to those among whom his work lies than he could be if he knew only as much about them as can be seen by the ordinary eye.

If, for example, his sight includes the auras of those around him, he can judge from what it shows him how best to deal with them, how to bring out their latent good qualities, how to strengthen their weaknesses, how to repress what is undesirable in their characters. Again, his power may often enable him to observe something of the processes of nature, to see something of the working of the non-human evolutions which surround us, and thus to acquire most valuable knowledge on all kinds of recondite subjects. If he happens to be personally acquainted with some clairvoyant who has been put under regular training he has of course a great advantage, in that he can without difficulty get his visions examined and tested by one upon whom he can rely.

Generally speaking, then, the course to be recommended to the untrained clairvoyant is that of exceeding patience and much watchfulness; but with this hope ever before his eyes, that assuredly if he makes use of the talent entrusted to him it cannot but attract the favourable notice of Those who are ever watching for instruments which can be employed in the great work of evolution, and that when the right time comes he will receive the training which he so earnestly desires, and will thus be enabled definitely to become one of those who help the world.

Special training should be arranged from early childhood for clairvoyant children. The modern system of education tends to suppress all psychic faculties, and most young people are overstrained by their studies. In Greece and Rome these psychic children were promptly isolated as vestal virgins or postulants for the priesthood, and specially trained. There is a natural tendency in the present day, apart from education, to repress these faculties. The best way to prevent the loss of these to the world is to put the boys into some sort of monastery where the monks know about the higher life and try to live it, for family life is not suitable for this development. Where such clairvoyance appears it ought to be encouraged, for many additional investigators are wanted for the Society's work, and those who begin young are likely to adapt themselves to it most readily.

People who are psychic by birth generally use the etheric double a great deal. People who possess what has sometimes been called "etheric sight" - that is, sight capable of observing physical matter in a state of exceedingly fine subdivision, though not yet capable of discerning the subtler matter of the astral plane - frequently see, when they look keenly at any exposed portion of the human body, such as the face or the hand, multitudes of tiny forms, such as dice, stars, and double pyramids. These belong neither to the thought-plane nor to the astral, but are purely physical, though of exceeding minuteness. They are simply the physical emanation from the body, which is always taking place - the waste matter, consisting largely of finely-divided salts, which is constantly being thrown out in this manner. The character of these tiny particles varies from many causes. Naturally loss of health often alters them entirely, but any wave of emotion will affect them to a greater or lesser extent, and they even respond to the influence of any definite train of thought.

Professor Gates is reported as saying (a) that the material emanations of the living body differ according to the states of the mind as well as the conditions of the physical health; (b) that these emanations can be tested by the chemical reactions of some salts of selenium; (c) that these reactions are characterised by various tints or colours according to the nature of the mental impressions; (d) that forty different emotion-products, as he calls them, have already been obtained.

People sometimes see animated particles quivering with intense rapidity, and dashing about in the air before them. This again shows the possession of much increased physical power, not of mental. It is unfortunately only too common for the person who gains for the first time a glimpse of astral or even of etheric matter to jump at once to the conclusion that he is at least upon the mental level, if not upon the nirvânic, and holds in his hand the key to all the mysteries of the entire solar system. All that will come in good time, and these grander vistas will assuredly open before him one day; but he will hasten the coming of that desirable consummation if he makes sure of each step as he takes it, and tries fully to understand and make the best of what he has, before desiring more. Those who begin their experience with nirvânic vision are few and far between; for most of us, progress must be slow and steady, and the safest motto for us is festina lente.

I should not advise anyone to allow himself to be thrown into mesmeric sleep for the purpose of gaining clairvoyant experiences. The domination of the will by that of another produces effects that few people realise. The will of the victim becomes weaker, and is more liable to be acted upon by others. In the scheme of things no man is forced to do anything; he is taught by receiving always the result of his actions; and it is better to allow clairvoyant powers to come gradually in the natural course of evolution, rather than to try to force them in any way.

We must not always assume that a man who sees something pertaining to higher planes is necessarily becoming clairvoyant. By clairvoyance, for example, we may undoubtedly see an apparition, but on the other hand there are various other ways in which a man may see or suppose himself to see something which to him would be exactly the same as an apparition.

The apparition of a dead person may be (a) one's own imagination, (b) a thought-form produced by another person, (c) or by the person seen, (d) an impersonation, (e) the etheric double of the person, or (f) the real person actually there. In the last case one of three things must have happened - that is, supposing that the apparition is a dead or sleeping person in his astral body, and that the man who sees him is himself in his physical body and wide awake. Either (a the dead man has materialised himself, in which case of course he is for the time a physical object, which may be seen by any number of people with ordinary physical sight; (b) the dead man is in his astral body, in which case only those possessing astral sight can perceive him; he has probably succeeded by some special effort in temporarily opening that sight for the person to whom he wishes to show himself, and is therefore most likely visible to that one person only, and not to any others who may happen to be present; or, (c) the dead man has mesmerised the living, so as to impose upon him the idea that he sees a figure which is not really visible to him, though it may be really present.

If the apparition be an etheric double, it will not stray far away from the dense body to which it belongs or used to belong. An unpractised apparition - one who is new to the astral plane - often shows traces of the habits of his earth-life. He will enter and depart by a door or a window, not yet realising that he can pass through the wall just as easily. I have even seen one squeeze through the crack of a locked door; he might as well have tried the key-hole! But he moves as he has been accustomed to move - as he thinks of himself as moving. For the same reason an apparition often walks upon the earth, when he might just as well float through the air.

It is a mistake to think that if you see a vision, it must necessarily mean something for you, or be specially sent to you. If you for the moment become sensitive, you see what happens to be there.

Suppose I am sitting in a room, and a curtain is drawn across the window, so that the street outside is invisible to me. Suppose the wind lifts the curtain for a moment, so that I get a glimpse of the street, I shall then see whatever happens to be passing at that moment. Let us imagine that I see a little girl in a red cloak, carrying a basket. That little girl is probably going about her own business, or perhaps her mother's; should I not be very foolish if I chose to fancy that she had been sent there especially for me to see, and began to worry myself as to what could be symbolised by the red cloak and the basket? A flash of clairvoyance is usually just the accidental lifting of a curtain, and generally what is seen has no special relation to the seer. There may occasionally be instances in which the curtain is intentionally lifted by a friend because something of personal interest is passing; but we must not be too ready to assume that that is the case.

Among the real psychic powers, however, which are attained by slow and careful self-development, there are some which are of very great interest. For example, for one who can function freely in the mental body there are methods of getting at the meaning of a book, quite apart from the ordinary process of reading it. The simplest is to read from the mind of one who has studied it; but this is open to the objection that one gets not the real meaning of the work but that student's conception of the meaning, which may be by no means the same thing. A second plan is to examine the aura of the book - a phrase which needs a little explanation for those not practically acquainted with the hidden side of things.

An ancient manuscript stands in this respect in a somewhat different position from a modern book. If it is not the original work of the author himself, it has at any rate been copied word by word by some person of a certain education and understanding, who knew the subject of the book, and had his own opinions about it. It must be remembered that copying (done usually with a stylus) is almost as slow and emphatic as engraving; so that the writer inevitably impresses his thought strongly on his handiwork. Any manuscript, therefore, even a new one, has always some sort of thought-aura about it which conveys its general meaning, or rather one man's idea of its meaning and his estimate of its value. Every time it is read by anyone an addition is made to that thought-aura, and if it be carefully studied the addition is naturally large and valuable.

This is equally true of a printed volume. A book which has passed through many hands has an aura which is usually better balanced than that of a new one, because it is rounded off and completed by the divergent views brought to it by its many readers; consequently the psychometrisation of such a book generally yields a fairly full comprehension of its contents, though with a considerable fringe of opinions not expressed in the book, but held by its various readers.

On the other hand, a book used in a public library is not infrequently as unpleasant psychically as it usually is physically, for it becomes loaded with all kinds of mixed magnetisms, many of them of a most unsavoury character. The sensitive person will do well to avoid such books, or if necessity compels him to use them he will be wise to touch them as little as may be, and rather to let them lie upon a table than to hold them in his hand.

Another factor to be remembered with regard to such book is that a volume written upon a special subject is most likely to be read by a particular type of person, and these readers leave their impress upon the aura of the volume. Thus a book violently advocating some sectarian religious views is not read except by persons who sympathise with its narrowness, and so it soon developes a decidedly unpleasant aura; and in the same way a book of an indecent or prurient nature quickly becomes loathsome beyond description. Old books containing magical formulae are often for this reason most uncomfortable neighbours. Even the language in which a book is printed indirectly affects its aura, by limiting its readers largely to men of a certain nationality, and so by degrees endowing it with the more prominent characteristics of that nationality.

In the case of a printed book there is no original copyist, so that at the beginning of its career it usually carries nothing but disjointed fragments of the thought of the binder and bookseller. Few readers at the present day seem to study so thoughtfully and thoroughly as did the men of old, and for that reason the thought-forms connected with a modern book are rarely so precise and clear-cut as those which surround the manuscripts of the past.

The third method of reading requires some higher powers, in order to go behind the book or manuscript altogether and get at the mind of its author. If the book is in some foreign language, its subject entirely unknown, and there is no aura around it to give any helpful suggestion, the only way is to follow back its history to see from what it was copied (or set up in type, as the case may be) and so to trace out the line of its descent until one reaches its author. If the subject of the work be known, a less tedious method is to psychometrise that subject, get into the general current of thought about it, and so find the particular writer required, and see what he thinks. There is a sense in which all the ideas connected with a given subject may be said to be local - to be concentrated round a certain point in space - so that by mentally visiting that point one can come into touch with all the converging streams of thought about that subject, though these are linked by millions of lines with all sorts of other subjects.

Another interesting power is that of magnification. There are two methods of magnification which may be used in connection with the clairvoyant faculty. One is simply an intensification of ordinary sight. It is obvious that when in common life we see anything, an impact of some sort is made upon the retina - upon its physical rods and cones. The effects there produced, or the vibrations set up, are transmitted, in some way by no means thoroughly understood, by the optic nerve to the grey matter of the brain. Clearly before the true man within can become conscious of what is seen, these impressions made upon the physical brain-matter must be transmitted from that to the etheric matter, from that in turn to the astral, and from that to the mental - these different degrees of matter being, as it were, stations on a telegraph-wire.

One method of magnification is to tap this telegraph-wire at an intermediate station - to receive the impression upon the etheric matter of the retina instead of upon the physical rods and cones, and to transfer the impression received directly to the etheric part of the brain By an effort of will the attention can be focussed in only a few of the etheric particles, or even in one of them, and in that way a similarity of size can be attained between the organ employed and some minute object which is to be observed.

A method more commonly used, but requiring somewhat higher development, is to employ the special faculty of the centre between the eyebrows. From the central portion of that can be projected what we may call a tiny microscope, having for its lens only one atom. In this way again we produce an organ commensurate in size with the minute objects to be observed. The atom employed may be either physical, astral or mental, but whichever it is it needs a special preparation. All its spirillae must be opened up and brought into full working order, so that it is just as it will be in the seventh round of our chain.

This power belongs to the causal body, so if an atom of lower level be used as an eye-piece a system of reflecting counterparts must be introduced. The atom can be adjusted to any subplane, so that any required degree of magnification can be applied in order to suit the object which is being examined. A further extension of the same power enables the operator to focus his own consciousness in that lens through which he looks, and then to project it to distant points. The same power, by a different arrangement, can be used for diminishing purposes when one wishes to view as a whole something far too large to be taken in at once by ordinary vision.

THE MYSTIC CHORD

Questions have often been asked as to the method by which a person at a distance of some thousands of miles can be instantly found by a trained clairvoyant. Apparently this remains somewhat of a mystery to many, so I will endeavour to give an explanation of the plan commonly adopted, though it is not easy to put it quite plainly. A clear expression of super-physical facts cannot be achieved in physical words, for the latter are always to some extent misleading even when they seem most illuminative.

Man's various forces and qualities, manifesting in his bodies as vibrations, send out for each vehicle what may be called a keynote. Take his astral body as an example. From the number of different vibrations which are habitual to that astral body there emerges a sort of average tone, which we may call the keynote of the man on the astral plane. It is obviously conceivable that there may be a considerable number of ordinary men whose astral keynote is practically the same, so that this alone would not suffice to distinguish them with certainty. But there is a similar average tone for each man's mental body, for his causal body, and even for the etheric part of his physical body; and there have never yet been found two persons whose keynotes were identical at all these levels, so as to make exactly the same chord when struck simultaneously.

Thus the chord of each man is unique, and it furnishes a means by which he can always be distinguished from the rest of the world. Among millions of primitive savages there may possibly be cases where development is as yet so slight that the chords are scarcely clear enough for the differences between them to be observed, but with any of the higher races there is never the least difficulty, nor is there any risk of confusion.

Whether the man be sleeping or waking, living or dead, his chord remains the same, and he can always be found by it. How can this be so, it may be asked, when he is resting in the heaven-world, and has therefore no astral or etheric body to emit the characteristic sounds? So long as the causal body itself remains, it has always attached to it its permanent atoms, one belonging to each of the planes, and therefore, wherever he goes, the man in his causal body carries his chord with him, for the single atom is quite sufficient to give out the distinctive sound.

The trained seer, who is able to sense the chord, attunes his own vehicles for the moment exactly to its notes, and then by an effort of will sends forth its sound. Wherever in the three worlds that man who is sought may be, this evokes an instantaneous response from him. If he be living in the physical body, it is quite possible that in that lower vehicle he may be conscious only of a slight shock, and may not in the least know what has caused it. But his causal body lights up instantly; it leaps up like a great flame, and this response is at once visible to the seer, so that by that one action the man is found, and a magnetic line of communication is established. The seer can use that line as a kind of telescope, or if he prefers he can send his consciousness flashing along it with the speed of light, and see from the other end of it, as it were.

The combination of sounds which will produce a man's chord is his true occult name; and it is in this sense that it has been said that when a man's true name is called he instantly replies, wherever he may be. Some vague tradition of this is probably at the back of the idea so widely spread among savage nations, that a man's real name is a part of him, and must be carefully concealed, because one who knows it has a certain power over him, and can work magic upon him. Thus also it is said that the man's true name is changed at each initiation, since each such ceremony is at once the official recognition and the fulfilment of a progress by which he has, as it were, raised himself into a higher key, putting an additional strain upon the strings of his instrument, and evoking from it far grander music, so that thence-forward his chord must be sounded differently. This name of the man must not be confused with the hidden name of the Augoeides, for that is the chord of the three principles of the ego, produced by the vibrations of the âtmic, buddhic and mental atoms, and the monad behind them.

In order to avoid such confusion we must keep clearly in mind the distinction between two manifestations of the man at different levels. The correspondence between these two manifestations is so close that we may almost consider the lower as the repetition of the higher. The ego is triple, consisting of âtmâ, buddhi, manas, three constituents each existing on its own plane - the âtmâ on the nirvânic, the buddhi on the buddhic, and the manas on the highest level of the mental. This ego inhabits a causal body, a vehicle built of the matter of the lowest of the three planes to which he belongs. He then puts himself further down into manifestation, and takes three lower vehicles, the mental, astral and physical bodies. His chord in this lower manifestation is that which we have been describing, and consists of his own note and those of the three lower vehicles.

Just as the ego is triple, so is the monad, and this also has its three constituents, each existing on its own plane; but in this case the three planes are the first, second and third of our system, and the nirvânic is the lowest of them instead of the highest. But on that nirvânic level it takes to itself a manifestation, and we call it the monad in its âtmic vehicle, or sometimes the triple âtmâ or triple spirit; and this is for it what the causal body is for the ego. Just as the ego takes on three lower bodies (mental, astral, physical), the first of which (the mental) is on the lower part of his own plane, and the lowest (the physical) two planes below, so the monad takes on three lower manifestations (which we commonly call âtmâ, buddhi, manas), the first of which is on the lower part of his plane, and the lowest two planes below that. It will thus be seen that the causal body is to the monad what the physical body is to the ego. If we think of the ego as the soul of the physical body, we may consider the monad as the soul of the ego in turn. Thus the chord of the Augoeides (the glorified ego in his causal body) consists of the note of the monad, with those of its three manifestations, âtmâ, buddhi, manas.

It must be understood that the chord cannot be accurately considered as sound in the sense in which we use that word on this plane. It has been suggested to me that an analogy which is in some respects better is that of the combination of lines in a spectrum. Each of the elements whose spectrum is known to us is instantly recognisable by it, in whatever star it may appear, no matter how great the distance may be - so long as the lines are bright enough to be seen at all. But the chord of which we have been speaking is not actually either heard or seen; it is received by a complex perception which requires the practically simultaneous activity of the consciousness in the causal body and in all the lower vehicles.

Even with regard to ordinary astral perception it is misleading (though practically unavoidable) to speak of "hearing" and "seeing." These terms connote for us the idea of certain sense-organs which receive impressions of a well-defined type. To see implies the possession of an eye, to hear implies the existence of an ear. But no such sense-organs are to be found on the astral plane. It is true that the astral body is an exact counterpart of the physical, and that it consequently shows eyes and ears, nose and mouth, hands and feet, just as the latter does. But when functioning in the astral body we do not walk upon the astral counterparts of our physical feet, nor do we see and hear with the counterparts of our physical eyes and ears.

Each particle in an astral body is capable of receiving a certain set of vibrations - those belonging to its own level, and those only. If we divide all astral vibrations into seven sets, just like seven octaves in music, each octave will correspond to a sub-plane, and only a particle in the astral body which is built of matter belonging to that subplane can respond to the vibrations of that octave. So "to be upon a certain sub-plane in the astral" is to have developed the sensitiveness of only those particles in one's astral body which belong to that subplane, so that one can perceive the matter and the inhabitants of that sub-plane only. To have perfect vision upon the astral plane means to have developed sensitiveness in all particles of the astral body, so that all the sub-planes are simultaneously visible.

Even though a man has developed the particles of one sub-plane only, if those are fully developed he will have on that sub-plane a power of perception equivalent to all of our physical senses. If he perceives an object at all, he will in that one act of perception receive from it an impression which conveys all that we learn down here through those various channels which we call the senses; he will simultaneously see, hear and feel it. The instantaneous perception which belongs to higher planes is still further removed from the clumsy and partial action of the physical senses.

In order to see how the chord helps the clairvoyant to find any given person, it must also be understood that the vibrations which cause it are communicated by the man to any object which is for some time in close contact with him, and therefore permeated by his magnetism. A lock of his hair, an article of clothing which he has worn, a letter which he has written - any of these is sufficient to give the chord to one who knows how to perceive it. It can also be obtained very readily from a photograph, which seems more curious, since the photograph need not have been in direct contact with the person whom it represents. Even untrained clairvoyants, who have no scientific knowledge of the subject, instinctively recognize the necessity of bringing themselves en rapport with those whom they seek by means of some such objects.

It is not necessary for the seer to hold the letter in his hand while examining the case, or even to have it near him. Having once held the letter and sensed the chord, he is able to remember it and reproduce it, just as any one with a good memory might remember a face after seeing it once. Some such link as this is always necessary to find a person previously unknown. We had recently a case of a man who had died somewhere in the Congo district, but as no photograph of him was sent by the friend who wrote about him, it was necessary first to seek that friend (somewhere in Scandinavia, I think) and make a contact in a roundabout way through him.

There are, however, other methods of finding people at a distance. One which is most effective requires higher development than that just described. A man who is able to raise his consciousness to the atomic level of the buddhic plane there finds himself absolutely in union with all his fellowmen - and therefore of course among the rest with the person whom he seeks. He draws his consciousness up into this unity along his own line, and he has only to put himself out again along the line of that other person in order to find him. There are always various ways of exercising clairvoyance, and each student employs that which comes most naturally to him. If he has not fully studied his subject, he often thinks his own method the only one possible, but wider knowledge soon disabuses him of that idea.

HOW PAST LIVES ARE SEEN

As a series of past lives of enthralling interest has recently been published in The Theosophist, many enquiries have been received as to the exact method by which the record of such lives is read by the investigators. It is not easy to explain the matter satisfactorily to those who have not themselves the power to see them, but some attempt at a description of the process may at least help students on the way towards comprehension.

To begin with, it is by no means easy to explain what the record is which is to be read. A suggestion leading towards an idea of it may perhaps be obtained by imagining a room with a huge pier-glass at one end. Everything which took place in that room would be reflected in that mirror. If we further suppose that mirror to be endowed with the properties of a kind of perpetual cinematograph, so that it records all which it reflects, and can afterwards under certain circumstances be made to reproduce it, we have advanced one stage towards understanding how the record presents itself. But we must add to our conception qualities which no mirror ever possessed - the power to reproduce all sounds as a phonograph does, and also to reflect and reproduce thoughts and feelings.

Then we must further try to understand what the reflection in a mirror really is. If two persons stand in relation to a mirror so that each sees in it not himself but the other, it is obvious that the same area of glass is reflecting the two images. Therefore if we suppose the glass to retain permanently every image which has ever been cast upon it (perhaps it actually does!) it is again clear that the same part of the glass must be simultaneously recording those two images. Move up and down and from side to side, and you will soon convince yourself that every particle of glass must be simultaneously recording every part of every object in the room, and that what you happen to see in it depends upon the position of your eye. Hence it also follows that no two people can ever see at the same moment exactly the same reflection in a mirror, any more than two people can see the same rainbow, because two physical eyes cannot simultaneously occupy exactly the same point in space.

What we have supposed to happen with regard to the particles of our mirror does really happen with regard to every particle of every substance. Every stone by the roadside contains an indelible record of everything that has ever passed it, but this record cannot (so far as we yet know) be recovered from it so as to be visible to the ordinary physical senses, though the more developed sense of the psychometrist perceives it without difficulty.

How is it possible, men ask, for an inanimate particle to register and reproduce impressions? The answer is that the particle is not inanimate, and that the life which ensouls it is part of the Divine Life. Indeed, another way in which one may attempt to describe the record is to say that it is the memory of the LOGOS Himself, and that each particle is somehow in touch with that part of that memory which includes the events which have taken place in its neighbourhood, or what we may call within sight of it. It is probable that what we call our memory is nothing but a similar power of coming into touch (though often very imperfectly) with that part of His memory which refers to events which we happen to have seen or known.

So we might say that every man carries about with him on the physical plane two memories of anything which he has seen - his brain-memory, which is often imperfect or inaccurate, and the memory enshrined in any unchanged particles of his body or of the clothes that he wears, which is always perfect and accurate, but is available only for those who have learnt how to read it. Remember also that the brain-memory may be inaccurate, not only because it is itself imperfect, but because the original observation may have been defective. Also that it may have been coloured by prejudice: we see, to a large extent, what we wish to see, and we can remember an event only as it appeared to us, though we may have seen it partially or wrongly. But from all these defects the record is entirely free.

It is obvious that a man's physical body can have neither a memory nor a record of a past incarnation in which it did not participate; and the same is true of his astral and mental bodies, since all these vehicles are new for each new incarnation. This at once shows us that the lowest level at which we can hope to get really reliable information about past lives is that of the causal body, for nothing below that can give us first-hand evidence. In those previous lives the ego in his causal body was present - at least a certain small part of him was - and so he is an actual witness; whereas all lower vehicles were not witnesses, and can only report what they have received from him. When we recollect how imperfect is the communication between the ego and the personality in the ordinary man, we shall at once see how entirely unreliable such second, third, or fourth-hand testimony is likely to be. One may sometimes obtain from the astral or mental bodies isolated pictures of events in a man's past life, but not a sequential and coherent account of it; and even those pictures are but reflections from the causal body, and probably very dim and blurred reflections.

Therefore to read past lives with accuracy the first thing necessary is to develope the faculties of the causal body. Turning those faculties upon the causal body of the man to be examined, we have before us the same two possibilities as in the case of the physical man. We can take the ego's own memory of what happened, or we can as it were psychometrise him and see for ourselves the experiences through which he has passed. The latter method is the safer, for even the ego, since he has seen these things through a past personality, may have imperfect or prejudiced impressions of them.

This then is the mechanism of the ordinary method of investigating past lives - to use the faculties of one's own causal body, and by its means to psychometrise the causal body of the subject. The thing could be done at lower levels by psychometrisation of the permanent atoms, but as this would be a much more difficult feat than the unfolding of the senses of the causal body it is not at all likely ever to be attempted successfully. Another method (which, however, requires much higher development) is to use the buddhic faculties - to become absolutely one with the ego under investigation, and read his experiences as though they were one's own - from within instead of from without. Both of these methods have been employed by those who prepared the series of lives which appear in The Theosophist, and the investigators have also had the advantage of the intelligent co-operation of the ego whose incarnations are described.

The physical presence of the subject whose lives are being read is an advantage, but not a necessity; he is useful if he can keep his vehicles perfectly calm, but if he becomes excited he spoils everything.

The surroundings are not specially important, but quiet is essential, as the physical brain must be calm if impressions are to be brought through clearly. Everything which comes down to the physical level from the causal body must pass through the mental and the astral vehicles, and if either of these is disturbed it reflects imperfectly, just as the least rippling of the surface of a lake will break up or distort the images of the trees or houses upon its banks. It is necessary also to eradicate absolutely all prejudices, otherwise they will produce the effect of stained glass; they will colour everything which is seen through them, and so give a false impression.

In looking at past lives it has always been our custom to retain full physical consciousness, so as to be able to make a note of everything while it is being observed. This is found to be a much safer method than to leave the physical body during the observations, and then trust to memory for their reproduction. There is however a stage at which this latter plan is the only one available, when the student, though able to use the causal body, can do so only while the physical vehicle is asleep.

The identification of the various characters encountered in these glimpses of the past sometimes presents a little difficulty, for naturally egos change considerably in the course of twenty thousand years or so. Fortunately, with a little practice it is possible to pass the record in review as rapidly or as slowly as may be desired; so when there is any doubt as to an identification we always adopt the plan of running quickly along the line of lives of the ego under observation, until we trace him to the present day. Some investigators, when they see an ego in some remote life, at once feel an intuition as to his present personality; but though such a flash of intuition may often be right, it may certainly also sometimes be wrong, and the more laborious method is the only one which is thoroughly reliable.

There are cases in which even after many thousands of years the egos of ordinary people are instantly recognisable; but that does not speak particularly well for them, because it means that during all that time they have made but little progress. To try to recognise twenty thousand years ago some one whom one knows at the present day is rather like meeting as an adult some one whom one knew long ago as a little child. In some cases recognition is possible; in other cases the change has been too great. Those who have since become Masters of the Wisdom are often instantly recognisable, even thousands of years ago, but that is for a very different reason. When the lower vehicles are already fully in harmony with the ego, they form themselves in the likeness of the Augoeides, and so change very little from life to life. In the same way when the ego himself is becoming a perfect reflection of the monad, he also changes but little, but gradually grows; and so he is readily recognisable.

In examining a past life the easiest way of all would be to let the record drift past us at its natural rate, but that would mean a day's work to look up the events of each day, and a lifetime spent upon each incarnation. As has been said, it is possible to accelerate or retard the passage of events, so that a period of thousands of years may be run through rapidly, or on the other hand any particular picture may be held as long as is desired, so that it may be examined in detail. The acceleration or retardation may perhaps be compared to the hastening or slackening of the movement of a panorama; a little practice gives the power to do this at will, but as in the case of the panorama, the whole record is really there all the time.

What I have described as the unrolling of the record rapidly or slowly at will is in reality a movement not of the record, but of the consciousness of the seer. But the impression which it gives is exactly as I have stated it. The records may be said to lie upon one another in layers, the more recent on the top and the older ones behind. Yet even this simile is misleading, because it inevitably suggests the idea of thickness, whereas these records occupy no more space than does the reflection on the surface of a mirror. When the consciousness passes through them, it does not really move in space at all; it rather puts on itself, as a kind of cloak, one or other of the layers of the record, and in doing so it finds itself in the midst of the action of the story.

One of the most tiresome tasks connected with this branch of enquiry is the determination of exact dates. In fact, some investigators frankly decline to undertake it, saying that it is not worth the trouble, and that a round number is sufficient for all practical purposes. Probably it is; yet there is a feeling of satisfaction in getting even details as accurate as possible, even at the cost of tedious counting up to very high numbers. Our plan is of course to establish certain fixed points and then use those as a basis for further calculation.

One such fixed point is the date 9,564 B.C., when the sinking of Poseidonis took place. Another is the date 75,025 B.C., for the commencement of the great previous catastrophe. In the course of the investigation of the lives of Alcyone we have thus established a number of points, up to the date of 22,662 B.C., and as those lives were worked backwards, and the intervals were therefore counted one by one and not all at once, the scheme was not too insufferably tedious, as it certainly would be with very large numbers. In certain cases astronomical means are also employed. A description of these different methods will be found in my book on Clairvoyance.

It is on the whole somewhat easier to read lives forwards than backwards, because in that case we are working with the natural flow of time instead of against it. So the usual plan is to run rapidly to some selected point in the past, and then work slowly forwards from that. It must be remembered that at first sight it is rarely possible to estimate accurately the relative importance of the minor events of a life, so we often skim over it first, to see from what actions or occurrences the really important changes flow, and then go back and describe those more in detail. If the investigator himself happens to be one of the characters in the life which he is examining, there opens before him the interesting alternative of actually putting himself back into that old personality, and feeling over again just what he felt in that ancient time. But in that case he sees everything exactly as he saw it then, and knows no more than he knew then.

Few of those who read the life-stories, which are often somewhat meagre outlines, will have any conception of the amount of labour which has been bestowed upon them - of the hours of work which have sometimes been given to the full comprehension of some trifling detail, so that the picture finally presented may be as nearly a true one as is possible. At least our readers may be sure that no pains have been spared to ensure accuracy, though this is often no easy task when we are dealing with conditions and modes of thought as entirely different from our own as though they belonged to another planet.

The languages employed are almost always unintelligible to the investigator, but as the thoughts behind the words lie open before him that matters little. On several occasions those who were doing the work have copied down public inscriptions which they could not understand, and have afterwards had them translated on the physical plane by someone to whom the ancient language was familiar.

A vast amount of work is represented by the sets of lives which are now appearing; may that labour bring its fruit in a more vivid realisation of the mighty civilisations of the past and a clearer comprehension of the working of the laws of karma and reincarnation. Since the first set of lives which appeared have culminated in the initiation of the hero in his present incarnation, they are surely a valuable study for those whose aspiration is to become the pupils of a Master of the Wisdom, for their own progress should be the more rapid when they have learnt how a brother has attained the goal towards which they are striving. This progress has been made the more easy for them because that brother has taken the trouble to record for us in that most admirable little book At the Feet of the Master the teachings which led him to that goal.

About a hundred and fifty of those who are at present members of the Theosophical Society are the prominent characters in the drama which lies before the readers of The Theosophist; and it is deeply interesting to note how those who in the past have often been linked by the ties of blood-relationship, though born this time in countries thousands of miles apart, are yet brought together by their common interest in Theosophical study, and bound to one another more closely by their love for the Masters than they could ever have been by any mere earthly connection.

There are two sources of possible error in examining the records clairvoyantly; first, personal bias, and secondly, limited views. There are fundamental differences of temperament, and these cannot but colour the views taken of other planes. The adept has a perfect perception of life, but below that level we are sure to have some prejudices. The man of the world magnifies unimportant details and omits all the important things, because he is in the habit of doing that in daily life; but on the other hand a man starting on the Path may, in his enthusiasm, lose for a time his touch with the ordinary human life from which he has emerged. Even then he has made a great advance, for those who see the inside of things are nearer to the truth than those who see only the outside.

The statements of clairvoyants may and must be coloured by opinions already formed, as was clearly the case with Swedenborg, who used a very narrow Christian terminology to describe the facts of the astral plane, and unquestionably saw many things through strong thought-forms which he had made in previous years. He started with certain definite preconceptions, and he made everything which he saw fit into those preconceptions. You know how it is possible down here on the physical plane to start with some preconception about a man and distort his most innocent words and actions to fit that preconception - to read into them ideas of which the unfortunate man never even dreamt. The same thing is possible on the astral plane if one is careless.

Theosophical investigators are thoroughly on their guard against this danger of personal bias, and use constant checks of all kinds to avoid it. To minimise the chance of error from this source the Masters usually select people of radically different types to work together.

Secondly, there is the danger of a limited view - of taking a part for the whole. For example, there has been much said of the corruption and black magic of later days in Poseidonis, but there existed there, at that very time, a secret society that was quite pure and had high aims. If it had happened that we had seen only this society, we might easily have thought of Poseidonis as a most spiritual country. It is possible, you see, that such limited views may be taken as applying to a whole region or community. Generalisations must be checked and verified. There is, however, a general aura of a time or a country, which usually prevents any great mistakes of this sort. A psychic who has not been trained to sense this general aura is often unconscious of it, and thus the untrained man falls into many errors. In fact, long continued observation shows that all untrained psychics are sometimes reliable and sometimes unreliable, and those who consult them always run a risk of being misled.

The records must not be thought of as originally inhering in matter of any kind, though they are reflected in it. In order to read them it is not necessary to come into direct contact with any particular grouping of matter, since they can be read from any distance, when a connection has once been made.

Nevertheless it is also true that each atom retains the record, or perhaps only possesses the power to put a clairvoyant en rapport with the record, of all that has ever happened within sight of it. It is by means of this quality that psychometry is possible. But there is this very curious limitation attached to it, that the normal psychometer sees by means of it only what he would have seen if he had been standing at the spot from which the object psychometrised has been taken. For example, if a man psychometrises a pebble which has been lying for ages in a valley, he will see only what has passed during those ages in that valley; his views will be limited by the surrounding hills, just as if he had stood for all those ages where the stone lay, and had witnessed all those things.

True, there is an extension of the psychometric power, by which a man may see the thoughts and feelings of the actors in his drama as well as their physical bodies, and there is also another extension by which, having first established himself in that valley, he may make it the basis of further operations, and so pass over the surrounding hills and see what lies beyond them, and also what has happened there since the stone was removed, and even what occurred before it in some manner arrived there. But the man who can do that will soon be able to dispense with the stone altogether. When we use the senses of the causal body on the counterparts of physical things, we see that every object is thus throwing off pictures of the past.

As we develop our inner consciousness and faculties, our life becomes a continuous one; we reach the consciousness of the ego, and then we can travel back even as far as the group-soul in which we lived the animal stage of our life, and look through animal eyes at the human beings of that period and the different world that flourished then. But there are no words to tell what is seen in that way, for the difference of outlook is beyond all expression.

Short of that continuous consciousness, however, there is no detailed memory - not even of the most important facts. For example, a person who knows the truth of reincarnation in one life does not necessarily carry his certainty over to the next. I forgot it myself, and so did Mrs. Besant. I did not know anything of it in this life, until I heard of it from outside, and then I instantly recognised its truth. Whatever we have known in the past will spring up in the mind in this way as a certainty when it is next presented before us.

As a child I used constantly to dream of a certain house, which I afterwards learned was a house which I had lived in a previous life. It was quite unlike any with which I was at that time familiar on the physical plane, for it was built round a central courtyard (with a fountain and statues and shrubs) into which all the rooms looked. I used to dream of it perhaps three times a week, and I knew every room of it and all the people who lived in it, and used constantly to describe it to my mother, and make ground-plans of it. We called it my dream-house. As I grew older I dreamt of it less and less frequently, until at last it faded from my memory altogether. But one day to illustrate some point my Master showed me a picture of the house in which I had lived in my last incarnation, and I recognised it immediately.

Any one may intellectually appreciate the necessity of reincarnation; but actually to prove it one must become, in the causal body, cognisant of the past and future. The only way of casting off the fetter of doubt is by knowledge and intelligent comprehension. Blind belief is a barrier to progress, but this does not mean that we are wrong in accepting intelligently the statements of those who know more than ourselves. There are no authoritative dogmas which must be accepted in the Theosophical Society. There are only statements of the results of investigation, which are offered in the belief that they will be as helpful to other minds as they have been to the investigators.

FORESEEING THE FUTURE

It is very difficult to explain how the future is foreseen, but there is no doubt whatever as to the fact. Apart from apparently accidental pictures and flashes of intuition, often effective but not under control, there are two ways in which the future may definitely be foreseen by means of the higher clairvoyance. One is quite readily explicable and comprehensible; the other is not explicable at all.

Even with only physical senses we may see enough to foretell certain things. If, for instance, we see a man leading an extravagant life of debauchery, we may safely predict that, unless he changes, he will presently lose both health and fortune. What we cannot tell by physical means is whether he will change or not. But a man who has the sight of the causal body could often tell this, because to him the reserve forces of the other would be visible; he could see what the ego thought of it all, and whether he was strong enough to interfere. No merely physical prediction is certain, because so many of the causes which influence life cannot be seen on this lower plane. But when we raise our consciousness to higher planes we can see more of the causes, and so can come much nearer to calculating the effects.

Obviously if all the causes could be perfectly seen and judged, all their results would be readily calculable. Perhaps none but the LOGOS can see all causes in His system, but an adept would surely be able to see all that could affect an ordinary man! so it is probable that by this method an adept could foretell the life of that man quite accurately. For the ordinary man has little will-power; karma assigns to him certain surroundings, and he is the creature of those surroundings; he accepts the fate marked out for him, because he does not know that he can alter it. A more developed man takes hold of his destiny and moulds it; he makes his future what he wills it to be, counteracting the karma of the past by setting fresh forces in motion. So his future is not so easily predicable; but no doubt even in this case an adept, who could see the latent will, could also calculate how he would use it.

That method of foretelling the future is entirely comprehensible, and it is clear that the chief events of any life could be prophesied along that line. But there is another way for which we cannot so easily account. One has only to raise the consciousness to a plane sufficiently high, to find the limitation which we call time disappearing, and the past, present and future spread out before us like an open book. How that can be reconciled with our freedom of action I am not prepared to say, but I can testify that the fact is so; when this sight is employed the future is simply there, down to the minutest detail. I believe myself that we are free to choose, though only within certain limits; yet a power, far higher than we, may well know how we shall choose. You know what your dog will do under certain conditions, but that does not in the least make him do it; so a power as much higher than man, as man is than the dog, may know quite well how man will use his fragment of free-will.

For it is only a fragment; the plan of the LOGOS is to trust us with a little freedom, and see how we use it. If we use it well and wisely, a little more is given to us; and so long as we continue to use it in harmony with His great intention of evolution, we shall find more and more freedom of choice coming to us. But if we are so foolish as to use it selfishly, so as to bring harm to ourselves and hinder His plan, we shall find ourselves cramped in our action and forced back into line. A child must have freedom to walk, even though that involves a risk of falling, or else he will never learn; but no one would let him make his experiment on the edge of a precipice. So we have freedom enough to do ourselves a little harm if we use it wrongly, but no freedom enough to destroy ourselves altogether.

Times of choice certainly come to us, but between those times we have often little option. When we have made our choice we must abide by its consequences. Looked at from above, human destiny seems rather like a network of railway lines. A man starts out on a locomotive, and chooses his line of rail; but when he has chosen it he must run along it, and cannot swerve to the right hand or the left until he reaches the first set of points. Then he may descend and set the points as he will, but having once set them and started on his way he must accept the consequences of his decision; he has no power to turn aside until the next point of choice comes in his way. We must not confuse free-will with freedom of action.

Now to possess fully the power of forecasting the future by either of the methods described means considerable development; but isolated pictures reflected from both of them may often be had at very much lower levels. What is called in Scotland second-sight appears to be an example; by that, a future event is often seen with quite a wealth of detail.

I remember reading of a case where a seer told a sceptic that a certain man known to them both would die at a given time, and furthermore gave a detailed description of his funeral, mentioning the pall-bearers by name. The sceptic ridiculed the whole prediction, but when the appointed time came the man indicated did die as had been prophesied. The sceptic was astonished, but still more annoyed, and he determined that the rest of the story should not come true, for he himself would interfere to falsify it. He therefore got himself appointed as one of the pall-bearers! but when the day came and the party was just about to start, he was called aside for a moment, and when he returned he found that the procession had already moved away, and that the pall-bearers were those who had been seen in the vision.

I have myself had similar pictures of scenes in the future - scenes of no interest to myself, and of no use so far as I could see; but they have always happened exactly as I had seen them, in every case where I have had the opportunity of verifying them.

The LOGOS has thought out the whole life of His system, not only as it is now, but as it has been at every moment in the past, and as it will be at every moment in the future. And His thought calls into existence that of which He thinks. These thought-forms are said to be on the cosmic mental plane - two whole sets of seven planes above our set of seven. He thinks out what He intends each of the planetary chains to do; He comes down to smaller details, for He thinks of the type of man for every root-race and sub-race, from the beginning of all, through the Lemurian, the Atlantean, the Aryan and the succeeding races. Thus we may say that on that cosmic mental plane the whole of the system was called into existence simultaneously by that thought - an act of special creation; and it must all be now simultaneously present to Him. So that it may well be that His mighty consciousness to some extent reflects itself even on very much lower levels, and somehow we sometimes catch faint glimpses of those reflection.

Fifth Section: Devas and Nature Spirits

THE AURA OF THE DEVA

The devas are a mighty kingdom of spirits, the next above humanity, just in the same way as the animal kingdom is the next one below it. You may think of them as great and glorious angels, but of course they are of many different kinds, and different degrees of evolution. None of them are so low down as to have physical bodies such as we have. The lowest kind are called kamadevas, and they have astral bodies, while the next higher variety have bodies made of lower mental matter, and so on. They will never be human, because most of them are already beyond that stage, but there are some of them who have been human beings in the past. When men come to the end of their evolution as men, and become something greater than human, several paths open before them, and one of these is to join this beautiful deva evolution.

Devas and men differ in appearance. For one thing devas are more fluidic - capable of far greater expansion and contraction. Secondly, they have a certain fiery quality which is clearly distinguishable from that of any ordinary human being. The only kind of human being with whom it might be possible to confound them would be the highly-developed - an arhat, for example, who had a large and well-arranged aura; but even then one who had seen both would not be likely to mistake them. The aura of the ordinary man is capable of a certain amount of temporary expansion. It has a definite size, which is the same as that of a section of the causal body, and as the causal body grows, that section becomes larger, and the man has a larger aura; but such increase comes only gradually.

If you remember the plates in Man Visible and Invisible, you will recollect that the ordinary man, as far as the causal body is concerned, is far from being fully developed. When you look at the causal body of the developed man, you will see that it is full of colour, so the first stages of improvement in the case of the ordinary man consists in its filling up, not its enlargement. He must get the ovoid filled with different colours, and then expansion begins.

If any sudden rush of feeling comes over the ordinary man, it shows itself, as depicted in the book, by the flashing in the aura, and out from it, of the colour of the quality expressed - rose for affection, blue for devotion or green for sympathy; and also in the pulsating bands of that colour, and in the general intensification of everything connected with that emotion. It does not do more than that for the ordinary man; an exceedingly vivid rush of affection, for example, fills the aura with rose and sends out thought-forms of that colour in the direction of its object; but it does not usually appreciably increase, even temporarily, the size of the aura.

The developed man, however, has already filled the causal body with colour, so in his case the effect produced by such a rush of affection or devotion or sympathy is not only to suffuse the body with colour and cause a great outrush of thought-forms, but also to produce a considerable temporary expansion, though the aura afterwards contracts to its normal size. Each such outrush of feeling makes the aura permanently just a little larger than before. The more it increases, the more power the man has to feel. Intellectual development also increases the aura, but in that case yellow is the predominant colour.

Remember that utterly unselfish affection or devotion belongs not to the astral but to the buddhic plane, and that is why when a wave of such feeling rushes over a man it causes great temporary expansion of his aura; yet it never increases to the same tremendous extent as with a deva. The fluctuations in the aura of a deva are so great as to be startling to those who are not used to them. One who recently did us the honour to pay us a visit at Adyar, to give us information about the foundation of the sixth root-race, had normally an aura of about one hundred and fifty yards in diameter; but when he became interested in the teaching which he was giving to us, that aura increased until it reached the sea, which is about a mile away from us.

No human being could feel sufficient emotion to produce such an increase as this. Even in the case of a Master the proportionate temporary enlargement would never be so great. I do not mean anything derogatory to the deva, when I say that the Master is steadier, and that the permanent growth of His aura would be as great as that of the deva, but the temporary expansion less in proportion. The texture of the deva's aura is, as it were, looser. The same extent of aura in a human being contains more matter, because it is more condensed or concentrated. The deva in question was no further advanced than an arhat, whose aura might probably extend a third of the distance. But it might easily happen that a clairvoyant who had not seen either before might realise only that he was surrounded by a cloud of glory in either case, and he probably would not know the difference.

Expansion and growth take place in the astral and mental bodies as well as in the causal. These three bodies are all of the same extent, although you must remember one is dealing with only sections, and even sections of sections. There used to be a theory afloat that the causal body of the ordinary was about the size of a pea, and that it gradually increased; but that is not correct. The undeveloped causal body is the same size as any other, until the expansion begins.

As I have said, the aura of a deva has fiery characteristics which are not easy to describe, though very readily recognisable. All of the colours are more fluidic, and of the nature of flame rather than of cloud. A man looks like an exceedingly brilliant, yet delicate cloud of glowing gas, but a deva looks like a mass of fire.

The human form inside the aura of a deva is very much less defined than in a man. He lives more in the circumference, more all over his aura than a man does. Ninety-nine per cent of the matter of a man's aura is within the periphery of the physical body, but the proportion is far less in the case of a deva. Devas usually appear as human beings of gigantic size. Somebody has suggested that there are devas who look as though they were feathered. There is some justification for this idea; I know exactly the appearance that that man was trying to describe, but it is not easy to put it into words. The great green devas whom I saw in Ireland have a very striking appearance, being enormous in size and most majestic. One cannot describe them accurately; in words it is only possible to approximate. The painters usually represent angels with wings and feathers, but I think where these are mentioned in the Christian scriptures they are always symbolical, for when real angels appear they are sometimes mistaken for human beings (as by Abraham, for example) ; so obviously they could not have had wings.

In many cases a deva may be distinguished by the form which he happens to be taking inside his ovoid. It is nearly always a human form. You remember that nature-spirits take human form almost invariably, but with a peculiarity of some sort - always a little odd. I should be disposed to say the same of the devas; but it would be wrong to think of their forms as in any way distorted, for they have a great dignity and majesty.

The devas produce thought-forms as we do, but theirs are not usually so concrete as ours until they reach a high level. They have a wide generalising nature, and are constantly making gorgeous plans. They have a colour-language, which is probably not as definite as our speech, though in certain ways it may express more.

As regards the size of the aura, that of an ordinary man extends about eighteen inches on each side of the body. If he puts his elbow against his side and stretches out his arm and hand, his finger-tips will be near the circumference. The average Theosophist may be a trifle larger than the quite uninterested person; but there are fine, large auras outside the Society as well. Intense feeling means a larger aura.

We may have a distortion of the aura - it may be a little out of shape. As I have explained before, most people have the small end of the egg upwards, but we who are students tend to grow larger at the top, because the characteristics which we are developing express themselves in matter which naturally floats in the upper part of the aura because of its specific gravity. The increased size of the aura is a prerequisite for initiation, and the qualifications should be visible in it. The aura of a Buddha is said in the books to be three miles in radius; at one stage below His, I have myself seen one which extends about two miles. It naturally increases with each initiation.

The devas do not come along our line of development, and do not take such initiations as we do, for the two kingdoms converge at a point higher than the adept. There are ways in which a man can enter the deva evolution, even at our own stage, or lower.

You ask if the devas are often near at hand and willing to teach men. They are usually quite willing to expound and exemplify subjects along their own line to any human being who is sufficiently developed to appreciate them. Much instruction is being given in this way; but most people have not prepared themselves for it yet, and so are unable to profit by it. We know nothing of any rule or limit for the work of the devas; they have more lines of activity than we can imagine.

There are usually plenty of them here at Adyar. We have many great advantages here, where the Masters come so frequently. In order to see them, all that is required is a little clairvoyance at the right moment. There is a stimulus from these Beings, which some feel in one way and some in others. Perhaps in the earlier incarnation of the Lord Gautama as the first Zoroaster, the fire which is one of the signs of His development may have been one of the reasons why He was mistaken for a deva. It is said that during meditation flames leapt from the aura of the Lord Buddha; but we must remember that an ordinary thought-form would often appear flame-like to a person who was not used to such things. The shining of the Christ at the transfiguration is a similar case.

There are plenty of glorious influences all around us here, but their effect upon each one of us can be in proportion to his receptivity. We can take from all this just what we make ourselves fit to take, and no more. A person who is thinking of himself all the while may bathe in this glowing magnetism for a year, and not be one iota the better for it. He may even be the worse; for these tremendously strong vibrations tend to intensify a man's qualities, and sometimes the undesirable are strengthened as well as the desirable; or he may be altogether upset, and become unbalanced and hysterical. To a man who is wise enough to take it, a stay at Adyar is an opportunity such as few men have ever had during history; but what we make of it depends entirely upon ourselves.

THE SPIRIT OF A TREE

The spirit of a great tree, such as a banyan, not infrequently externalises itself, and when it does so it usually takes on a gigantic human form. I have noticed one near here, for example, whose form is about twelve feet high, and looked like a woman the last time I saw it. Its features were quite clear, but its form was misty. There are also nature-spirits which cling round a tree, and do not at all like to be disturbed. I have heard it said that nature-spirits do not cling round the trees which man fells for timber; but such observations as I have been able to make do not bear out this contention, and it seems to me that it must have been invented by men who wished to destroy the tree without feeling any unpleasant twinges of conscience.

Although it takes so fine a form, the spirit of a tree is not individualised, nor even within measurable distance of individualisation. Nevertheless, it is already much higher than the lower forms of animal life, and when it passes into the animal kingdom it will come straight into some of the mammalian groups. It has its likes and dislikes, and these show in its aura, though the colour and definition are naturally altogether vaguer and dimmer than in the case of an animal. Indeed, in animals who glow with affection its colour is often remarkably strong; stronger in the case of some animals than that which is shown by some human beings, because it is so much more concentrated and one-pointed.

The strong attraction which some people feel for particular kinds of trees or animals depends often upon the line of animal and vegetable evolution through which those people have risen.

Sixth Section: The World And The Races Of Men

THE BUILDING OF THE SYSTEM

Our solar system has seven planes which, when taken together, form the lowest of the great cosmic planes. There was a time when this cosmic plane consisted only of what was to it atomic matter, that is to say, of the bubbles in koilon. That was the condition existing on what we may call the site of the solar system. When the Solar LOGOS chose to manifest Himself, when He came forth out of eternity into time, and wished to form this system, He commenced first of all by defining an area, the limit perhaps of His own aura.

Within that area He began His work upon the bubbles in koilon (which seem to have been already constructed, probably by some still greater LOGOS) using them as the atoms of our highest plane, and creating the universe in seven breaths. For example, He did not make the physical-plane matter directly from the astral-plane matter, but withdrew into Himself some of the matter of the astral plane and then breathed it out again in a new combination. Thus there is what is sometimes called a fresh tanmatra as well as a fresh tattwa for each plane.

The shortest and clearest definition of these words which I have ever heard was given by the late T. Subba Rao. He said:

"The tanmatra is the modification in the consciousness of the LOGOS, and the tattwa is the effect produced in matter by that modification. You have seen how on a sandy shore a little wave comes quietly in, runs up on the sand and retires. But it has left behind it a tiny ridge to mark its limit. If the tide is rising, the next wave which comes in goes a little further up the beach, makes its mark in turn and then retires. You may think of the tanmatra as imaged by that wave, which is the temporary modification of the ocean, and you may think of the little ridge made in the sand as symbolising the tattwa."

The meaning of the word tattwa appears to be "thatness," or "inherent quality."

Though the atoms of the various planes as we descend are thus not made directly from one another it is nevertheless true that the atoms of the lower planes could not be made as they are unless the bubbles of which they are composed had already had the experience of passing through all the others above. The atom of the second plane already consists of forty-nine of these bubbles, and the atom of the third or nirvanic plane of two thousand four hundred and one. This proportion persists all the way down, so that the same energy which makes forty-nine astral atoms makes only one physical atom, the bubbles being arranged differently.

If we could take a physical atom and put it back plane by plane up to the highest, it would be found to consist of about fourteen thousand million of these bubbles. But when the LOGOS is making the planes, the matter of one plane is drawn up and disintegrated down to the original bubbles, and then recombined to make the matter of the next lower plane. It is probable that the force by which some greater LOGOS formed the bubbles in koilon is what Madame Blavatsky calls fohat, for you remember that that is spoken of as digging holes in space, and the holes may be these infinitesimal bubbles, instead of solar systems, as we at first supposed.

I do not know whether each bubble is rotating round its own axis or not. Remember, it is not like a soap-bubble, which is a film of water with an outer and inner surface, enclosing air inside it; it is like a bubble in soda-water, which has only one surface, where the air meets the water. To the highest sight that we can as yet bring to bear upon it, it appears to be absolutely empty, so we cannot tell whether there is any interior motion going on in it or not. It seems to have no proper motion of its own, but it can be moved as a whole from without, singly or en masse, by an exertion of the will. No two of these bubbles ever under any circumstances touch each other.

The drawing of the physical atom which is given in the frontispiece to *The Ancient Wisdom* is not quite accurate; it is far too flat - too much like a locket in appearance. The drawing given in Occult Chemistry is far better. The atom in reality is nearly globular, and its projecting points lie almost on the surface of a sphere. It looks somewhat like a wire cage, composed of ten endless wires, which lie completely separate and never touch one another - that is, if any one of them were taken out and uncoiled, and laid out flat, it would be a circle. The arrangement is rather complicated, and a diagram is necessary in order to make it clear. A model would be still better, but no one has yet had the time or the patience to make one.

By reference to the illustration in Occult Chemistry it will be seen that three of these ten wires are thicker than the rest, for in them the seven sets of spirillae do not fit accurately over one another (as they do in the other wires), because in every seven hundred turns there are four more atoms. This means an increase of one in every one hundred and seventy-five bubbles, and it is this which makes those three seem larger than the rest. A scientific man, in criticising the Koilon article, said that in dealing with such minute particles it was impossible to be so accurate, but that is only because he did not understand that it is a mere question of counting and comparison.

The atom has three movements of its own: (1) rotation on its axis; (2) an orbital motion, for it is continually running round in a small circle; (3) a pulsation like a heart, a constant expansion and contraction. These three movements are always going on, and are unaffected by any force from outside. A force from outside - a ray of light for example - will set the atom as a whole moving violently up and down, the phase of this movement being proportional to the intensity of the light, and its wave-length being determined by the colour of the light. A curious feature is that when this happens one of the seven minor wires of the atom begins to glow - the which corresponds to the colour of the light which is setting the whole atom in motion.

The atom exists because of the force which the LOGOS is pouring through it, precisely as a little revolving column of dust and leaves, at the corner of the street, exists because of the whirling wind which made it. The existence of matter depends therefore absolutely upon the continuance of an idea in the mind of the LOGOS; if He chose to withdraw His force from the physical plane - to cease thinking it - every physical atom would instantly disintegrate, and the whole physical plane would disappear in an instant like the light of a candle when it is blown out.

Besides this force which holds the atom together in its spiral form, a number of the forces of the LOGOS are also playing round its coils - or perhaps we should rather say, one of His forces is playing at a number of different levels. There are seven orders of this force, which are eventually, at the end of the seventh round, to play fully round the seven sets of spirillae; but some of them are not yet in activity, since this is only the fourth round.

There is some reason to believe that what the scientific people call electrons may be what we call astral atoms, for they have said that in a chemical atom of hydrogen there are probably somewhere between seven hundred and a thousand of these electrons. Now it happens that in a chemical atom of hydrogen there are eight hundred and eighty-two astral atoms. This may of course be only a coincidence, but that seems somewhat improbable. If this suggestion be true it follows that in some of their experiments our scientific men must be actually disintegrating physical matter, and throwing it back on to the astral plane; in which case it would seem that they must presently be forced to admit the existence of astral matter, though they will naturally think of it as nothing but a further subdivision of physical matter.

I do not know whether in such cases the disintegrated physical atoms re-form themselves; but in our experiments, when by an effort of the will the physical atom is broken up into astral or mental atoms, it means only that for a moment the human will is set against the divine will which formed that atom. It requires a distinct effort to hold the atom temporarily in a different form, and the moment that the human will is withdrawn the divine will re-asserts itself and the physical atom is there once more. This, however, seems to apply only to the breaking up of the ultimate atoms of the plane; when for experimental purposes we break up a chemical atom into physical ultimate atoms, it remains in that condition, and does not return to its original state.

In interstellar space (between solar system) we are given to understand that atoms lie far apart and equidistant; and I believe that that is their normal condition when undisturbed. That is what is meant by speaking of the atoms as free. Within the atmosphere of a planet they are never found in at all that state, for even when not grouped in forms, they are at any rate enormously compressed by the force of attraction.

A man has a causal body on the atomic mental plane, but the mental atoms composing it will be crushed together by attraction into a very definite and quite dense shape, even though they are in no way altered in themselves, and are not grouped into molecules. Such a body could exist comfortably on its own atomic plane in the neighbourhood of a planet, where the atomic matter is in the compressed condition; but it would not at all be able to move or function in this far-away space where the atoms remain absolutely free and uncompressed.

The conditions in interplanetary space are probably not exactly the same as in interstellar space, for there may be a great deal of disturbance due to cometic and meteoric matter, and also the tremendous attraction of the sun produces a considerable compression within the limits of his system. Indeed, the vortex made in the first place by the LOGOS is of course still in action; and part of its action was to draw in matter from the surrounding space and compress it. I have no information upon the question as to whether atoms floating within the limits of the solar system would or would not be necessarily all vivified by elemental essence. It seems to me most probable, however, that only those atoms which make the mental, astral and physical bodies (the latter of course, including the atmosphere and the lower varieties of ether) of the sun and the various planets and comets would be so vivified.

At any rate, as we began by saying, the LOGOS chooses His area - an area of size stupendous beyond our comprehension. Astronomy tells us that the distance between solar systems is so enormous as to be out of all proportion to the systems themselves. It is nevertheless probable that the LOGOI of those systems are actually in touch with one another, and that the solar system existing in the centre of each of these inconceivably vast spheres represents the condensation of matter which was originally scattered throughout the whole of that prodigious area, in a condition of the minutest possible subdivision - perhaps in the condition of the ultimate bubbles which are atoms of our highest plane.

At a certain stage in that condensation or compressed - a stage when the radius of His globe still extent far beyond the orbit of the outermost planet of our system as it is to-day - He sets up within it a whirling motion accompanied by intense electrical action, thus making a kind of colossal vortex in many dimensions. The compression of the whirling mass is continued through what to us would be untold ages, in the course of which He breathes the seven breaths of which we have previously spoken, and thereby groups the bubbles into the atomic matter of the various planes. Eventually there comes a point at which He sends through it a kind of electrical shock, which precipitates it into a lower condition of matter, so that instead of being a mere aggregation of atoms it becomes definitely a combination of then, usually a mass of glowing hydrogen.

Here we have the nebular stage, through which various systems in our universe are at this moment passing, as may be seen by means of any large telescope. As our nebula revolved round its axis it gradually cooled, contracted and flattened down, so that eventually it became rather a huge revolving disc than a sphere. Presently fissures appeared in this disc and it broke into rings, presenting somewhat the appearance of the planet Saturn and its surroundings, but on a gigantic scale. At a chosen point in each of these rings a subsidiary vortex was set up, and gradually much of the matter of the ring was gathered into this. The concussion of the fragments generated an amount of heat which reduced them to a gaseous condition and thus formed a huge glowing ball, which gradually, as it cooled, condensed into a planet.

The planet formed upon the ring in this particular part of the system was, however, not the earth but the moon. We think of the moon as the satellite of the earth, comparing it in our minds with the satellites of Mars, Jupiter or Saturn; but in reality the comparison is unfair, for the moon is more companion planet than a satellite. No other satellite in the solar system bears at all the same proportion to its primary as the moon does to the earth, even though it is now much smaller than it used to be, as will be presently explained. It was the one physical planet of the lunar chain, and our present humanity inhabited it in the distant past, although we were then a stage further back, and were in the animal kingdom.

The earth came into existence when the active life of the moon was already over. A new vortex was set up not far away from the moon, and the rest of the matter of the ring was gradually gathered into it.. The resultant collisions once more produced a ball of glowing gas, which enfolded the body of the moon and very soon reduced it to a similar condition. As this combined mass gradually cooled, condensation took place round the two vortices, but by far the larger part of the matter was attracted to the new one which became the earth, leaving the moon a much smaller body than it had been and altogether denuded of air and water

The moon was still, from the intense heat, in a plastic condition like hot mud, and the earth in its earlier stages was subject to the most tremendous volcanic convulsions. In the course of these, enormous masses of rock, often many miles in diameter, were thrown up into space to vast distances in all directions. The majority of these fell back upon the earth, but some of them struck the moon while still in its plastic condition and produced upon it many of those huge depressions which we now call lunar craters. Any one who will take the trouble of throwing a few small pebbles into mud at the right stage of consistency will find that be obtains in that way an effect precisely similar to that which we observe upon the surface of the moon. Some of the lunar craters are really craters, but not many.

The moon is now like a vast cinder, hard but porous, of a consistency not unlike that of pumice-stone, though harder. Hardly any physical action of any sort is now taking place upon the surface of the moon. It is probably slowly disintegrating, and we are told that in the course of our seventh round it will break up altogether, and its matter will be used (with presumably some of our own) to build a new world which will be the only physical globe of the next incarnation of our chain. To that new globe whatever remains of the earth will act as a satellite.

The moon has often been described in Theosophical literature as the eighth sphere, because it is not one of the seven planets of our chain upon which evolution is taking place. It is therefore what is called a "dead end," a place where only refuse gathers, and it is a kind of a dust-heap or waste-paper-basket to the system - a kind of astral cesspool into which are thrown decaying fragments of various sorts, such as the lost personality which has torn itself away from the ego, who has allowed it to slip out of his grasp in the manner which I explained in the first volume of this book, in the article on Lost Soul.

THE PLANETARY CHAINS

Our solar system at the present moment contains ten chains, each consisting of seven globes, and these are evolving side by side, though at different stages. Seven of them are represented upon the physical level by one or more globes, but the three others exist only on higher levels. The number of globes on the physical plane which a chain has at any given time depends upon the stage of its evolution. The globes of each chain present us with a small cycle of evolution descending into denser matter and then ascending out of it, and in an exactly analogous manner the successive incarnations of a chain also descend into denser matter and then ascend out of it. Our own chain is at the present moment at its lowest level of materiality, so that of its seven planets three are on the physical plane, two on the astral and two on the lower mental.

We usually employ the letters of the alphabet to denote these globes in their order; so we should represent the present condition of affairs by saying that globes A and G are on the lower mental plane; globes B and F on the astral, and globes C, D, and E upon the physical level, C and E being smaller than D. It will be observed that in travelling round the chain the life-wave is steadily involving itself more and more in matter as it descends from A to D, but is rising again and casting off successive veils of matter as it passes from D to G.

This is the condition of affairs during the fourth and most material incarnation of each chain. But in the third and fifth incarnations each chain has its first and seventh planets on the higher mental, its second and sixth on the lower mental, its third and fifth on the astral, and only one planet, the fourth, on the physical plane. The second and sixth incarnations of each chain are one stage higher; their fourth planet is upon the astral plane, while the third and fifth are upon the lower mental, the second and sixth upon the higher mental and the first and seventh at the buddhic level. The first and seventh incarnations of a chain are one stage higher still, in that their lowest planets are on the lower mental plane and their first and seventh planets at the stage which we call nirvanic.

It is not easy for us to attach any meaning to the idea of a planet upon planes so exalted as the nirvanic or buddhic, and we are perhaps scarcely justified in using the term. All that we mean is that there is a certain location in space where the evolution of certain groups of monads is taking place through agencies which work on those exalted levels.

Each of these seventy planets may be regarded as having a definite location in space and as revolving round, or in some way depending upon, our sun. Of these seventy planets only twelve are physical, and even of those twelve one is not yet recognised by science and two others have only lately been discovered.

The existence of Vulcan was accepted by some astronomers a century ago, but as it cannot now be found, the scientific men of the present day hold that the earlier observations were incorrect. No astronomer had dreamt of the two planets beyond the orbit of Neptune at the time when they were first mentioned in Theosophical writings, but now their existence is admitted in consequence of the deflections which they have produced in certain cometary orbits.

Madame Blavatsky says that Neptune is not in our solar system, but there can be no question that it revolves round our sun. Madame Blavatsky therefore must have been speaking in some occult or symbolical sense when she used those words. From the occult point of view also, the Neptunian chain is clearly part of our system, being one of the ten chains which compose it; so we are unable at the moment to attach any meaning to Madame Blavatsky's statement. That does not in the least imply that it is really meaningless or inaccurate.

We have frequently found that passages in her writings, which we had been for a long time compelled to put aside as incomprehensible and apparently contrary to known facts, had nevertheless a definite meaning and a certain sense in which they were true, though these were discoverable only when (by penetrating to higher planes) fresh aspects of the subject were brought into view. No doubt in due time this will prove to be the case with this enigmatical statement about Neptune.

Besides those on the seventy planets of which we have spoken, there are other evolutions taking place, every inch of place being utilised. Even in the koilon itself there may be an evolution going on of which we know nothing and can imagine nothing. We know as yet so little of this marvellous system to which we belong; all this teaching of Theosophy which has so changed our lives is but the lifting of a tiny corner of the veil. All space is filled with life, and there are even lower orders than that of the physical plane. It sometimes happens that a human being comes into touch with that lower evolution, but that is always undesirable. Yet it would be a great mistake to speak of the inhabitants of this lower world as wicked. Certainly that evolution brings harm to us if we become entangled with it, but that is because it is not meant for us.

Of the seven chains that have physical planets, taking them in order, beginning with the nearest to the sun and working outwards, we have first Vulcan, with only one physical planet, which is small and must be very hot. The Vulcan chain is in its third incarnation, but we are given to understand that its scheme of evolution is not destined to bring the entities concerned with it to as high a level as will be ultimately attained by the inhabitants of our own planet.

Mercury is the next planet, and belongs to the earth-chain.

Venus is the only physical planet of the chain of which it is a part. It is in the seventh round of its fifth incarnation, and it represents the most advanced degree of evolution yet attained by humanity in this solar system. Being so far advanced, it has been to able to afford assistance to other and less developed evolutions; from it, as we know, descended the Lords of the Flame, who gave so great a stimulus to the progress of humanity in the middle of our third root-race.

It is a remarkable fact that the astronomers of a hundred and fifty years ago recorded several observations of a satellite of Venus, whereas now it is quite certain that no such orb exists. The usual supposition is that those earlier astronomers erred. But this is scarcely likely in view of the number and character of the witnesses, and also their repeated observations. It was seen by astronomers as well known as Cassini and Short, in 1761, and that not once but many times, and with different telescopes. It was observed by Scheuten during the whole of its transit along with Venus in the same year; it was seen four times by Montaigne, and again in 1764 by Rödkier, Horrebow and Montbaron. It was estimated to have a diameter of about two thousand miles. It is surely more probable that all these astronomers were right in their observations, for we are told that in our seventh round the moon will disintegrate and we shall be left without a satellite. It may be only a coincidence that Venus is in its seventh round, but it is a curious one.

The next planets are our Earth and Mars, and these two, along with Mercury, are the three physical planets of a chain which is in its fourth incarnation. Our Earth is the lowest and most material of the series - planet D, while Mars is our planet C and Mercury our planet E. A good many of the more advanced members of our present humanity were not upon the planet Mars when the life-wave last swept over it, as will be explained later; but the great bulk of the human race has certainly passed through a series of incarnations on that planet, and we have left behind us many traces of our occupation, of which the present inhabitants are abundantly availing themselves. When our present occupancy of the earth ends for a time, we shall all pass on to the somewhat less material life of the planet Mercury, where the average level of consciousness may be somewhat more extended than it is here, since ordinary humanity will then possess what is now called etheric sight. There are no grounds whatever, so far as I know, for the statement made by a recent writer that the real names of Mercury and Venus have been interchanged. Indeed, we know a great deal about these planets which makes the idea inconceivable.

Next come the asteroids - material which will make a world some time; but we do not count them now.

The giant of the solar system, Jupiter, has a chain of its own. It is in an early stage of its evolution, being very much too hot for life, such as we know, to exist on its surface; but its satellites are inhabited. Its surface has seas of molten metals, and similar conditions exist on all the outside giant planets. It has a density about that of water, if you take the whole mass; but what we see is really the outside of a mass of cloud thousands of miles in depth - so we get a false estimate of the actual size of the planet itself. The Jupiter scheme is at present in the second round of its third incarnation. We are told that this system will eventually raise its humanity to an extremely high level.

Next we come to Saturn, with its wonderful system of rings and satellites. It is the only physical planet of its chain. It also is in an early round of its third incarnation, and we understand that the development connected with it is slower than most of the others, but that it will ultimately reach exalted levels.

As to the schemes to which the outer planets Uranus and Neptune belong, we have but little information, though we know that the latter is in its fourth incarnation, because of the fact that to it belong also the two other physical planets whose orbits lie outside its own. The conditions existing on all these gigantic outer members of the solar systems must be altogether so entirely different from those on the small inner planets that it is practically impossible to form any idea of the sort of life which must be lived by their inhabitants, even in the future when the globes have cooled down.

SUCCESSIVE LIFE-WAVES

The conception of the successive life-waves which pour out from the LOGOS should not be a difficult one, yet it frequently happens that some confusion seems to arise in the mind of the student in connection with it.

Perhaps this comes partially from the fact that the term "life-wave" has been employed in our literature in three distinct senses. First, it has been used to denote the three great outpourings of Divine Life by means of which our solar system came into existence - by which its evolution is carried on. Secondly, it has been applied to the successive impulsions of which the second outpouring is formed; and it is in this sense principally that I shall employ the term now. Thirdly, the expression has been accepted as signifying the transference of life from one planet of our chain to another in the course of evolution.

A life-wave of this third type does not at all correspond to the life-wave of the second type, but consists of synchronous portions of seven of the latter, treated as though they constituted a single entity. As we all know, we have with us at the present time seven kingdoms in manifestation - the human, the animal, the vegetable, the mineral, and the three elemental kingdoms which precede the mineral.

We must realise that all these are manifestations of the same life - the one life of the LOGOS manifesting in that second great outpouring which comes from His second aspect after the primitive matter has been prepared for its reception by the action of the first outpouring which comes from the third aspect (see The Christian Creed, p. 40). That second outpouring comes forth in a series of successive waves, following one another as the waves of the sea follow one another. Each of these waves has reached its present stage by passing through all the earlier stages, and in each of those it has spent a period of time corresponding to the life of a chain of seven worlds, sometimes called a manvantara.

This Sanskrit word manvantara literally means the period between two Manus, and so it might be applied at various levels. We see from *The Secret Doctrine* that each root-race has its Manu, a great adept who takes charge of it, and superintends its formation and growth. But there is also a Manu for the world-period which includes the seven root-races; and yet again there is a still greater Manu who superintends the progress of the life-wave (using that term in its third sense) through all the seven planets of the chain; and since one complete journey through all those seven globes has been called a round, He is spoken of as the Round-Manu.

Seven such rounds complete one life-period for a planetary chain - one incarnation of the chain, as it were; and over this enormous period there is a Great One who presides, and to Him also this title of Manu is accorded. Higher still there is One who presides over the seven successive chains, which may be regarded as the seven incarnations of our chain, making one complete scheme of evolution; but He is usually spoken of not as a Manu, but as the LOGOS of seven chains, or sometimes as the Planetary LOGOS. So we have here a graduated hierarchy of mighty adepts, extending up to Divinity itself.

It is obvious, therefore, that the term manvantara might indicate various periods of time, corresponding to the levels at which it was employed; but in our Theosophical literature it has generally been used to indicate the duration of one chain - the time occupied by the life-wave in making seven rounds. To the greater period of the seven successive incarnations of the chain, the name of mahamanvantara (which means simply great manvantara) has sometimes been given.

The following table may be of use to our students, as summarizing the system of evolution:

7 Branch Races make - One Sub-race.
7 Sub-races make - One Root-race.
7 Root-races make - One World-period.
7 World-periods make - One Round.
7 Rounds make - One Chain-period.
7 Chain-periods make - One Planetary Scheme.
10 Planetary Schemes make - Our Solar system.

It is scarcely practical for us at present to endeavour to estimate in years the exact length of these enormous expanses of time. In exoteric Hindu books definite numbers are given, but Madame Blavatsky tell us that it is impossible to rely fully upon these, as other and esoteric considerations are involved, which the writers do not take into account. We have no direct information upon these points, but there is some reason to suspect that the time of the rounds is not an invariable quantity, but that some are shorter than others. It has been thought that those in front of us will probably not be so long as those through which we have passed; but here again we have no certain information, and it seems useless to speculate.

At all these stages there are always seven life-waves in action. In every one of these chains is a human kingdom, and it is always accompanied by its brothers, an animal, a vegetable and a mineral kingdom. But each of these is steadily evolving; so that the life-wave which is ensouling the animal kingdom of the present day will in the next chain have arrived at the human level and will provide the causal bodies for the humanity of that chain. In the same way the life-wave which ensouls our vegetable kingdom now will ensoul the animal kingdom then, and so on.

It of course follows from this that we were the animal kingdom of the moon-chain, and the vegetable kingdom of the chain previous to that, That is not precisely an accurate method of expression, because we as separate egos did not exist then; but that wave of essence which in the first chain ensouled the mineral kingdom, in the second chain the vegetable, and in the third chain the animal, has now been employed in the formation of those causal bodies which we are inhabiting at the present day.

What then will be the future progress of that wave, and how will it appear in the next chain? It will not appear there at all, for we must remember that at the close of this human evolution man finds always before him the seven paths which open the way to still further development. I have tried to explain these, so far as they may at present be described, in the concluding chapter of Invisible Helpers.

I need not repeat here what I then wrote, but I may add to it a fragment of information which has since come to my knowledge. One of those paths, which we had then to leave blank, leads to what we have called a staff appointment. Every general has, quite apart from the regular officers who hold various commands under him, a special set of officers who form his staff, whose duty it is to be in personal attendance upon him, and to be ready at any moment to do anything that he may require, or to fill any vacancy that may occur. The Solar LOGOS also has His staff - a number of adepts who are not in the service of any particular chain, yet ever prepared to be sent to the aid of any that need assistance. To join this body is one of the seven possibilities which lie before him who has "reached the further shore."

When the time comes for our chain to disintegrate and for the life from it to pass into the fifth chain, we shall already have moved on to a stage beyond the human, along one or other of these seven paths. Consequently the humanity which will commence as primitive man in the fifth chain will not be ourselves at all, but will be the wave next behind us - that which is ensouling our present animal kingdom.

In the same way our vegetable monad will have evolved a stage higher, and will ensoul the animal kingdom of that new chain; while the life-wave which is now animating the mineral kingdom will by that time have risen to the level of the vegetable kingdom. Thus we see that of the seven life-waves which we now know, six will be present in the fifth chain, but each will have gained a stage in its development.

Our present human life-wave, having obtained the object of its immersion into matter, has passed out of this series of chains altogether, though some of those who were its members may still retain a voluntary connection with it for the purpose of helping its evolution. But since each of our waves has moved on a stage, how is the place of the hindmost supplied? Are we to suppose that the first elemental kingdom will no longer be represented in the new chain? By no means; for we find that a fresh life-wave from the LOGOS is following close behind the others, and so this new influx completes the seven.

Precisely the same process has taken place in connection with each chain in succession. In each of them one life-wave has attained its goal, and passed off through seven channels to some entirely higher form of manifestation; and each of those behind it has moved forward one stage, and place of the hindmost has in each case been filled by a fresh influx of life from the LOGOS.

Each of these waves enters in each chain-period at the lowest level of the kingdom which it is ensouling, and passes out of that kingdom at its highest point. A fresh influx of life from the LOGOS enters the first elemental kingdom in each chain, and there are six such influxes in our scheme, so that we have altogether thirteen successive life-waves at work in this scheme of seven chains, though never more than seven of them are in operation simultaneously. All are moving steadily onward but always preserving the same distance between them, and we can take up any particular wave at any point in its progress and follow it backwards or forwards as we desire.

Take for example the seventh of these waves. It enters into the first incarnation of the chain as the first elemental kingdom; in the second chain it has reached the level of the second elemental kingdom, and in the lunar chain it ensouls the third. In our present chain it animates our mineral kingdom, while in the fifth and sixth chains it will ensoul respectively the vegetable and animal kingdoms. In the seventh chain it will arrive at the level of humanity, and will then pass off through its seven channels, as the other humanities have done. We have then the complete history of this life-wave before us, from the time when it emerged into manifestation in the first elemental kingdom, until it is again attaining divine levels at the end of its appointed evolution.

We have not before us in our scheme the complete evolution of any other wave than this. If, for example, we trace back our own life-wave, we shall find that it ensouled the animal kingdom in the moon-chain, the vegetable kingdom in the second chain, and the mineral kingdom in the first chain. Where then did it gain the evolution of the three elemental kingdoms? For it must obviously have advanced through those stages before it manifested as the mineral. It has passed through them in some previous scheme of chains - we know not where or when. It is evident that the only entirely new impulse is that first chain of our scheme was the seventh life-wave, for all the others which form part of that first chain had already gone through some portion of their evolution in anterior schemes of worlds. Its humanity must evidently have passed through the six antecedent stages in that unknown past, and it came here only to acquire the finishing touch to its education which prepared it to pass off along the seven paths which lay open before it.

But our life-waves stretch onward into the future as well as back into the past. The eighth wave, for example, which entered for the first time in the second chain as a fresh impulse from the Divine Life, has no time in our scheme of evolution to reach the human level. In our present chain it is ensouling the third elemental kingdom, and causing us a great deal of trouble in the shape of desire-elementals. In the seventh chain that wave will be ensouling the animal kingdom, and it will therefore attain humanity in the first chain of some unknown scheme of globes, hidden at present in the womb of the future.

Naturally the remaining waves, from the ninth to the thirteenth, are also unfinished, so that out of all the waves which use our scheme as the theatre of their evolution only one finds time to complete all its stages - a fact which, if we can realise all that it involves, gives us a deeply impressive illustration of the vastness of the resources of nature, a glimpse into the illimitable eternities through which, never hastening yet never resting, her unfoldment proceeds with such splendid precision.

Now that we have clearly in our minds the steady progress of these life-waves, we must immediately proceed to modify our conception by the introduction into it of another important factor. In each case of transference from one kingdom to another, there is always a certain part of the life-waves which does not succeed in passing, and is therefore left behind. We may perhaps understand that most easily if we begin by thinking of the future of our own humanity.

We know that the goal set before us is the attainment of that level of initiation which has been called adeptship - the position of the asekha, "the one who has no more to learn" with regard to our planetary chain. But we also know that it will not be the whole of humanity that will succeed in this lofty aim, but only a certain part of it. We are told that in the middle of the next round a separation will occur between those souls who are strong enough to undertake the higher stages of evolution and those who are not.

This separation has been prefigured by the many legends of a "last judgment" at which the future destiny of the souls for this aeon would be decided. The diseased imagination of the mediaeval monk, always seeking an opportunity to introduce grotesquely exaggerated horrors into his creed in order to terrify an incredibly ignorant peasantry into more liberal donations for the support of Mother-Church, distorted into "eternal damnation" the perfectly simple idea of aeonian suspension.

Those who are left behind at this period have sometimes been described as "the failures of the fifth round," though perhaps even this is somewhat too harsh a term. There may well be some among them who by greater exertion might have qualified themselves to pass onward, and these are rightly spoken of as failures; but the majority will be left behind simply because they are too young to go on, and so not strong enough for the more difficult work.

The facts of the case may be stated quite simply. The lower classes of monads passed only gradually from the animal kingdom into the human during the earlier half of our present chain-period. Some of them are still, consequently, at an early stage of the human evolution, and are therefore exceedingly unlikely to overtake the classes which are so far in advance of them. We have been given to understand that it is just possible for even the lowest savage to reach before the middle of the fifth round the level necessary for continued evolution, but in order to do this he must never once fail to take advantage of each opportunity as it is offered to him, and the number who will do this will be infinitesimally small. It is calculated that the proportion who will be prepared to go on will amount to about three-fifths of the total population of the earth (not merely of the physical population, it will be understood, but of the total number of egos who constitute the human life-wave evolving through this chain) while the remaining two-fifths will be left behind.

The surroundings in the world at that time will be specially adapted for the rapid progress of the more advanced egos, and will therefore be wholly unsuitable for entities at a much lower stage of evolution, as the gross vibrations of violent passion and of strong coarse feelings which are necessary for the development of the inert and half-formed astral body of the savage will be no longer available. We can easily imagine many ways in which this unsuitability would show itself. In a world of high intellectual and spiritual development, where war and the slaughter of animals have long been things of the past, the existence of savage races, full of undisciplined passions and desire for conflict, would obviously introduce many serious difficulties and complications; and though no doubt means might be devised for their repression, that very repression would debar them from the activities requisite for their early stage of evolution.

Obviously, therefore, the kindest and best thing to do with those who are thus backward is simply to drop them out from this evolution, and let them prepare to take their place in next year's class - in the next planetary chain. Such entities will not suffer in any way; they will simply have a very prolonged period of rest in such heaven-life as they may be capable of appreciating, and no doubt, even though their consciousness during this period will probably be but partially awakened, a certain amount of inner progress will be going on.

From that condition they will descend into the earlier stages of the evolution of the next chain, and will be among the leaders of primitive humanity there. We should not think of them as in any way put back, but merely as assigned to the position to which they really belong, where their progress is easy and certain. It is to this class that Madame Blavatsky referred when she spoke of vast numbers of "lost souls" ; though this term "lost souls," when employed in this connection, sometimes misleads students who have not yet grasped the full splendour and certainty of the evolutionary scheme.

We may think then of each life-wave in its passage through the chain as breaking up into wavelets. Consider what will be the progress made by our own life-wave. Broadly speaking, this represents the animal kingdom of the moon, though the failures of the lunar humanity have naturally joined it, and may be expected to be among its leaders.

The whole of the wave which ensouled that lunar animal kingdom should theoretically have entered humanity during the earlier part of this chain, and should by the end of the seventh round attain the goal appointed for it.

We who are now human beings in this chain ought all of us to attain adeptship, and pass away from this scheme of evolution altogether by one of the seven paths which open before the adept, while what is now our animal kingdom ought by the end of this chain to attain individualisation, and therefore to be ready to furnish the humanity for the next chain, the fifth of the scheme.

We know, however, that two-fifths of our humanity will fall out in the middle of the fifth round, because it is obviously too far behind the rest to enable it even with the greatest efforts to attain the goal during this chain. This two-fifths will enter the next chain along with the members of our present animal kingdom, and will therefore constitute part of that future humanity.

One of the great reasons why the division between the more advanced and the less advanced must be made in the middle of the fifth round is that the later races will be in much closer touch with the adepts and the great devas than we are now. It will therefore be necessary for them to hold themselves always in an impressible condition, in readiness to receive and respond to an outpouring of influences. This in its turn requires that they shall live a peaceful and contemplative life, which would be an impossibility if there were still left in the world savage races who would attack and kill the man in a state of contemplation. The more powerful vibrations of that time would not rouse the higher nature of the savage, but would only stimulate and intensify his lower passions, so that he would gain nothing by being on earth at that period, while he would make impossible the progress of the more developed people.

But the other three-fifths of our present humanity, which may be described as successful in so far as it does not drop out at the day of judgment in the fifth round, will yet not all of it succeed, in the sense of attaining the asekha level.

It is thought that probably about one-fifth of the whole number (that is to say, one-third of those who have not dropped out) will fully achieve ; but that means that two-thirds of the successes will still at the end of our chain of worlds have further work to do, before they have reached the level intended for them. They also will have to enter the next chain, though they will not need the earlier stages of its evolution: so they will probably appear at about its middle point, much as the higher classes of monads who came over from the moon entered our present evolution at its middle point. The matter will, however, be complicated for them by the fact that, just as on this chain the point set before us for attainment is higher than that of the moon-chain, so will the level of achievement expected on the fifth chain be higher than ours. With that, however, we have no concern for the moment.

The actual distribution at the end of our planetary chain will probably be into several well-defined classes, somewhat as follows; though obviously each of these might be further subdivided:

Those who, having intelligently studied evolution and determined to take the shorter and steeper Path to the goal, have already attained adeptship in previous rounds.

Those who attain the asekha level in the seventh round. These are the highest class of the men who have moved along with the ordinary stream of evolution - the vanguard of those who have followed the usual path. They may be taken as corresponding, for our chain, to the first class of the moon-men.

Those who have fallen short of this perfect attainment, but yet have succeeded in reaching the arhat level in the seventh round. They correspond for our chain to the second class of the moon-men, and will need very few births in the next incarnation of the chain before they also gain the level of liberation.

Those who, while they passed the examination at the middle of the fifth round, have not yet succeeded in raising themselves above the three lower levels of the Path Proper. These may perhaps be taken to correspond for our chain with the animal-men of the moon, who had only just contrived to separate themselves from the animal kingdom, and consequently had much preparatory work to do in the new chain.

Those who, while they succeeded in attaining humanity in our earth-chain, yet failed to raise themselves sufficiently to justify their continuance in that chain after the middle of the fifth round. There will, no doubt, be several subdivisions or classes among these.

Those who have failed altogether to gain the level of humanity. These will be some of the very lowest of the monads, who had only just reached the animal kingdom on the moon, and have been slowly rising during the earth-chain, but have not succeeded in attaining individualisation.

It is not only in the case of humanity that we find this failure to attain the destined level. The same thing appears to happen in connection with every kingdom all through the course of evolution. While the majority of each wave of monads fulfil the destiny appointed for them, there is in each a minority who fall behind, and a much smaller minority who run far in advance of that destiny. For example, just as a few men are now rising far above their fellows and attaining adeptship, so a few animals are even already breaking away from their group-souls and becoming individualised, though the great body of the animal life-wave will arrive at individualisation only towards the end of the seventh round, and will form the humanity of the fifth chain. The men who are approaching adeptship are always those who are in close touch with the existing adepts as Their pupils; the animals who are approaching humanity are usually those who are in close touch with the existing humanity as pets specially developed in affection and intelligence.

In the earlier days of the Theosophical teaching we supposed that even if an animal by specially rapid development should become individualised here and now, he would still have to wait until the next chain before he could secure a human body. Later investigations, however, have shown us that exceptions to this rule are at this stage still possible, and that animals who are fortunate enough to attain individualisation during this present world-period may be accommodated with primitive human bodies at the commencement of the occupation by our life-wave of the next planet in our present chain. It is obvious that the number of animals prepared to take advantage of this (which, so far as we can see, appears likely to be their final opportunity of entering the human life of this chain) must be relatively exceedingly small; but still it is a possibility which we must take into account if we wish correctly to comprehend the course of evolution.

I have once seen a case in which there were special features that made an even earlier incarnation possible - a case of an animal which had shown in earth-life not only great intelligence, but also unusually strong devotion to his human friend, a devotion which of course continued in the astral life and was even stronger there than ever. The animal's power of definite thought was such that during life he frequently travelled great distances in his astral body when asleep, to visit his master on his journeys. In this case definite progress was made in the astral life after death, and the response to our efforts was much greater than we had hoped, for the astral life gave us a better opportunity than was possible on the physical plane to grasp the exact limits of the animal's lines of thought. They were few, narrow and curiously limited; but yet they extended much further along their lines than one would suppose.

Certain new lines of thought opened up in the astral life, and the developments were exceedingly interesting. An almost immediate incarnation in this world was clearly possible, but there were some curious combinations which made the matter difficult to arrange. The animal would have been a primitive savage in many ways, and yet could only have been incarnated in immediate personal relation with his master, for whom his attachment was so strong that it would have been impossible to keep him away from him This presented serious difficulties, but still they might somehow have been overcome, but for the fact that it was impossible to guarantee the sex of the savage!

Presumably among the animals that succeed there will also be various classes, corresponding in a general way in this evolution to the various classes of monads in the lunar evolution; and some of the animal essence at present ensouling the lowest forms of life will certainly fail to attain the human level in this chain, and will therefore correspond in the animal kingdom to our "failures of the fifth round." As to whether these forms also will disappear from the earth at that same period in the fifth round we have no direct information, but analogy would seem to require that this should be so. The same differentiation into classes, according to the measure of success achieved, has been observed in connection with all the lower kingdoms, so that in reality each life-wave ought to be symbolised as breaking up constantly into ripples or wavelets, some of which in time join the preceding or succeeding waves, though the majority move steadily along their appointed course.

The seven life-waves which ensoul our seven kingdoms have always for their principal field of action the planet to which the attention of the LOGOS is for the moment directed; but a certain small proportion of their action is always manifesting in the other worlds of the chain also. Thus, although the attention of the Planetary LOGOS is now fixed upon our earth, there are yet representatives of all the kingdoms simultaneously existing upon every one of the six other globes of our chain. These are often described as the seed from which the forms will develope when the life-wave reaches the planet - that is to say, when the special attention of the Planetary LOGOS is turned to it once more.

These forms have remained in existence upon their respective planets ever since they were first filled by the lunar animal-men in the first round, and in this way the trouble of what might be called fresh creation for each globe in each round is avoided. The life ensouling these forms during the comparative obscuration of those planets is still part of the great wave, and is still moving onward in connection with it. It serves other functions besides that of providing the seed for the incoming wave, since it is also employed as a means of more rapid evolution for certain classes of monads.

It is by the special treatment thus given that it is possible for the second-class monad to overtake the first class and become one of its members. Under certain conditions of strong desire for advancement, if he is seen to be striving with exceptional vigour to improve himself, he may be separated from the great masses of his fellows on this planet, and passed by the authorities into what is called the Inner Round, and may take his next incarnation among the limited population of Mercury. In that case he will spend there about the same time that he would otherwise have devoted to incarnations in one root-race, and will then pass on to the astral planet F. After a similar stay there he will be transferred to globes G, A and B successively, and then to Mars and to the Earth.

As in each of these spheres he will have made a stay about equivalent to the normal period of a root-race, the life-wave will have left the Earth before his return, but he will overtake it upon the planet Mercury, and will then join the ranks of the first-class monads and share the remainder of their evolution and their varied opportunities of more rapid development. Entities engaged upon this special line of evolution form the majority of the small population of Mercury and Mars at the present time. In the latter planet there is also a certain residuum of primitive mankind which was unprepared to pass on when the life-wave left for the Earth - a race which represents a stage of humanity lower than any at present existing within our cognisance. It will probably be extinct long before we reach Mars in the fifth round, since there appear to be no other egos needing manifestation at that level for the moment.

In the same way we find that all the kingdoms are represented upon the astral and mental globes. It is not very easy for us to grasp with our physical consciousness what can be the condition of the life of the lower kingdoms on these higher planes; the idea of the evolution of a mineral on the mental plane, for example, suggests nothing readily comprehensible to the ordinary mind. We may perhaps help ourselves towards the understanding of it by remembering that every mineral must have its astral and mental counterparts, and that the special types of matter which form these are also on their respective planes manifestations of the mineral monad, and we may suppose that through such manifestations that monad is evolving during its existence on these loftier levels.

The group-soul must always contain within itself latent possibilities connected with the higher planes through which it has descended; and it may be that in those stages of evolution these potentialities are being developed by some method quite outside those with which we are familiar. Without the unfolding of psychic faculties we cannot expect to understand in detail the hidden growth in these exalted spheres of finer matter; the important point is that we should realise that although the great life-wave resides only upon one globe of our group at a given time, the remaining planets are by no means dormant, and useful progress is continually being made in every part of our chain.

I have tried to make the above description of the successive life-waves as clear as possible; but lest it should still present some difficulties to the mind of a reader unaccustomed to the study of this system of cosmogony, I append a little diagram which I think may be of assistance. The vertical columns indicate the successive incarnations of the chain; the horizontal divisions represent the various kingdoms of nature; the diagonal arrows are the successive waves of evolution which have come forth from the LOGOS. The arabic numbers attached to each of these arrows apply to those arrows only, and not to the squares in which they happen to come. It will be seen that there are thirteen of these arrows. Their length appears to vary, but that is only because we are regarding them solely from the point of view of our own scheme of evolution.

Within the limits of that scheme arrow No. 1 appears to cross only one kingdom - the human. That does not at all mean that the wave represented by that arrow has not passed through the six previous stages; it means only that those six previous stages have been experienced in some other scheme. Just the same thing is true at the opposite corner of the diagram. Arrow No. 13 crosses only one kingdom - the first elemental; it will inevitably in due course have to pass through all the other kingdoms, but it cannot do so in this scheme of evolution, because that is already at an end. So far as our diagram is concerned it appears in that one kingdom only.

If we take the column representing any one chain - let us say the fourth, which denotes our present stage of evolution - we shall find in running the eye down it that seven arrows pass through it, indicating the seven kingdoms now existing around us. We can follow any one of those arrows either backwards or forwards, and so can trace any of our kingdoms either in the past or in the future. We should note that waves 1 to 6 come to us from some other scheme of evolution, while waves 7 to 13 are fresh emanations from the LOGOS.

THE MONADS FROM THE MOON

Those who have studied the Theosophical system are aware that we divide humanity into various classes according to the age of the ego, and the degree of his development. Transaction No. 26 of the London Lodge gives this arrangement very clearly, and it is also to be found in Chapter XII of *The Ancient Wisdom*; but our students will see that the author of the last-named work has altered the numbering of the classes so as to bring it more nearly into agreement with that adopted in *The Secret Doctrine*.

Mrs. Besant separates from the rest those entities to which the London Lodge Transaction had given the titles of the first and second classes, and calls them solar monads, so that she begins her list of the lunar monads with those that the Transaction had called the third class, and to it she gives the name of the first class; consequently in *The Ancient Wisdom* the fourth class of the Transaction is called the second and the fifth becomes the third. Madame Blavatsky's fourth class covers Mr. Sinnett's sixth and seventh, while the remainder of her classes includes entities which he did not take into account at all. His classification dealt only with members of the lunar animal kingdom, which would become human on our earth-chain; hers took in everything which passed over from the lunar chain to this. Her fifth class represents the vegetable kingdom of the moon, and her sixth class its mineral kingdom, while her seventh includes all three of its elemental kingdoms.

Since the writing of *The Ancient Wisdom* and *The Pedigree of Man*, Mrs. Besant has thought it advisable to adopt clearly descriptive English names in place of those which have previously been used. To those who fully succeeded upon the moon-chain, and attained the arhat level prescribed for them, she gives the title of Lords of the Moon. Those whom she had previously called solar monads (whom Mr. Sinnett had described as first and second class pitris) are now to be called moon-men of the first and second orders respectively. The first order of moon-men has many sub-divisions, as we shall see directly. What she previously called the first-class monads (Mr. Sinnett's third class) are now described as lunar animal-men. Her second, third and fourth classes (corresponding, as above stated, to Mr. Sinnett's fourth, fifth, sixth and seventh) are now described as the first, second and third divisions of the lunar animals. This completes the list of the entities constituting our present humanity, as Madame Blavatsky's lower classes (of which Mr. Sinnett took no account) will not attain the human level in the present chain.

These classes are arranged in the order of their advancement, and they differ not only in appearance but also in the methods by which that advancement is attained. Among other points there is great difference in the length of the intervals between successive incarnations, and in the way in which these intervals are spent; but this part of the subject will be treated in the section on reincarnation.

To understand how these classes are distinguished we must remember that for each chain of worlds a definite level of attainment is laid down, and to reach that is to gain full success. In our present chain of worlds the level assigned is that of the asekha adept, but in the moon-chain it was the fourth step of the Path, that of the arhat. Those who fully attained that on the lunar chain had achieved the purpose of the LOGOS, and so were free to take one or other of the seven paths which always open before the perfected humanity of each chain.

Below them were people standing at many different stages, whom we must to some extent attempt to classify. Broadly speaking, the animal kingdom of one chain makes the humanity of the next. Our present humanity is composed of the successful portion of the animal kingdom of the moon-chain, plus those members of the lunar humanity who failed to reach the required level.

We have already attempted to show into what classes men must inevitably distribute themselves at the end of evolution upon our own earth-chain. A similar arrangement existed at the end of the lunar chain.

Those who had attained the arhat level were the full successes, and they passed off along one or other of their seven paths. We do not certainly know that these are the same as the seven which open before our own adepts, but at least one of them shows decided resemblance; for just as some of our adepts will remain in close touch with the next chain and incarnate on it in order to help its inhabitants in their evolution, so one of the seven classes of the Lords of the Moon stayed to help us in our chain. The members of this class are those called in *The Secret Doctrine* the Barhishads.

Moon-men (first order). Next below this level comes a large and diversified group to which we are at present giving the title of moon-men (first order), though for convenience in following out the several destinies of its subdivisions it will probably be found necessary presently to assign separate names to them. It includes some who, though they had not succeeded in reaching the arhat level, were on some of the lower steps of the Path; others who had not yet gained that Path, though they were approaching it; the failures who had dropped out of the lunar humanity (corresponding to the two-fifths of our humanity who will drop out in our fifth round) ; and the most advanced representatives of the lunar animal kingdom, who had succeeded in fully developing the causal body. We may later give distinctive names to these subdivisions, but for the present we will merely number them.

Those who, although they had not attained arhatship, were already upon one or other of the various steps of the Path. These also, like the Lords of the Moon, have long ere this attained adeptship and passed away altogether from the field of our consideration.

Those of the lunar-chain animal kingdom who attained individualisation in the fourth round of the moon-chain. All these also have by this time attained adeptship. The Masters best known to us in connection with Theosophical work belong to this class, and in it we may also include the majority of those who became arhats under the influence of the preaching of the Lord Buddha .

Those who attained individualisation in the fifth round of the moon-chain. These are now the distinguished people of the world - not by any means only those whom the world calls distinguished, but those who, along one line or another, are considerably in advance of their fellows. In our Theosophical ranks this means those who are either already on the Path or approaching it; in the outer world it means men who are either great saints or of specially high intellectual or artistic development.

Those who attained individualisation in the sixth round of the moon-chain. We have here a fairly large class of people, distinctly gentlemen, persons of refined feeling, with a high sense of honour, and rather above the average in their goodness, intellect, or religious feelings. Typical instances of this class are our country gentlemen and professional men, our clergy or our officers in the army and navy. They have strength, but they are by no means free from the possibility of using their power wrongly. They may not do at all what people around them think they ought to do, and therefore they may often not be considered respectable; but at least they will do nothing low or mean.

Those who attained individualisation in the seventh round of the moon-chain. The members of this class do not differ greatly from those of the last, except that they are somewhat nearer the average in goodness or intellectual development or religious feeling. They turn their intelligence to rather more material ends, as city merchants perhaps. They represent the great division which we commonly call the upper middle class - gentlemen still, yet with a life slightly less elevated than that of the professional man.

All these classes which have been mentioned are in reality subdivisions of one class - the first order of the moon-men - and all the way through they melt into one another by almost indistinguishable gradations, so that the lowest ego of any one of them differs but little from the highest ego of the next class below. Not only are the lines between them thus not clearly marked, but there is even a good deal of interpenetration. Egos belonging by right to the mercantile class get astray among the professions, while those of the higher type find themselves forced into business. As they say in India: "In these days castes are mixed."

I have divided them according to the round of the lunar chain in which they became human. When that happens in any of the earlier rounds it usually means that the newly-formed ego proceeded to take human incarnations in the next following round. For example, those who were individualised in the fourth round of the moon-chain came into human incarnation in the middle of the fifth, and continued to incarnate through the remainder of the fifth, the whole of the sixth, and half of the seventh. In the same way those individualised in the fifth round took up their series of human incarnations in the middle of the sixth; and those individualised in the sixth took birth in the seventh. Those individualised in the seventh round had their first experience of human life on the earth-chain, and of course had to be correspondingly primitive on their arrival here.

Moon-men (second order). Below this huge class comes the second order of the moon-men, whose members, having been individualised at a somewhat earlier stage in their animal life, had not yet fully developed a causal body, but had already what might be described as the skeleton of such a vehicle - a number of interlacing streams of force which indicated the outline of the ovoid that was yet to come. These egos had consequently a somewhat curious appearance, almost as though they were enclosed in a kind of basket-work of the higher mental matter.

At the present day these are represented by the great mass of the bourgeoisie; what is usually called the lower middle class, a typical specimen of whom would be the small shop-keeper or shop-assistant. This class may be described as on the whole well-intentioned, but usually narrow, conventional and dull. They often make a fetish of what they call respectability. A man who is deadly respectable usually does nothing whatever that counts, either for good or for ill. He may go on at a dead level of monotony for many lives, guiding himself always by the canon of what he supposes other people will think of him.

We may sometimes see a bourgeois soul even in the higher classes, and when such souls attain power in any country, it indicates that that country is engaged in expiating its evil karma. The reign of such a king as George III. in England was the karma of the murder of king Charles I. and of the other horrors of puritanism; and the result was the division between England and America, which is only now being healed. Since people of this level cannot learn the lesson of any particular sub-race as rapidly as the higher classes, they usually take many incarnations in each before passing on to the next.

Lunar Animal-men. The next group we call the lunar animal-men - those egos who had individualised from the earliest stage of the animal kingdom at which individualisation was possible. They consequently commenced their human life without anything which could properly be called a causal body, but with the monad floating above a personality to which it was linked only by certain threads of nirvanic matter. It was they who in the first round filled the forms made by the Lords of the Moon, and thus did pioneer work for all the kingdoms.

In considering them we come at last to what are called the working-classes, who make the enormous majority of humanity in every country. Why they alone should receive the honourable title of workers is not clear, for they would assuredly rebel with promptitude and vigour if they were called upon to work as many hours a day as does any successful man of the higher classes; but it is usually taken to signify those who work with their hands rather than with their heads. The particular type with which we are dealing at the moment - those who were animal-men on the moon - may be said to work with both, for they are the skilled workmen of the world - belonging to the proletariat, but representing the best class of it; men of determination and good character, self-respecting and reliable.

Below that again we have three classes, whose members had not yet succeeded in breaking away from their group-souls, and were consequently not then individualities, though they had every prospect of becoming so during our present earth-chain. These are still labelled as animals.

First-class Moon-animal. These attained humanity during the second round of the earth-chain, and are at the present day represented by the vast mass of unskilled labour, on the whole well-meaning but usually careless and improvident. Along with them we must group the higher types of savages - men like the Zulus and some of the better kinds of American Indians and negroes.

Second-class Moon-animals. This is a lower type which gained individuality only in the third round the earth-chain. We see it exemplified now in savages of comparatively mild type, in some of the hill-tribes of India, and among ourselves in the wastrels, the unemployable, the drunkards, and many of the slum-dwellers of our great towns.

Third-class Moon-animals. These are the lowest specimens of humanity, but little removed even now from the animal kingdom, which they left only during the earlier world-periods of this present round, or even in the earlier races on this earth. It is represented now by the lowest and most brutal of savages, and among ourselves by habitual criminals, by bomb-throwers and wife- and child-beaters. To this group also may be added a few of those who at various stages were individualised through hatred or fear.

Below all these come the three classes which furnish our present lower kingdoms; the lunar vegetable kingdom, which is now our animal; the lunar mineral, which is now our vegetable; and the lunar elemental kingdoms, the most advanced of which has become our mineral kingdom.

It is to those whom we have called the animal-men that the pioneer work on the earth-chain was assigned. Although on the moon they broke away from the animal kingdom, and must therefore be considered as potentially human, on the first globe of the first round of our earth-chain they entered into evolution not at the human level but at that of the first elemental kingdom. They passed rapidly from that into the second and third, and then successively through the mineral, vegetable and animal kingdoms until they reached the human.

In each of these kingdoms they established the forms, taking the idea of them from the minds of the Lords of the Moon, who, on behalf of the LOGOS, were directing the evolution of that globe. We might rather say, perhaps, that these primitive entities flowed into the moulds made by the instructors, and materialised these moulds for the use of those who followed them; for close behind them all the time was pressing the next class of monads - the highest of those who had not yet in the lunar chain broken away from the group-souls. And behind them in turn came all the rest.

When our animal-men had completed this work on the first globe in that first round, they moved on to the second globe and repeated exactly the same process there in denser matter; when that was finished they passed to the third, and then to the fourth, and so on, running again through the tedious evolution from the first elemental kingdom up to the human in each of the globes, in order that the forms might be duly prepared for those that followed. At the end of the first round their task was over, and they entered the first globe of the second round at the level of primitive humanity, though it was so primitive that the advantage is scarcely a perceptible one.

In the course of that second round the first class of the lunar animals had reached the human level, and the same thing happened in the third round to the second class of lunar animals; but here a fresh complication is introduced by the entry in the middle of the third round of the second order of moon-men, who had succeeded on the moon-chain in setting up a kind of framework for the causal body. Coming in at this stage, they soon pushed themselves to the front and took the lead.

Students will remember that the fourth world-period of the fourth round differs from all the rest in that it is to some extent a recapitulation of all the earlier stages. A large number of entities appear to have been on the brink of individualisation, but could not quite attain it in the ordinary course of evolution before that middle point of the fourth round when the door was to be shut. A special opportunity was therefore given to them, and the conditions of the first, second and third rounds were reproduced in miniature in the first, second and third root-races of this present world-period.

If we examine humanity as it appeared on Mars in this fourth round, we find that it did not differ radically in appearance from that of the present day; and this is true of all its root-races from the first to the seventh. But if we look at the humanity of the first root-race on our own globe in this present round, we shall see that its members are utterly unlike any kind of men that we know. They are mere drifting masses of cloud - just the men of the first round over again. In the same way men of our second root-race have the curious formless pudding-bag appearance which had not until then been seen on any world of our chain since the second round. In the third root-race came over again all the business of the descent into denser matter and the separation of the sexes which had distinguished middle of the third round.

All this was done only for the sake of backward entities, and it must not be forgotten that only they took part in it - which accounts for the sin of the mindless, the extreme degradation of the forms, and other things. None of the humanity of previous rounds (and previous parts of this round) appeared during that period at all; all its members came in only when the changes in the middle of the third root-race had brought matters back to something resembling the conditions to which they were accustomed - though even then the physical vehicles were of so low a type that some of the arrivals declined to occupy them. The whole of the plan of the earlier races of this globe was in fact the offering of a final opportunity to the laggards, and it was to a large extent successful. Many entities who had not been fully able to take advantage of these conditions in those earlier rounds were able to do something with them now, especially with the aid of the tremendous impetus given to evolution by the descent of the Lords of the Flame from Venus.

In this fourth round the third class of lunar animals attained their individuality, and in the middle of the third root-race on this globe the less developed of the first order of moon-men began to return to incarnation also. From that time until the middle of the Atlantean period, and perhaps even somewhat beyond it, the monads of that first order came rapidly into incarnation, and of course at once took up a position in the forefront of evolving humanity.

It is hoped that this attempt at explanation will facilitate the work of those who are studying this most interesting subject. There is, it is true, much complication in detail, but the broad principles are clear, and a student who keeps those in mind will soon grasp the scheme as a whole.

THE EARTH-CHAIN

We have just passed the middle point of the evolution of our chain of worlds. There are to be seven rounds - seven journeys round the seven globes. Three of those journeys have been completed, and we are now on the fourth (the middle) globe of the fourth round. The middle point of our world-period ought to be the culmination of the fourth or Atlantean root-race, and as we are now at a comparatively early period in the history of the fifth root-race it is evident that we have only just passed that middle period. We do not know, however, whether the middle point in evolution corresponds to the middle point in time, for we do not know whether all the rounds or all the race-periods are of the same length. As I have mentioned before, the probabilities seem to be that they differ, perhaps even differ considerably; and there is reason to hope those lying in front of us may be somewhat shorter than those which are behind us.

As I have already said, it is useless even to speculate on the actual length in years of these enormous periods. Some years ago we took considerable pains to verify one of the remote dates given in *The Secret Doctrine*, that of sixteen and a half million years since the separation of the sexes in the middle of the third root-race. We found that separation to be a long process which extended over more than million years and was taking place at different times in different parts of the world. Selecting a time when it seemed to have been fairly achieved, we calculated from that time to the present by observing certain astronomical changes, and our result was within a hundred thousand years of Madame Blavatsky's. As this was an observation made years after her death, and by methods absolutely different from any that I have known her to use, I think we may accept it as a very good corroboration.

From what we saw in the course of that enquiry we came to the conclusion that all those earlier radical changes in the constitution of man extended over really enormous periods of time, but that the later changes connected with the development of civilisations passed much more rapidly, so that these latter could be counted by thousands of years, while the former required actually millions. Without then pledging ourselves to anything in the way of dates as regards the earlier part of this stupendous evolution, let us glance rapidly over the work done so far in this earth-chain.

Before the solar system was brought into manifestation, the LOGOS formed the entire scheme of it in His mind, and by doing so brought it all simultaneously into existence upon His mental plane. At what level that mental plane may be we cannot tell; it may be what we call the mental cosmic plane, or it may be higher still. To it Madame Blavatsky, so far as it concerns our solar system, has given the name of "the archetypal world," and the Greeks seem to have called it "the intelligible world." All that we hear or read as to an instantaneous creation of the whole system out of nothing refers to this formation of cosmic thought-forms.

Indeed, from one point of view it seems as though we were in truth an expression of the Planetary LOGOS Himself, and as though the evolution were taking place within His body, as though the globes were centres in that body, or rather, not the globes that we see, but the spirit of them - their higher principles. From this point of view globe A would be the expression of His brain or mental body, and all these forms would exist in His mind. For our mental plane is not only the third subdivision of the lowest cosmic plane; it is also at the same time the lowest subdivision of an aspect or manifestation of the LOGOS. We may take it that He manifests Himself along seven lines or through seven aspects, and that each of these that we call planes is the lowest form of one of these aspects, so that the atomic part of our mental plane is really the lowest subplane of the mental body of the Planetary LOGOS.

Before the Manu of a chain or of a round commences the task appointed for Him, He examines the part of that mighty thought-form which refers to His work, and brings it down to some level within easy reach for constant reference. The same thing is done at a somewhat lower level by the Manu of each world and of each root-race . Each Manu at His own level has before Him the model towards which He has to build, and He endeavours to make His race or His world, as the case may be, as nearly as possible an exact copy of what the LOGOS intended it to be. As He has to build with existing materials He can usually approach the required perfection only by degrees; and so the earlier efforts at the formation of a race, for example, are often only partially successful.

In the first round of the earth-chain the Manu in charge brought down all the archetypes for the whole of the chain. Although many of these will not be fully perfected down here until the seventh round, the germs of all of them were already there even in the first round. For every kingdom in nature He selected a certain set of forms, which He wished to have vivified during the first round, with the view of developing from them at later stages everything which the LOGOS wished the earth-chain to produce. The scheme of these forms, materialised down to a level where they could use them, was handed over to certain of the Lords of the Moon, who were entrusted with the work of setting the activities of the first chain in motion. They made these forms in each of the seven worlds of that first round, and as they made them the animal-men from the moon entered them, solidified and used them, and from them generated others which could be inhabited by the moon-animals which occupied the stages below them.

On each of the planets these lunar animal-men began at the lowest level, with the forms necessary for the first elemental kingdoms. Then they passed through in rapid succession the second and third elemental kingdoms, and then the mineral, vegetable and animal until they reached the human. Having done this on each planet they attained humanity for the last time on the seventh planet of the lunar chain. Since then they have rested from that particular kind of labour, for on the second round and afterwards they were human from the beginning.

The conditions during that first round were different from any that have prevailed since. First, the life was in all cases a stage higher, for when the planets were first brought into existence they were at the same level as those of the moon-chain. Globes A and G, for example, which are now on the lower levels of the mental plane, were then the theatre for life belonging to the higher levels. The globes themselves were built even then of the lower mental matter, but it was not in a condition to be inhabited by beings at its own level - not sufficiently condensed nor sufficiently at rest. Globes B and F, though composed of astral matter, were then utilised only for forms of lower mental matter.

Mars and Mercury were still in a condition largely gaseous and etheric, and only astral bodies were employed by the entities who lived their lives upon these two planets. Our own planet D already contained a good deal of solid physical matter, but in a condition of heat so intense that there were still lakes and seas and even showers of molten metal, so that it would have been quite impossible for people with bodies in the slightest degree like ours to live there at all. The inhabitants, however, used only vehicles of etheric matter, and therefore were not at all incommoded by these conditions. In the interval between the first and the second round the matter of the various globes had time to settle down into a more orderly condition, so that each of them could be inhabited by entities using vehicles at the level its of its own matter.

It is difficult for us to imagine what the evolution of that first chain can have been; it is even difficult for those of us who have repeatedly watched it to give any account of it in words upon the physical plane. It is by no means easy to realise even the present condition of globe A. We can understand that the men of that globe are living in their mental bodies, and we can imagine to some extent that the group-souls of animals and vegetables may somehow or other exist at such a level; but what can a mineral be upon the mental plane? It would correspond to our thought of a mineral. Yet perhaps we should be wrong to assume that such a thought-form as we could make of gold would be the only representative of gold on that level; the thought-form which exists there is that of the Manu, and is moulded by a power altogether beyond comparison with that of our mentality.

Every article which exists on the physical plane must also exist in a certain sense upon all the planes above it, since it is a manifestation of the divine life, and must therefore have its connecting link through all the planes. It must be on these higher correspondences of the minerals that certain effects are produced which constitute for them the evolution of those less material globes; but the idea is not one which can readily be explained or made to gear in with the conceptions of the physical brain. It is the bringing down of the mind-energies flowing from the LOGOS - from His cosmic mental plane to that prakritic mental which is our mental plane. It is His idea of a mineral, materialised as low down as our thought of the etheric body of a mineral.

When the whole thing was brought down upon globe D in the first round the etheric body of a mineral was formed, but even then it was not a whole etheric body, because at this early stage only some of the sub-planes were fully vivified. The very atoms also were more sluggish, since only one set of spirillae was in activity. In each round an additional force was poured into the atoms, and that brought an additional set of spirillae into play, so that now as we are in the fourth round we have four sets of spirillae in activity; but even now our atom is as nothing in comparison with that which will exist in the seventh round, when all the sets of spirillae will be fully working, and the entire atom will be what the LOGOS intends it to be.

The man of globe A in the first round can hardly be called a man at all; he is a thought. He is what will some day be a mind-body - the germ of a mind-body, bearing perhaps the same relation to its later possibilities as the embryonic form of an infant after the first month bears to the fully developed human body. He has marvellously little consciousness at this early stage.

As we have said, on the astral globe B in the first round everything was brought down to the lower mental level and fixed definitely there, with a little commencement of astralisation. On Mars men had definite astral bodies, but they were as yet imperfect, for only matter of certain subplanes was then to be had. A little touch of etheric matter was also introduced, though only certain kinds of ether were available. On the Earth in this round men had etheric bodies, but they were mere drifting shapeless clouds, though towards the end of the world-period they began to aggregate around themselves gaseous matter as well as etheric. They appear to have absorbed from the intensely heated surrounding atmosphere whatever they required in the way of nutriment.

They seem to have had a succession of manifestations which I suppose we must take as corresponding to races - apparently, however, only root-races, for there were but seven; and one incarnation (if we can call it an incarnation) for each individual lasted through the whole race. It appears, however, that the world-periods were enormously longer then even than they are now, but it is not easy for us, with our ideas of what life means, to understand how these most primitive of men could contrive to evolve at all. The condition of the world has already been described, but we may note that some of the chemical elements were already beginning to combine. By the end of the world-period the temperature was considerably reduced, perhaps to about a thousand degrees Fahrenheit on the average, though it remained much hotter than that in certain districts, and in others it had even got down to the level of boiling water.

On globe E (Mercury) they had apparently only the three higher ethers - not four as they had had upon the earth. But they had obviously progressed, and were much more alive than they had been, though even now their consciousness seemed amoebalike. Nevertheless, it is clear that man was already beginning in a blind way to work both upwards and downwards - downwards to densify his lower vehicles and upwards to make them more conscious. Primitive though everything was, it is clear that each globe was an advance on that which had preceded it. But in all cases it appears that he had not yet the full consciousness even of any subdivision of matter in which he happened to be working. The impression given rather is that each subdivision was again subdivided, and that he was able to use only this fraction of a part.

There seems little to be said with regard to evolution on globes F and G, except that there for the first time we begin to notice the curious phenomenon of failures. On every globe from the first a certain small portion of each kingdom had been intentionally left behind, in order to act as seed for the next occupation of the planet in the following round. If this were not done all the trouble of making the forms afresh would have to be undertaken on each globe in each round; whereas by the present scheme a certain population is always left on each planet, from which the race can be reproduced in the next round when necessary.

The great wave of life moves from planet to planet, as the LOGOS wills it. When He fixes His attention upon one globe, the life flames out there and evolution pushes rapidly forward. When he withdraws His eyes from it the life fades away, the wheels of progress slacken and the wave passes on to the globe to which His attention has been turned. But the life does not die out altogether.

A small population, human, animal, vegetable, still remains, but does not increase. It usually maintains its numbers at about the same level through the untold millions of years until that planet is entered again. When the life-wave reaches it once more, when a vast number of egos are ready to incarnate in it, the stagnant race suddenly becomes wondrously prolific, and great changes and vast improvements of alls kinds are quickly introduced, and vehicles are soon evolved fit to receive the coming inrush of a far more highly evolved humanity. Meantime the small and comparatively torpid race has been providing for those who are engaged in the inner round to which I have already referred. As I have said, in the earlier globes of the first round this seed was purposely left behind; but towards the end of that round there were egos who did not achieve quite what was expected of them - who were not fit to go on to globe G at the time when the normal evolution of globe F was over.

Such entities were left behind, and worked on steadily among the remnant, passing perhaps, in, process of time, to join the remnant of globe G; possibly also, by means of some extraordinary impulse, occasionally being able to hurry on to try to overtake the life-wave, but more often continuing to lag behind, until they are overtaken by the life-wave on its next journey round the globes. In this latter case they usually find themselves in a class of monads lower than that to which they had previously belonged. This process is a kind of reversal of the procedure of the inner round. In the inner round the ego runs on ahead of the life-wave, and by making an extra journey round the globes raises himself one class higher. These laggards fall behind the life-wave and, by losing one round, drop into an inferior class. A certain proportion of these failures appear on every planet and in all the various kingdoms - mineral essence that ought to have reached the vegetable level, vegetable life that should have touched the animal, animal life that should have becomes individualised.

No matter of the lower planes is ever carried over from planet to planet. When, for example, we leave this planet in order to incarnate upon Mercury, only the egos will be carried over. Those egos will draw round themselves mental and astral matter belonging to their new planet, and they will obtain physical bodies by entering the baby vehicles provided by some of those who are already inhabiting Mercury.

Just at first those vehicles will be of but poor quality, no doubt; but it will not be the first-class monads who require them, for it is a law of this system of evolution that those who reach the highest level on one planet are never born in the early races of the next planet. They do not need such primitive evolution as those early races would give, and so they join the evolution of the planet when a certain proportion of its people have evolved to somewhere near their level, and can provide them with fitting vehicles.

Exactly the same thing happens as egos pass from chain to chain. The most developed of the lunar inhabitants are not found in the first round of the earth-chain, but come in only in the middle of the fourth. The egos who incarnate in the first root-race on any planet are those who have not progressed beyond the middle of the evolution on the previous planet, just as it was the animal-men from the moon who did all the work in this first round of the earth-chain of which we have been speaking.

In connection with this first round it may be well to explain the apparent difference which exists between the Theosophical teaching and the theories of Darwin. In this first round, when form appeared for the first time so far as our planetary chain is concerned, the human shape was evolved from the animal, just as the Darwinian theory suggests, though it is also true that in our present fourth round the process was reversed, and the human form existed on this globe before those of any of the mammals which we now know.

For the inconceivably slow process of natural selection from accidental variation we substitute an intelligent direction both of the selection and of the variations; for we hold that the forms evolved only in order that they may be a fitter expression for the evolving life within. Our attitude towards Darwinism is that we agree in broad outline with its discoveries, but carry them much further, since we propound a spiritual as well as a material evolution.

In the second round the forms made in the first round were already there, so that it was not necessary to repeat the building process. Each subplane of each plane is divided into seven, so that in each plane there are forty-nine subdivisions. In this second round man was working at and through the first and second subdivisions of each of the subplanes, so that while he had matter of all the planes in him it was only the two lower subdivisions of the two lower sub-planes that were active. Man may be said to be building his lower quaternary gradually through the earlier half of his evolution.

In this second round the races were much more definite, and were clearly distinguishable one from another. Men were no longer mere drifting clouds of etheric or gaseous matter, but had succeeded in developing a certain amount of solidity, though they were still unpleasantly jelly-like in consistency and indeterminate in shape. Madame Blavatsky compares them to pudding-bags, because of the curious shapeless projections which they had instead of arms and legs. At the beginning of the round they put out these projections temporarily, just as an amoeba does; but constant repetition of the process at last made the projections permanent, and moulded them into some approximation to the form into which they were destined finally to settle. Many of these people were so light and tenuous that they were able to drift about in the heavy atmosphere of the time. Others rolled along rather than crept, but none of them were able to maintain themselves in an upright position without assistance.

Man was still lamentably incomplete as regards his higher vehicles. He had what he considered a mind, and something else that might stand for a feeble astral body, but his consciousness was still dim and vague and he had little thinking power; he was all instincts and almost no reason.

In this round the animal-men maintained and improved their human position, and by the end of it the first class of the animals had definitely attained humanity. Just as all the archetypes of the mineral kingdom had been fully brought down in the first round, though not yet fully worked out, so were all the vegetable archetypes brought down in this second round, though it was long after that before they were all realized. It is probably chiefly to the vegetation of this period that we owe our coal deposits.

In the course of the third round we come to more comprehensible conditions. Even in the earlier globes man became more human in shape than he had been before, though even then he was still cloudy, gigantic and far from beautiful. On Mars in this third round man had for the first time what may be called a recognizably human body, though at first it was still etheric, and more like some kind of reptilian monkey than like man as we know him now. He was still somewhat jelly-like, and if one pressed in his skin by a poke of the finger the hole remained for a long time before it filled out again. He had rudimentary bones - more gristle perhaps than bone, but he was not stiff enough to stand, and so he lay about groveling and wallowing in the soft warm mud at the sides of the rivers.

Mars had much more water then that it has now, and much of the country was pretty, though the vegetation was peculiar. The atmosphere was what we should now consider unbreathable - full of chlorine and quite suffocating. All the animal archetypes were brought down in this round, though many of them were not worked out until the middle of our present round.

On the earth in the third round great changes took place. Even from the beginning men were more compact and began to try to stand upright, though they were still shaky and uncertain, and always fell back to all-fours when pursued or frightened. They began to have hair and bristles upon the body, but they were still loose and flabby. Their skins were dark and their faces scarcely human; strangely flattened with eyes small and set curiously far apart, so that they could see sideways as well as in front. They had the lower jaw very heavily developed, and practically no forehead, but just a roll of flesh like a sausage where the forehead should have been, the whole head sloping backwards curiously.

The arms were much longer in proportion than ours, and could not be perfectly straightened at the elbows, a difficulty which existed with the knees also. The hands and feet were enormous and misshapen, and the heels projected backwards almost as much as the toes did forwards, so that the man was able to walk backwards as rapidly and certain as in the other direction. This curious form of progress was facilitated by the possession of the third eye at the back of the head, which still remains to us in a rudimentary form as the pineal gland.

Even yet men had scarcely any reason, but only passions and instincts. They knew nothing about fire, and were unable to count. They ate chiefly certain slimy creatures of reptilian nature, but they also dug up and ate some kind of primitive truffle, and I have seen them tearing off the tops of gigantic tree-ferns in order to eat the seeds.

Towards the middle of the occupation of this planet the separation of the sexes took place, and soon after that the second order of moon-men began to come into incarnation. They were in the first place born of the existing humanity, but they soon established a new type for themselves, becoming smaller, more compact, lighter in colour and generally speaking much more what we should now call human in appearance.

There was constant war between them and the earlier and more gigantic inhabitants, who caught and ate them whenever opportunity offered, but the later arrivals, having much more intellect, were presently able to dominate their gigantic congeners, and to keep them in some sort of order. Indeed, practically the whole of the world presently passed into their control, and the earlier races had either to adapt themselves to the more civilized life or to be driven off into the less desirable parts of the country.

The world was still far from being as quiescent as at the present time. Earthquakes and volcanic outbursts were still painfully common, and life was distinctly precarious. The configuration of the land was entirely different, and mountains seem to have attained stupendous heights, unknown to us now. There were enormous waterfalls, and great whirlpools were also common.

When the race passed on to Mercury we find on the whole a decided improvement. Much more affection appeared, and men showed distinct traces of unselfishness, sharing their food instead of snarling over it as they had frequently done at the earlier stages. The presence of the moon-men had given a great impetus to progress, and though the bulk of humanity were still very animal and undeveloped, traces of co-operation and rudimentary civilization already began to appear. There is not much to be said with regard to the sixth and seventh planets, so we will turn to the consideration of our present fourth round.

On globe A in this fourth round mind became definite on the lower mental level, and so we may say that in this round man began really to think. The result at first was by no means good. In the previous rounds he had not been sufficiently developed to originate thought-forms to any great extent, and so the elemental essence of the globes had been affected only by the thoughts of the devas, which left everything harmonious and peaceful. Now that man began to interject his selfish and jarring thoughts, this comfortable condition was very largely disturbed. Strife, unrest and disharmony were introduced, and the animal kingdom drew decisively apart from man, and began to feel fear and hatred towards him.

All the archetypes for humanity were brought down at the beginning of this round - among others, archetypes of races which have not yet come into existence. From examining these it is possible to see what the men of the future will be like. They will have finer vehicles in every way, and will be distinctly more beautiful in appearance, expressing in their forms the spiritual forces.

When the life-wave reached Mars in this fourth round, it found in possession of the planet, besides the ordinary seed-humanity, another and most unpleasant race, which is spoken of in *The Secret Doctrine* as the "water-men, terrible and bad." They were descended from the type which had been left behind in the previous round as not fit to make progress, and they had since then been engaged in developing the evil side of their nature. They were the usual half-reptile, half-ape, but with a horrible tarantula-like appearance about the eyes, and a fiendish delight in cruelty and evil. They seem also to have had a certain amount of low-class mesmeric power, and were a kind of primitive edition of the Malakurumbas as described by Madame Blavatsky in her account of the hill tribes of the Nilgiris.

When the life-wave came around, the incoming humanity soon established itself sufficiently strongly to free itself from the fear of these monstrous savages. It was to resist possible attacks from them that the first fortifications were erected by man, and it was also to be able to defeat their malignity that men began first to build primitive cities and live together in considerable numbers. At first they built them principally of wood and mud, though sometimes of piles of unhewn stone.

At this period some of the Lords of the Moon incarnated among them and taught them many things - among others the use of fire, which, however, they did not yet know how to produce for themselves. The greater Beings lighted their fires for them, and then they kept them perpetually alight. Very early a stringent law was made that a public fire should always be kept burning in a building specially dedicated to it, and the young girls who could not as yet either work or fight were usually left to watch it. From this no doubt arose the first idea of a sacred fire ever to be kept burning as a religious duty, and of the appointment of vestal virgins to guard it.

Sometimes, however, it happened that, from a great flood or tempest or some other catastrophe, a whole district was left for a time without fire, and then the people often had to travel far in order to obtain and carry back to their homes this prime necessity. Some bold spirit conceived the idea of obtaining fire in such an emergency from the crater of a volcano, and many lives were at one time and another lost in such attempts. This was in the fourth root-race.

The men of the fifth root-race were comparatively advanced, for they built their houses of hewn stone, though without mortar. They were a proud and warlike people, but had some curious ideas. They appear to have had no initiative whatever, and they regarded anything new with horror, as exceedingly immoral and repulsive. They had no perseverance, and even yet but little reasoning capacity. Everything was done on impulse, and nothing was under control in any way, so long only as it was nothing new. Yet in many ways they would compare favourably with some races which exist on earth now.

The men of the sixth race were a much more powerful set of people, with a considerable amount of will and determination. They soon dominated the fifth, taking up its civilisation and carrying it much further. They succeeded in subduing the whole of the planet and brought it under one rule, although the enormous majority of its inhabitants belonged to the fifth race. These people had much more mind than the others, and possessed some inventive genius, but it was their tendency to do everything by fits and starts, and not take up a piece of work and carry it through. There was some psychic development among them, but it was usually uncontrolled. Want of control, in fact, was a permanent characteristic of this Martian civilisation. Everything was erratic, even though the people were capable in certain ways.

The people of the seventh race in turn got the power into their hands, not by force, but rather by superior mental development and cunning. They were not so warlike as the sixth, and they were always smaller in number, but they knew more in many ways than the sixth. They were coming nearer to modern ideas; they had a more definite sense of right and wrong; they were less fierce and more law-abiding; they had a definite policy and lived according to it.

Their supremacy was entirely intellectual, and they possessed to a high extent the art of combination. Their social polity seems to have been something like that of ants or bees, and in some ways they would compare favourably with many races of the present day. It was in this race that we first noticed writing as a fairly common accomplishment They knew something of art, for they had both statues and pictures, though totally different in every way from ours. They were also the first race who took the trouble to make good roads.

I believe that I have already explained why the earlier races of our present world-period differ from all the rest. We were in fact recapitulating the first, second and third rounds for the benefit of those monads who, though considerably behind the rest, could by a special effort of this sort be helped to overtake them. During the third root-race was repeated all that had happened in the middle of the third round - the materialisation of men on to the physical plane and their separation into sexes. After this had been fully achieved, and a reasonable continuity of form had been arrived at, a number of special efforts were made, by the authorities in charge of the evolution, to consolidate humanity and set it definitely on its way to the higher spiritual advancement which lies before it on the upward arc of the chain.

The first step was the descent of seven of the leading Lords of the Moon, in order to provide vehicles for the seven great types or rays of men. We are told in *The Secret Doctrine* how each stood on his own lot, and cast off shadows which were inhabited by the men of the lower race. This somewhat mystical statement means simply that these great men duplicated, by an effort of the will, their own etheric doubles; in fact, they materialised round themselves an additional etheric double, made it permanent and then stepped out of it.

The other entities of lower race who were just being brought down to the physical level eagerly seized upon these vehicles, entered them and tried to use them. Not being yet fully adapted to them, they found it difficult to maintain their position, and were constantly slipping out. As soon as this happened, some other entity would seize the etheric body, and slip into it as though it were an overcoat, only presently to find it slipping from him in turn, and to see it seized by somebody else. Many of these etheric doubles were made, and by degrees the less developed people learnt how to inhabit them permanently, so that the process of further materialisation could be undertaken, and in this way gradually bodies were produced which served to express the seven great types and their sub-types.

The bodies of the children of these entities were by no means equal to those of their fathers, but still certain types were established, and however much the forms deteriorated they were still habitable. As soon as these lines were definite the special classes of monads from the moon, who had been individualised at an earlier stage for the purpose, were brought down to take possession of them. These were the three classes who had been individualised on globes A, B and C of the lunar chain, and I have already described how the first of these classes, the orange-coloured group, refused to do its duty precisely because the forms were still in so unsatisfactory a condition. Because of this refusal the forms destined for them had to be occupied by an altogether lower class; and the consequence was that, instead of maintaining the advancement which had been gained by so much effort, the forms were allowed to drop back again into a condition even worse than before. Their undeveloped possessors even intermingled with some of the animal forms. This is what Madame Blavatsky called the sin of the mindless, and the result of it gave us various types of anthropoid apes.

The fifth, sixth, and seventh subraces of the third root-race were much more what we should now call human than their predecessors. The description previously given of a third-round man would fit aptly enough the man of the fifth Lemurian subrace. These have been often spoken of as the egg-headed people, from the resemblance of their skulls to an egg with the small end up. They had still but little forehead, and the eyes were set near the top of the egg.

The men of the sixth subrace were chiefly remarkable for their colour. They were no longer black or brown-black like the fifth subrace, but blue-black shading towards the end of the race into a distinct but rather livid blue.

The seventh subrace, beginning as grey-blue, passed down through various greyish shades into a kind of grey-white. A fair idea of the type of their faces may be obtainable from the statues which they themselves erected, some few of which still remain upon Easter Island. They had long horse-like faces, the trip of the nose being at first above the centre, and at the end of the race exactly in the centre, of a line drawn from the top of the forehead to the chin. The forehead was still a mere roll of bone, though growing a little higher towards the end of the subrace.

They had thick clumsy lips and broad and flat noses, characteristics which have survived in a less aggravated form among the negroes who are perhaps now their nearest representatives.

No race of pure Lemurian blood now exists; though the pigmies of Central Africa appear to represent a long-isolated fragment of the fourth subrace, decreased to their present stature during millions of years in accordance with that curious law which appears to impose diminution of size upon the last relics of a dying race. Most negro tribes have a considerable admixture of Atlantean blood; in the case of the Zulus, for example, we have in general build and bearing a close representative of the Tlavatli subrace of the Atlanteans, although the colour and some of the faces are Lemurian. The men of this seventh subrace were great builders in a rough cyclopean fashion, and they had also a certain rude idea of art.

It was during the period of this third root-race that there occurred one of the greatest events connected with human evolution - the descent of the Lords of the Flame from Venus. It has already been mentioned that Venus is considerably further advanced in evolution than our earth-chain, and in consequence of that fact many of her adepts are able to move freely about the solar system, and to go and offer assistance wherever it is needed.

The determined effort had been made to bring up the backward members of our humanity, by affording the additional opportunity to those who needed it of running once more through such evolution as the first, second and third rounds can give; and when that was over this further tremendous stimulus of the descent of these Great Ones was brought to bear as a final effort, to individualise as large a number as possible of the more backward entities before what is called "the shutting of the door," the period when for the sake of further evolution no more entities could be admitted from the animal kingdom into the human.

This band of Great Ones then arrived from Venus and at once took charge of evolution. Their Leader is called in Indian books Sanat Kumara, and with Him came three lieutenants and some five and twenty other adepts as assistants. About a hundred ordinary human beings who were in some way affiliated to these Great Ones, or perhaps had been individualised by Them, were also brought over from Venus, and merged into the ordinary humanity of the earth.

It is these Great Ones who are spoken of in *The Secret Doctrine* as projecting the spark into the mindless men and awakening the intellect within them. We must not allow ourselves to be misled by this rather curious expression into supposing that the Lords threw some part of Themselves into the human bodies. They acted rather in the nature of a magnetic stimulus; They shone upon the people as the sun shines upon flowers, and drew them up towards Themselves, and so enabled them to develope the latent spark and to become individualised.

Another point worthy of notice is that none of the Lords from Venus took incarnation in our humanity at all. They did not (and indeed could not) take human bodies; They build for Themselves instead vehicles like the highest ideals of the human form in appearance, yet absolutely unlike it in that they were uninfluenced by time and incapable of change or decay. I have myself seen several of these marvellous vehicles, and although they have been worn upon this earth for sixteen million years they still remain precisely as on the day when they were made. They must be regarded as a kind of permanent materialisation; bodies built like statues, and yet to the sight and the touch presenting the appearance of ordinary living men.

I know that in *The Secret Doctrine* Madame Blavatsky mentions some of the sons of mind, who came to this earth to help, as incarnating among the people whom they were trying to benefit; but she applies this title to the Lords of the Moon as well as to the Lords of the Flame, and it was the former only who entered into ordinary human bodies and so for the time became part of another race. The great Lords of the Flame have done Their work long ago, and most of Them have passed away from us to take up Their tasks elsewhere. Only a very few still remain with us, holding some of the highest offices of the Hierarchy which works for the good of humanity.

But for the help kindly given to us by these great Leaders the world would have been a very different place to-day. Without Them not only would millions, who became human under the impetus which They gave, be still in the animal kingdom, but all the rest of humanity would be far behind the position in which it now stands. This fourth round is that which is especially destined to the development of the desire-principle in man; it is only in the next or fifth round that he is intended to devote himself to the unfolding of the intellect. Owing, however, to the stimulus given by the Lords of the Flame the intellect has already been considerably developed, and we are therefore for a whole round in advance of where we should have been but for Their help. At the same time it should be said that the intellect of which we are now so proud is infinitesimal compared to that which the average man will possess at the culminating point of the next or fifth round.

Among other plans for the helping on of evolution, the Lords of the Flame brought from Their planet certain additions to our kingdoms. They imported wheat as a specially desirable food-stuff for humanity, and they also brought in bees and ants - the former to modify the vegetable kingdom and assist in the fertilisation of flowers, as well as to provide a pleasant and nutritious addition to human food. It will be noted that both bees and ants live in a manner quite different from that of the purely terrestrial creatures, in that with them a group-soul animates the entire ant or bee community, so that the community acts with a single will, and its different units are actually members of one body in the sense in which hands and feet are members of the human frame. It might indeed be said of them that they have not only a group-soul but a group-body also.

Our human evolution has attempted to imitate all these importations, but with somewhat indifferent success. In imitating bees we have produced wasps; and in imitating ants we have produced what are commonly called "white ants," as well as curious little ant-flies which are almost indistinguishable from them. The nearest that we have been able to get to wheat is rye, but the crossing of the wheat with other native terrestrial grasses has given us oats and barley.

After this comes the history of the mighty Atlantean race, to which even to-day belong the majority of earth's inhabitants. Towards the middle part of this race came in the first order of moon-men, ship-load after ship-load of them, each taking their places just where they could themselves evolve best, and where they could be of the greatest use to the rest of evolving humanity, to the forefront of which they naturally immediately gravitated.

Later than the great Atlantean race came the wonderful history of the Aryans - a grand civilisation built up by the great Manu Vaivasvata. Although as yet comparatively in its youth, it already dominates the world, but its greatest glory lies still in advance of us. Soon, under another Manu even better known to us, the sixth root-race will be born. But the story of all this will be found in Mrs. Besant's new book *Man; Whence, How and Whither*, which contains details of the results of all the recent investigations into the subject.

MODES OF INDIVIDUALISATION

Those who have been following the recent discoveries and investigations will remember that in an article not long ago I mentioned the existence, within one of the great classes of monads, of two types which, though equal to one another in development, differ greatly in their intervals between lives, one of them habitually taking nearly double the length of heaven-life which is customary with the other. As the amount of spiritual force generated is roughly equal in the two cases, it follows that one type of man must exhaust that force more speedily than the other. Into the same portion of time, as we measure it, he compresses a double amount of bliss; he works as it were at higher pressure, and therefore concentrates his experience and gets through nearly twice the amount in any given period, so that his seven hundred years is fully equivalent to the twelve hundred of a man of the other type.

The fundamental difference between these two varieties results from the way in which, in each case, individualisation was attained. We know that the monad manifests itself upon the nirvanic plane as the triple spirit, and that, when an ego is called into existence as an expression of this triple spirit, its manifestation is arranged in a certain well-recognised form which has frequently been explained in our literature. Of the three aspects one, the spirit itself, remains upon its own plane; the second, the intuition (or, as our President has now decided to call it, the itself through the matter of the buddhic or rational pure reason) puts itself down one stage and expresses plane;* the third, intelligence, puts itself down two planes, and expresses itself through matter of the upper part of the mental plane.

* Our President has recently decided to endeavour as far as possible to replace

the Sanskrit terms in our literature by English words; from this point onwards, therefore, I shall use the words "pure reason" in place of "buddhi," and "rational plane" instead of "buddhic plane".

The personality is also triple in its manifestation, and is an accurate reflection of the arrangement of the ego; but like all other reflections, it reverses itself. The intelligence reflects itself in the lower mind on the lower part of the same mental plane: the pure reason mirrors itself in the astral body, and, in some way much more difficult to comprehend, the spirit in turn reflects itself upon the physical plane.

It is obvious that, when an ego is formed, all three of these manifestations of the spirit must be called forth, but the first connection may be made through any one of the three. It has previously been explained that individualisation from the animal kingdom usually takes place through association with the humanity of the period. Such examples of it as we occasionally see taking place round us at the present time will serve as instances for us. Some particular domestic animal, well treated by its human friends, is stimulated by its constant contact with them up to the point where it breaks away from the group-soul to which it has previously belonged. The process has been fully described in Man Visible and Invisible and The Christian Creed, and I need not repeat that description here. But a point which is not mentioned in those earlier works is the possibility that the first connection may be made in various ways - between the lower mind and the higher; between the astral body and the pure reason; or between the physical body and the spirit itself.

A domestic animal (when well treated) usually developes intense affection for its master, and a strong desire to understand him, to please him, and to anticipate what he is going to do. Sometimes, for a few minutes, the master turns affectionate thought upon the animal, or makes a distinct effort to teach him something; and in these cases there is a direct and intentional action passing from the mental or astral body of the master to the corresponding vehicle of the animal. But this is comparatively rare, and the greater portion of the work is done without any direct volition on either side, simply by the incessant and inevitable action due to the proximity of the two entities concerned. The astral and mental vibrations of the man are far stronger and more complex than those of the animal, and they are consequently exercising a never-ceasing pressure upon the latter.

We can see therefore that the character and type of the master will have a great influence on the destiny of the animal. If the master be an emotional man, full of strong affections, the probability is that the development of any domestic animal of his will be chiefly through its astral body, and that the final breaking of the link with the group-soul will be due to some sudden outrush of intense affection, which will reach the rational aspect of the floating monad belonging to it, and will thus cause the formation of an ego. If, on the other hand, the master be unemotional and if the chief activities in his nature are of the intellectual type, it is the nascent mental body of the animal which will be stimulated, and the probabilities are that individualisation will be reached because that mental development rises to a level too great to permit any longer of enfoldment within the group-soul. In yet another case, if the master be a man of great spirituality or of intensely strong will, while the animal will develope great affection and admiration for him, it will yet be the will within the animal which is principally stimulated. This will show itself in the physical body by intense activity, and indomitable resolution to achieve whatever the creature may attempt, especially in the way of service to his master.

It is difficult to rid oneself of the idea that the distance between the spirit and the physical body must be far greater than that between the lower mind and the intelligence, or between the astral and rational bodies. But this is not really so, for it is not a question of distance in space at all, but of the conveying of a sympathetic vibration from the reflection to the original. When we think of it in this way; it is obvious that each reflection must be in direct connection with its original, whatever the distance between them may be - in closer connection than it is with any object which is out of the direct line, no matter how much nearer in space the latter object may be.

The desire of the animal to rise constitutes a steady upward pressure along all these lines, and the point at which that pressure finally breaks through the restrictions, and forms the required link between the monad and its personality, determines certain characteristics of the new ego which thus comes into existence. The actual formation of the link is usually instantaneous if the first connection is made through affection or will, but it is much more gradual when it is a case of mental development; and this also makes a considerable difference in the current of the future evolution of the entity.

In the course of the recent investigations we discovered that, out of a great mass of people who were individualised practically simultaneously at a certain point in the moon-chain, those who had attained individualisation gradually by intellectual development came into incarnation upon earth roughly about one million years ago, and have since taken between any two lives an average interval of about twelve hundred years; whereas those who had attained individualisation through an instantaneous uprush of affection or will did not come into terrestrial incarnation until about four hundred thousand years later, though as they have since taken an average interval between lives of about seven hundred years their condition at the present time is practically the same.

I cannot emphasise too strongly that this difference of interval must not in the least be supposed to indicate that those who came in later generate less of spiritual force during their earth-lives. If there be any difference, it appears to be in favour of the men of shorter interval, for they (being as a rule more devotional) seem to be able to generate even more force in a given space of time than the others. Perhaps it would express the facts still better to say that they produce in a way a different kind of force; probably both are necessary, each as a complement to the other. The difference of interval between lives means merely that they take their bliss in a much more concentrated form, and therefore work out the result of an equal expenditure of force in much less time. Indeed, it appears very much as though the period of their respective entries upon terrestrial life had been arranged especially in order that, after running through about the same number of incarnations, they might arrive at the same point, and be able to work together.

Later investigations have convinced us that there is far greater flexibility with regard to these intervals between lives than we at first supposed. It is quite true that the amount of force which a man has to work out, first in the astral plane and then in the heaven-world, is precisely what he has developed during his earthly life - plus of course such further force of the same kind as he may generate during his astral or heaven-lives respectively. But it is evident that the rate at which this amount of force exhausts itself is by no means always the same. The necessity of bringing groups of people into incarnation together, in order not only that they may work out mutual karmic inter-relations, but also that they may all learn to labour together towards one great end, is evidently a dominant factor in regulating the rate of the expenditure of force.

A study of the lives of Alcyone will show that this must be so, since it is unquestionable that a number of people, living each his or her own life, must inevitably generate widely-varying amounts of spiritual force; yet in life after life of that entrancing story it is contrived that these people shall come back together, in order that they may pass through similar preparatory experiences, and that the bonds of affection between them may be knit so strongly that they will be incapable of misunderstanding or mistrusting one another, when the strain of the real work comes upon them in the future.

Besides the differences in the mode of individualisation which I have just mentioned, there are also differences in the degree of individualisation, which corresponds to the stage of development at which it takes place. It has been explained in Theosophical literature that as an animal group-soul gradually evolves within its own kingdom it breaks up into smaller and smaller subdivisions. Quadrillions of flies or mosquitoes are attached to one group-soul, millions of rats or mice, hundreds of thousands of rabbits or sparrows. But when we come to such animals as the lion, the tiger, the leopard, the deer, the wolf or the wild boar, only a few thousand will be found to belong to one soul, while among domesticated animals such as sheep and oxen the number is smaller still.

Individualisation is possible only from seven kinds of animals - one for each of the seven great lines or types. Of these we already know certainly the elephant, the monkey, the dog and the cat; and the horse is possibly a fifth. Up to each of these heads of types leads a long line of wild animals, which has not yet been fully investigated; but we know that wolves, foxes, jackals and all such creatures culminate in the dog, and lions, tigers, leopards, jaguars and ocelots in the domestic cat. When we reach these seven individualisable animals we find usually only a few hundred attached to each group-soul, and as their development continues the souls break up rapidly. The pariah dog of India or Constantinople is nothing but a half-tamed wolf, and a thousand of such creatures may well represent only one soul; but in the case of the really intelligent pet dog or cat one soul hovers over not more than ten or a dozen bodies.

Now it makes much difference at what stage of this higher animal life individualisation takes place, and this is dependent largely upon the opportunities which offer themselves. Even a pariah dog is presumably capable of individualisation, but it could be only a very low type of individualisation. The animals of the moon-chain were not the same as those of to-day, and so we cannot draw exact parallels; but assuredly the pariah dog could at most individualise into nothing more than a separated fragment of the group-soul with a monad hovering over it, connected perhaps by a line or two of spiritual matter - corresponding therefore to the animal-men from the moon, who led the way in filling the forms in the first round. On the other hand the really intelligent and affectionate pet dog or cat, whose owner looks after him properly and makes a friend of him, would certainly, when he individualised, obtain a causal body at least equivalent to that of the first order of moon-men, while various intermediate types of domestic animals would produce the basket-work causal body, such as that obtained by the second order of the moon-men.

It will be seen therefore that the amount of real work done in the attainment of any given level is practically always the same, though in some cases more of it is done in one kingdom and less in another. It has already been made abundantly clear, in the course of our investigations, that entities attaining to the culminating point in one kingdom do not enter the lower levels of the next higher kingdom. The life which ensouls an oak-tree, a banyan, or a rose-bush will pass directly into the mammalian order when it enters the animal kingdom; whereas the life which leaves the vegetable kingdom at a much lower level may pass into the stage of insects and reptiles.

In just the same way, a being who reaches the summit of intelligence and affection possible in the animal kingdom will overleap the absolutely primitive conditions of humanity, and will show himself as a first-class individuality from the beginning of his human career; whereas one who leaves the animal kingdom at a lower level will quite naturally have to begin correspondingly lower down in the scale of humanity. This is the explanation of a remark once made by one of our Masters, when referring to the cruelty and superstition shown by the great mass of humanity: "They have individualised too soon; they are not yet worthy of the human form."

The three methods of individualisation which I have already mentioned, through the development of affection, intellect, and will, are the normal lines which we may suppose to have been intended in the scheme of things. Individuality is, however, occasionally attained in certain other ways which we may perhaps define as irregular methods, since it would seem that they can scarcely have been part of the original plan.

For example, at the beginning of the seventh round of the moon-chain a certain group of beings were at the point of individualisation, and were drawn towards it by their association with some of the perfected inhabitants whom we call the Lords of the Moon. An unfortunate twist, however, entered into their development, and they began to take so great a pride in their intellectual advance, that that became the prominent feature in their character, so that they were working not to gain the approval or affection of their masters, but to show their advantage over their fellow-animals, and to excite their envy. It was this latter motive which pushed them on to make the efforts which resulted in individualisation, and so the causal bodies which were formed showed almost no colour but orange. The authorities in charge of that stage of evolution nevertheless allowed them to individualise, apparently because if they had been permitted to continue their evolution in the animal kingdom any further, they would have become worse instead of better. We have therefore the extraordinary spectacle of a detachment of egos (what we have lately been calling a ship-load), numbering about two millions, who had individualised themselves entirely by pride, and who, though clever enough in their way, possessed but little of any other quality.

The fruitage of the first, second and third globes of the seventh round of the lunar chain was intended to play a certain part in the development of humanity on the earth. At a certain stage in the development of that planet we know that seven of the Lords of the Moon - one belonging to each great type - descended to the earth and began to cast off etheric bodies for the shaping of the new race. The entities who occupied these vehicles intermarried, and when their descendants became numerous these three ship-loads of egos were called upon to descend and occupy these vehicles, and thus establish the type of the humanity that was to come. "One-third refuses; two-thirds obey." It was the members of this orange-coloured ship-load from planet A of the lunar chain who declined these lowly vehicles, while the golden-coloured egos from globe B and the rose-coloured group from globe C accepted the conditions, entered into the vehicles, and fulfilled their destiny.

The future career of these orange-coloured egos showed clearly enough the undesirability of the line along which they had come, for not only did they refused to take the primitive bodies which were assigned to them (thus leaving them to be occupied by very much lower animal types, and so leading to the sin of the mindless), but all through their history their arrogance and unruliness caused constant trouble to themselves and to others who were infected by their foolishness. Eventually the law of evolution forced them to occupy bodies in many respects considerably worse than those which had at first been offered to them; and though that lesson taught them something, and they seem to have recognised that a mistake had been made, even when they mingled with ordinary humanity we find them invariably in opposition, and perpetually making trouble by standing upon their own dignity at inopportune moments. By constant collision with natural laws the great majority of them have by degrees been driven more or less into line with the rest of humanity; but even now we may distinguish some of them by the occasional recrudescence of their old objectionable characteristics; they are still "turbulent and aggressive, independent and separative, prone to discontent and eager for change," as our President has described them.

Some few of the cleverest of them have made no inconsiderable mark upon human history, for they developed into the celebrated "Lords of the Dark Face" of Atlantis, of whom we read so much in *The Secret Doctrine*; and later such special distortions became world-devastating conquerors, caring nothing for the thousands who were slain or starved in the course of the gratification of their mad ambition, or (later still) equally unscrupulous American millionaires, well called by their parasites "Napoleons of finance."

Another abnormal method in which individuality has been gained is through fear. In the case of animals who have been cruelly treated by man, there have been cases in which the cunning developed by strenuous efforts to understand and avoid the cruelty has caused the breaking away from the group-soul, and produced an ego possessing only a very low type of intellectuality - an ego who, when he puts himself down into the lower planes, must inevitably, because of the nature of his permanent atoms, draw round him mental and astral vehicles capable only of expressing the less desirable passions.

A variant of this case is the type of ego in which the attitude caused by the cruelty has been rather that of intense hatred than of fear. That force also is strong enough to develope such intelligence as may be necessary to injure the oppressor, and in that way also individuality has been secured. It is not difficult to imagine the kind of human being that would be produced along such lines as these, and this is the explanation of the existence of the fiendishly cruel and blood-thirsty savages of whom we sometimes hear, of the inquisitors of the Middle Ages, and of those who torture children in the present day. Of them it is distinctly true that they have come into humanity far too soon, and are displaying under its guise an exaggerated form of some of the very worst characteristics of the most unpleasant types of animals.

Yet another variant is the entity who is individualised by an intense desire for power over others, such as is sometimes shown by the chief bull of a herd. An ego developed in such a way often manifests great cruelty, and appears to take pleasure in it, probably because to torture others is a manifestation of his power over them.

On the other hand those who have been individualised at a comparatively low level along one of the regular lines - as by affection - provide us with a type of equally primitive but joyous and good-natured savages - savages, in fact, who are not savage but kindly, as are many of the tribes to be found in some of the islands of the Southern Seas.

As we look at these early stages of our development upon the Moon-chain, it often seems as though the mode of individualisation of an ego depended upon mere chance - upon "the accident of environment." Yet I do not believe that this is so; even for animals the environment is not accidental, and there is no room for chance in a perfectly-ordered universe. I should not be surprised if further investigation should reveal to us that the very mode of the individualisation was somehow pre-determined either for or by the monad himself, with a view to preparation for whatever portion of the great work he is to undertake in the future. There will come a time when we shall be part of the great Heavenly Man - not in the least as a myth or a poetic symbol, but as a vivid and actual fact, which we ourselves have seen. That celestial body has many members; each of these members has its own function to fulfil, and the living cells which are to form part of them need widely-different experiences to prepare them. It may well be that from the dawn of evolution the parts have been chosen - that each monad has his destined line of evolution, and that his freedom of action is concerned chiefly with the rate at which he shall move along that line. In any case our duty is clear - to push ahead as rapidly as we can, watching ever to discern the divine purpose, living only to fulfil it, striving always to help onwards the great scheme of the LOGOS by helping our fellowman.

THE SEVEN TYPES

The seven great types or rays do not correspond to the planes, for each type is to be found upon all the planes. One may symbolize the planes as horizontal, as they are usually represented in Theosophical diagrams; and then if we proceed to draw seven vertical columns cutting across the seven planes at right angles, those columns will symbolize the types. This will cut up our diagram into forty-nine square, and in reality each of these forty-nine has also forty-nine subdivisions in the same manner, because each plane has seven sub-planes, and each type has seven sub-types, which are produced by the influence upon it of each of the other types in turn. A diagram which clearly explains this may be found in *The Secret Doctrine*, Vol. iii. p. 483.

There are seven great types of men, coming out from the seven great Planetary LOGOI. Each of us belongs to one of these, but each has also a sub-ray from one of the other types.

If a man belongs to the blue or devotional type, and has the wisdom ray as his sub-type, he will be wise in his devotion; but if his sub-ray be also devotional, he may be blindly devoted having no discrimination, and therefore unable to see any blemish in the object of his worship.

Yet though each of us, as has been said, has come out through one or other of the seven Planetary LOGOI, it does not at all follow that he will return through the same LOGOS. Each of the great root-races will produce as its flower and result what is called in the sacred books a Heavenly Man, one mighty Being who actually includes within Himself all those members of the root-race who have made themselves worthy of such inclusion - includes them precisely as our physical body includes millions of cells. True, we have all of us incarnated in other root-races, but we belong to that root-race in which we finally succeed in attaining adeptship, and it will be of the Heavenly Man which represents that race that we shall form a part.

For each root-race there is a Manu and a Bodhisattva, and these are respectively the brain and the heart of the Heavenly Man of the root-race. We who work in the Theosophical Society are most of us following along one or other of these two lines, and so we shall find ourselves grouped round one or other of those centres in that glorious future. But in the Heavenly Man, as in the man on earth, there are seven centres, and each of these centres is represented by an official of the Occult Hierarchy. Some men will be drawn to one of these centres, and some to another, so that there is the fullest possibility of development for all possible types and dispositions.

These Heaven-born Men so formed are the true inhabitants of the solar system, the mind-born sons of the Planetary LOGOI, destined themselves to be the Planetary LOGOI of the future, and of them we shall be living, conscious component parts; and yet at the same time each of us will have the fullest liberty and the highest possible activity. Incomprehensible, of course, to our present power of thought, but utterly true, nevertheless. Well for us if we can attain our level and take our part along with the great Masters who are the leaders of our Society. If that be too high for us at present, there will be other opportunities in the future - others, and yet others, stretching away in endless vistas. Yet those of us who are earnest students in this Society have now a glorious opportunity, of which we should do well to take the fullest advantage; for if we lose it who knows how many lives of hard work it will take us to earn such another? Soon the Teacher of angels and men will show Himself upon earth once more; happy are we in that we are allowed to help (even though it be ever so little) to prepare the way for His coming; happier yet will be those of us who shall see Him face to face, who will be privileged to work under Him in the service of humanity when that day of the Lord shall dawn!

STRAY NOTES ON RACES

The Irish Race

The Irish are not of Atlantean stock, but belong to the fourth sub-race of the fifth root-race. It is true that Ireland was part of the Atlantean continent, and that the earliest inhabitants were of the Rmoahal, the first sub-race of the fourth root-race; but no recognisable trace now remains of these aborigines, who were a small dark people somewhat of the type of the Laplanders of the present day. Nor is there much now left to bear witness to the first invasion from Africa of a host led by an Ethiopian queen; but there are still some tokens of the next arrivals - a race called the Firbolgs - big, hairy-faced men who appear to have come down from Iceland - probably people of the same stock as the Ainus of Japan. The great majority of the Irish nation (not counting the Scottish immigrants of Ulster) is composed of the descendants of two races - the Tuatha-de-Danaan and the Milesian. The Tuatha-de-Danaan were men of the Caucasian stock, practically identical with the early Greeks, and they reached Ireland by a circuitous northern route, having moved up gradually through Russia, and round by Sweden and Norway, in the manner of the curious slow, wholesale migrations of those earlier days. They were a handsome race with oval faces, clear complexion, mostly dark hair, and deep blue or almost violet eyes. Sometimes the hair was lighter and the eyes were grey, but the other type was the more common, and one may often see it exactly reproduced among the Irish peasants of to-day.

The Tuatha-de-Danaan were not only so much handsomer, but also intellectually and spiritually so very much in advance of the mixed race which they found in Ireland that they were regarded by the latter as of celestial lineage, and to this day tradition speaks of them as a race of gods who ruled Ireland during a golden age, which is by no means so entirely legendary as historians generally suppose. Ireland was unquestionably the seat of a high civilisation and a centre of philosophy and learning while the neighbouring island of England was largely covered by dense forests and peopled by naked savages who painted themselves blue.

The Tuatha-de-Danaan reigned in Ireland through many ages of power and great glory, but their civilisation waned in time, as all others do, and at last they were overcome by an invasion of the Milesians from Spain - a race far inferior to them in culture, spirituality and general development, but having the rude physical strength of youth and much knowledge of the lower magic. These were a bullet-headed people, rugged and often positively ugly of face, with light or vividly red hair - a type which may also still be seen sometimes among the peasantry of the southern part of the country almost in its original purity. Far inferior as they were to the Tuatha-de-Danaan, the Milesians were still a variant of that same fourth sub-race of the Aryans; and since these two types are its main constituents, it is to that sub-race that we must assign the Irish of the present day - Celts, near of kin to the Highlander of Scotland, the Welshman, the Cornishman or the Breton.

At present there is unfortunately a wide-spread poverty and general lack of prosperity among the Irish nation in its native Erin - a condition of affairs which the Irish usually attribute to oppression by the conquering English. This "oppression," so far as it is a fact, and not a figment of the imagination, comes from the radical difference between the two races, which causes a curiously complete lack of mutual understanding. The stolid matter-of-fact Anglo-Saxon cannot possibly comprehend the point of view of the imaginative and poetical Irishman, and the motives of the latter are always a sealed book to the former.

The average English peasant lives almost entirely upon the physical plane, and his thought runs naturally along lines connected with his every-day interests and experiences. The average Irish peasant of the south and west lives very much upon the astral plane, and cares comparatively little about physical conditions so long as he has the accustomed astral atmosphere about him. His thoughts are usually far away from the mechanical daily round, and occupied with legends of the past, or with the stories of saints and angels and fairies.

I well remember the plaintive amazement of an English landlord who, shocked at the condition of some of the cabins on his estate, had built for his labourers neat little staring brick cottages with all the latest improvements. With great difficulty he persuaded some of the peasants to try the new dwellings upon which they looked with such strong disfavour, but after a day or two every one of them went back again to the old cabins with their mud floors and leaking roofs, vowing that there was no home like the old home, with all its inconveniences. The truth was that they thought so little of the physical that these inconveniences were hardly felt at all, and weighed as nothing in the balance against the comfortable homelike feeling of the astral radiations of the old walls, to which they had been accustomed from childhood. But the Englishman knew nothing about astral vibrations, and could only marvel at the stupidity and obstinacy of people who actually preferred a miserable and unquestionably filthy old hovel to a new and clean cottage.

The drunkenness which is so sadly common among the peasantry is largely referable to the same cause; it is not physical but astral sensation which is sought, and to some extent obtained, by means of the absorption of alcohol. The average Irish peasant may perhaps drink more than his English compeer, but his thoughts are on the whole far purer and more elevated. To him all women are sacred for the sake of the Virgin Mother to whom he prays, and statistics show that crimes against the weaker sex are far rarer in Erin than in Albion. The Englishman endeavours to be accurate; the Irishman cares little for accuracy, but prefers to say rather what is most courteous, or what he thinks will please. In a word, they represent two different sub-races; their development runs along quite different lines, and only the wisest and most liberal of each can possibly understand and make allowance for the peculiarities of the other.

It is probable that many causes combine to produce the poverty and general lack of prosperity of the Irish. Without raising any of the vexed questions about which party opinions clash, the occultist may examine with interest at least one cause which is never suspected by those who discuss the subject in this prosaic twentieth century; and that is the working of a curse pronounced against the race (or perhaps one should rather say a spell laid upon it) no less than two thousand years ago at the time of the Milesian conquest. Students of early Irish history will remember how persistently it is stated that the invading Milesians were able to hold in thrall the distinctly superior race which they had overcome, because they cast upon it the glamour of a great illusion. This legend has a basis of fact. The priests of the Milesian religion were well acquainted with certain types of magic, and as the country was conquered they occupied it with strongly magnetised centres. They established one of these every few miles, until they had a net-work of them covering the whole southern and western part of the land, and even now, after the lapse of two thousand years, a strong influence radiates from them.

Great crowds of nature-spirits of a certain type are still irresistibly attracted to these centres, gambol round them and are permeated by their influence, and unconsciously become its ministers, and spread it all over the country wherever they go.

The spell which the Milesian priests laid upon the people was two-fold - the curses of disunion and lethargy - that they should never be able effectively to combine together, but always quarrel among themselves, and that they should apathetically submit to the domination of whoever wielded or inherited the magnetic power. If any English ruler had ever known enough of magic to understand and utilise this heritage of the Milesian priests, the history of Ireland might have been different. As the Anglo-Saxon is usually blankly ignorant and blatantly incredulous with regard to all that side of nature, a very curious thing has happened. Consciously or unconsciously the Roman Church has come into that heritage, and profits by what still remains of the power of that ancient spell, and her rule is unquestioned through all the districts where long ago those priests of an older faith established their magnetic centres.

The Spanish Race

The whole question of racial Karma is a difficult one, and I do not think that we have as yet sufficient information at our command to enable us to speak definitely upon the subject. This much is certain - that whenever we find markedly unusual conditions surrounding a race, we may conclude that the Manu in charge of that portion of evolution has in hand a number of egos who need just those conditions for their progress. The law of cause and effect must obviously govern national as well as individual affairs, though its action is complicated by the fact that the egos who form the race when the effect arrives are usually not those who were there when the cause was set in motion.

For example, it may be not unreasonable to suppose that the fact that Spain has somewhat ignominiously lost the whole of South America and Mexico, has a definite karmic relation to the awful cruelty and rapacity shown in her conquest of those countries; yet we imagine that the Spaniards who suffered loss when those countries freed themselves can hardly in all cases have been reincarnations of those who wrought such appalling havoc under Cortes and Pizarro. On the other hand, it is very probable that some of them may have been, for we know that people of the lower classes return very much sooner than those of the first class, and usually have to incarnate several times in the same branch-race before they have learnt all its lessons.

The Jewish Race

The peculiar conditions of the Jewish race exist primarily because at this particular stage the Manu needs them for the proper training of some of the egos under his care. We can only guess at the racial karma which made those conditions possible. Perhaps the explanation is to be found in the fact that the Jewish race is descended from those Atlantean Semites who were drawn away into Arabia, apart from their fellows, by the Manu of the Fifth root-race when he was making his first segregation. That first attempt was not wholly successful, and a second segregation took place into the Gobi district, from which in due time was produced the first sub-race of the new root-race. When a second sub-race was needed, the Manu sent emissaries to the descendant of those who had been left behind in Arabia, hoping to mingle with theirs the blood of the new root-race; but they were so strongly impressed with the idea (which he himself had originally implanted in them) that they were a chosen race, set apart from the world and forbidden to intermarry with others, that in the name of his own teaching they now rejected his overtures, and he had to seek elsewhere for what he wanted.

The particular sub-race from which the Jewish nation is directly descended had moved across from Arabia to the Somali Coast, in order to avoid conquest by those who followed the new teaching of the Manu. They then split off even from that dissenting band, and made their way along the shores of the Gulf of Aden and the Red Sea, until they entered upon the territory of Egypt. The Pharaoh of the time received them hospitably, and assigned them a tract of land on which to dwell, and they settled down there for some centuries; but as a later Pharaoh sought to levy from them some impost to which they objected, and also to force them to perform for him certain unpaid labour, as his other subjects did, they protested against his claims, and continued their migration by crossing the Sinaitic desert and settling themselves in southern Syria, dispossessing, after much fighting, other robber tribes of much the same blood as themselves.

The karma of that rejection has left them ever since a race apart, the same egos to a large extent incarnating again and again in that line instead of passing from race to race in the usual way. Whether some blind perception of this difference may help to account for the treatment they have received at the hands of other races I cannot definitely say, but it may also be partially due to the fact that because of the tradition of that original selection by the Manu they have always had a feeling somewhat similar to that of the Brahmans - that they are superior to all the rest of the world; and the rest of the world has not always appreciated the attitude which they adopted in consequence of that belief.

They were originally a nomad tribe like the Bedouin Arabs, and lived largely by robbery, their deity being confessedly but a private tribal god who fought against the gods of other nations and was perpetually vaunting himself as superior to them, although it will be remembered that in one case he was not able to overcome certain other races "because they had chariots of iron" (Judges, i. 19).

Just like all other elemental tribal deities, he required constant sacrifices of blood, and in order that he might receive plenty of these he was always exceedingly jealous lest any of his followers should desert him, and make their offerings to other deities. The requiring of blood-sacrifices is an invariable criterion as to the status of a deity; no entity in the least deserving of respect or worship ever made such an abominable demand. It will be found that he often suggested mean and dishonourable plans - which is quite a common thing for a tribal deity to do, but would of course be utterly impossible for any higher entity.

The carrying away into captivity in Babylon of a number of these turbulent people was quite the best thing that could happen to them. They then for the first time came into contact with a highly civilised race, and for the first time heard of a supreme God of whom everything was part. Then they characteristically tried to identify their own tribal deity with this Supreme Being, and so caused much confusion. When they returned from this captivity they rewrote their scriptures from the memory of the older men, and then they put into them a certain admixture the higher ideas about a supreme deity.

The Founder of Christianity took possession of a Jewish body; all the earlier teachers of the religion were of the same race, and so, unfortunately, they brought over into Christianity this mixed conception of a god who is full of irreconcilable characteristics, being at the same time jealous, cruel and revengeful, and yet omniscient, omnipresent and compassionate. Even at the present day the Christian church still reads in its highest service the ridiculous old Jewish commandments, with which is incorporated the statement of the jealousy of the deity, while in another part of the very same service she acclaims him as "God of God, Light of Light, very God of very God." If the Christians could only have left these primitive Jewish conceptions alone, and taken with reference to God the teachings of their Founder, who spoke of Him always as the Father in heaven, many of the troubles of the Church would have been avoided.

The Atlanteans

The Atlanteans had as a race no sense of the abstract, and were unable to generalise; for example, they had no multiplication table; arithmetic was to them a system of magic, and a child had to learn elaborate rules without ever knowing the reason for them. For example, he was taught that if 8 came beneath 8 in the particular form of magic which we now call addition, the figure 6 must be noted as the result, and the next figure to the left-hand side in the result must be increase by 1. If however the particular magic happened to be subtraction, a cipher was the result; if it was division the figure 1 appeared; if it was multiplication the figure 4 was the result, and the next figure to the left must be altered by 6. But he never knew that 8 plus 8 equals 16, or that 8 times 8 equals 64! A similar elaborate set of rules had to be memorized for every conceivable position of all the figures up to 10. These four sets or types of mathematical magic had to be learnt just as though they were four conjugations of a verb. Most of their calculations, however, were made by means of machinery - a kind of abacus or framework something like that now used by the Chinese and Japanese, by means of which it is even now possible to make quite elaborate calculations - as, for example, to take the square root of any number.

The Atlanteans were clever at amassing facts, and had prodigious memories; also they invented a good deal of quite complicated machinery, though most of it would seem to us now quite clumsy in its action. We see another curious trace of their limitations in the religion which the Egyptians inherited from them. They had observed and noted most of the types of elemental essence and nature-spirits, and they had named them all, and invented special forms of spells for each, by which it could be controlled; and they went on elaborately learning all these, with the feeling that if any but the right spell was applied to a particular elemental, he would probably prove destructive. Yet they never realised that the force behind the spells was in every case the human will, and that a determined exertion of that, without any spell at all, would have been equally effective in all these different places. The Book of the Dead contains great numbers of these, and only that portion of it which it was thought would be needed by each dead person was placed along with him in his tomb.

The Turanian sub-race of the Atlanteans made a series of experiments in what is now called democracy, and carried it to even wilder lengths than its most rabid exponents at the present day have yet suggested. The results were so utterly intolerable that the whole race broke up into anarchy and chaos; and China even now bears the impress of the violent reaction in the direction of aristocratic government which followed. The Turanians had their animal passions very strongly developed, and were in many ways not what we should call pleasant people.

MARS AND ITS INHABITANTS

The present condition of the planet Mars is by no means unpleasant. It is a smaller planet than the Earth and more advanced in age. I do not mean that it is actually older in years, for the whole chain of worlds came into existence - not simultaneously indeed - but within a certain definite area of time. But being smaller it lives its life as a planet more quickly. It cooled more rapidly from the nebulous condition, and it has passed through its other stages with corresponding celerity. When humanity occupied it in the third round it was in much the same condition as is the Earth at the present time - that is to say, there was much more water than land on its surface. Now it has passed into comparative old age, and the water surface is far less than that of land. Large areas of it are at present desert, covered with a bright orange sand which gives the planet the peculiar hue by which we so readily recognize it. Like that of many of our own deserts, the soil is probably fertile enough if the great irrigation system were extended to it, as it no doubt would have been if humanity had remained upon it until now.

The present population, consisting practically of members of the inner round, is but a small one, and they find plenty of room for themselves to live without great effort, in the equatorial lands, where the temperature is highest and there is no difficulty as to water. The great system of canals which has been observed by terrestrial astronomers was constructed by the second order of moon-men when they last occupied the planet, and its general scheme is to take advantage of the annual melting of enormous masses of ice at the outer fringe of the polar snow-caps. It has been observed that some of the canals are double, but the double line is only occasionally apparent; that is due to the fore-thought of the Martian engineers. The country is on the whole level, and they had great dread of inundations; and wherever they thought that there was reason to fear too great an outrush of water under exceptional circumstances the second parallel canal was constructed to receive any possible overflow and carry it away safely.

The actual canals themselves are not visible to terrestrial telescopes; what is seen is the belt of verdure which appears in a tract of country on each side of the canal only at the time when the water pours in. Just as Egypt exists only because of the Nile, so do large districts on Mars exist only because of these canals. From each side of them radiate at intervals water-ways, which run some miles into the surrounding country and are then subdivided into thousands of tiny streamlets, so that a strip of country a hundred miles in width is thoroughly irrigated. In this area are forests and cultivated fields, and vegetation of all sorts starts forth in the greatest profusion, making upon the surface of the planet a dark belt which is visible to us even forty million miles away when the planet is at its nearest and favourably situated.

Mars is much farther from the centre of the system than we are, and consequently the sun appears to its inhabitants scarcely more than half the size that it does to us. Nevertheless the climate of the inhabited portions of the planet is very good, the temperature during the day at the equator being usually about 70° Fahrenheit, though there are not many nights in the year when there is not a touch of frost. Clouds are almost unknown, the sky being for most of the year entirely clear. The country is therefore to a large extent free from the unpleasantness of rain or snow. The Martian day is a few minutes longer than our own and their year is nearly twice as long as ours, and the variation of the seasons in the inhabited part is but slight.

In physical appearance the Martians are not unlike ourselves, except that they are considerably smaller. The tallest men are not above five feet in height and the majority are two or three inches shorter. According to our ideas they are somewhat broad in proportion, having very great chest capacity - a fact which may possibly be due to the rarity of the air and the consequent necessity of deep breathing in order fully to oxygenate the blood. The whole civilised population of Mars is one race, and there is practically no difference in features or complexion, except that, just as among ourselves, there are blondes and brunettes, some of the people having a faintly yellowish skin and black hair, while the majority have yellow hair and blue or violet eyes - somewhat Norwegian in appearance.

They dress mostly in brilliant colours, and both sexes wear an almost shapeless garment of some very soft material which falls straight from the shoulders down to the feet. Generally the feet are bare, though they sometimes use a sort of metal sandal or slipper, with a thong round the ankle.

They are very fond of flowers, of which there is a great variety, and their towns are built on the general plan of the garden-city, the house usually being one-storeyed only, but built round inner courtyards and straggling over a great deal of ground. These houses look exteriorly as though built of coloured glass, and indeed the material which is used is transparent, but it is somehow so fluted that while the persons inside enjoy an almost unimpeded view of their gardens, no one from outside can see what is going on in the house.

The houses are not built up in blocks, but the material is melted and poured into moulds; if a house is to be built, a sort of double mould of it is first made in metal faced with cement, and then the curious glasslike substance is melted and poured into this mould, and when it is cold and hardened the moulds are taken away, and the house is finished except for a certain amount of polishing of the surface. The doors are not exactly like ours, since they have no hinges or bolts, and are opened and shut by treading on certain spots in the ground, either without or within. They do not swing on hinges, but run back into the wall on each side. All these doors and all furniture and fittings are of metal. Wood seems to be used scarcely at all.

There is only one language in use over the whole planet, except for the few savage tribes, and this language, like everything in their world, has not grown up as ours have done, but has been constructed in order to save time and trouble. It has been simplified to the last possible extent, and it has no irregularities of ant sort. They have two methods of recording their thoughts. One is to speak into a small box with a mouthpiece on one side of it, something like that of a telephone. Each word so spoken is by the mechanism expressed as a kind of complicated sign upon a little plate of metal, and when the message has been spoken the plate falls out and is found to be marked in crimson characters, which can easily be read by those who are familiar with the scheme. The other plan is actually to write by hand, but that is an enormously more difficult acquirement, for the script is a very complicated kind of shorthand which can be written as rapidly as one can speak. It is in this latter script that all their books are printed, and these latter are usually in the shape of rolls made of very thin flexible metal. The engraving of them is exceedingly minute, and it is customary to read it through a magnifier, which is fixed conveniently upon a stand. In the stand there is machinery which unrolls the scroll before the magnifier at any desired rate, so that one reads without needing to touch the book at all.

On every hand one sees signs of a very old civilisation, for the inhabitants have preserved the tradition of all that was known when the great life-wave of humanity occupied the planet, and have since added to it many other discoveries.

Electricity seems to be practically the sole motive power, and all sorts of labour-saving machines are universally employed.

The people are on the whole distinctly indolent, especially after they have passed their first youth. But the comparatively small size of the population enables them to live very easily. They have trained various kinds of domestic animals to a far higher condition of intelligent co-operation than has yet been achieved upon earth, so that a great deal of servant's and gardener's work is done by these creatures with comparatively little direction.

One autocratic ruler governs the whole planet, but the monarchy is not hereditary. Polygamy is practised, but it is the custom to hand over all children to the State at a very early age to be reared and educated, so that among the vast majority of the people there is no family tradition whatever, and no one knows who are his father and mother. There is no law compelling this, but it is considered so decidedly the right thing to do and the best for the children that the few families who choose to live somewhat more as we do, and to educate their children at home, are always regarded as selfishly injuring their prospects for the sake of what is considered mere animal affection.

The state is thus in the position of universal guardian and schoolmaster, and the school authorities of each district are instructed-carefully to sort the children according to the aptitudes which they display, and their line of life is decided for them in this manner - a very wide range of choice, however, being allowed the individual child as he approaches years of discretion. But children who show at the same time great intellect and wide general capacity are set apart from all the rest, and trained with a view of becoming members of the ruling class.

The King has under him what may be called viceroys of large districts, and they in turn have under them governors of smaller districts, and so on down to what would be equivalent here to the head-man of a village. All these officials are chosen by the King from this group of specially educated children, and when the time of his own death is considered to be approaching it is from the already appointed officials that he chooses his successor.

They have brought their scientific medical studies to such perfection that disease has been eliminated, and even the ordinary signs of the approach of old age have been to a large extent got rid of. Practically no one appears old, and it would seem that they hardly feel old; but, after a life somewhat longer than our own the desire to live gradually fades away, and the man dies. It is quite customary for a man who is losing interest and feels that death is approaching (this corresponds to what we should call a centenarian) to apply to a certain scientific department which corresponds to what we might call a school of surgery, and ask to be put painlessly to death - a request which is always granted.

All these rulers are autocratic, each within his own sphere, but appeal to a higher official is always possible, though the right is not frequently exercised, because the people usually prefer to acquiesce in any fairly reasonable decision rather than to take the trouble involved in an appeal. The rulers on the whole seem to perform their duties fairly well, but again one gets the impression that they do so not so much from any pre-eminent sense of right or justice as to avoid the trouble that would certainly ensue from a flagrantly unjust decision.

One of the most remarkable things about this people is that they have absolutely no religion. There are no churches, no temples, no places of worship of any sort whatever, no priest, no ecclesiastical power. The accepted belief of the people is what we should call scientific materialism. Nothing is true but what can be scientifically demonstrated, and to believe anything which cannot be so demonstrated is regarded as not only the height of folly, but even as a positive crime, because it is considered a danger to the public peace.

Martian history in the remote past was not unlike our own, and there are stories of religious persecutions, and of peoples whose beliefs were of so uncomfortable a nature that they forced them not only into feverish energy for themselves, but also into perpetual interference with the liberty of thought of other people. Martian public opinion is quite determined that there shall never again be any opportunity for the introduction of disturbing factors of that sort, and that physical science and the lower reason shall reign supreme; and though there, as here, events have occurred which material science cannot explain, people find it best to say nothing about them.

Nevertheless on Mars, as in other places, there are a certain number of people who know better than this, and many centuries ago a few of these joined themselves together into a secret brotherhood to meet and discuss such matters. Very gradually and with infinite precaution, they took other recruits into this charmed circle, and so came into existence, in this most materialistic of worlds, a secret society which not only believed in superphysical worlds but practically of their existence, for its members took up the direct study of mesmerism and spiritualism, and many of them developed a good deal of power.

At the present time the secret society is very widely spread, and the head of it at this moment is a pupil of one of our Masters. Even now after all these centuries its existence is not officially known to the authorities, but as a matter of fact they have something more than a suspicion of it, and they have learnt to fear it. None of its members are actually identified as such, but many are strongly suspected, and it seems to have been observed that when any of these strongly suspected people have in the past been injured or unjustly put to death, the persons who were concerned in bringing about that result have invariably died prematurely and mysteriously, though never in any case has their death been traceable to any physical-plane action on the part of the suspected member. Consequently, although such a belief is no doubt somewhat of an infringement of the principles of pure reason by which everything is supposed to be governed, it has come to be generally understood that it is safest not to pry too closely into the beliefs of people who seem to differ in some degree from the majority, so long as they do not openly make profession of anything which would be considered subversive of the good morals of materialism.

Driven far away from the pleasant equatorial regions into inhospitable lands and impenetrable forests, there still exist some remnants of the savage tribes who are descended from those left behind when the great life-wave left Mars for the earth. These are primitive savages at a lower stage than any now living on the exterior of our earth, though bearing some resemblance to one of our interior evolutions.

Some at least of the members of the secret society have learnt how to cross without great difficulty the space which separates us from Mars, and have therefore at various times tried to manifest themselves through mediums at spiritualistic séances, or have been able, by the methods which they have learnt, to impress their ideas upon poets and novelists.

The information which I have given above is based upon observation and inquiry during various visit to the planet; yet nearly all of it might be found in the works of various writers within the last thirty or forty years, and in all such cases it has been communicated or impressed by someone from Mars, although the very fact of such impression was (at least in some cases) quite unknown to the physical writer.

Of our future home, Mercury, we know much less than of Mars, for visits to it have been hurried and infrequent. Many people would think it incredible that life such as ours could exist on Mercury, with a sun that appears at least seven times as large as it does here. The heat, however, is not at all so intense as would be supposed. I am informed that this is due to the presence of a layer of gas on the outskirts of the Mercurian atmosphere, which prevents most of the heat from penetrating. We are told also that the most destructive of all possible storms on Mercury is one which even for a moment disturbs the stability of this gaseous envelope. When that happens a kind of a whirl-pool is set up in it, and for a moment a shaft of direct sunlight comes from the sun through its vortex. Such a shaft instantly destroys whatever life comes in its way, and burns up in a moment everything combustible. Fortunately such storms are rare. The inhabitants whom I have seen there are much like ourselves, though again somewhat smaller.

The influence of gravity both on Mars and Mercury is less than half what it is on earth, but while on Mars I did not notice any particular way in which advantage had been taken of this. I observed Mercury that the doors of the houses were quite a considerable height from the ground, needing what for us would be a respectable gymnastic feat to reach them, though on Mercury it is only a slight spring that is required. All the inhabitants of that planet are from birth possessed of etheric sight; I remember that the fact was first brought to my notice by observing a child who was watching the movements of some crawling creature; and I saw that when it entered its abode he was still able to follow its movements, even when it was deep down under the ground.

Seventh Section: Reincarnation

THREE LAWS OF HUMAN LIFE

The ordinary ego is by no means yet in a position to choose a body for himself. The place of his birth is usually determined by three factors , or perhaps it would be better to say by the combined action of three forces. First comes the law of evolution, which cause an ego to be born under conditions which will give him an opportunity of developing exactly those qualities of which he stands most in need. But the action of this force is limited by the second factor, the law of karma. The ego may not have deserved the best possible opportunity, and so he has to put up with the second or third best. He may not even have deserved any great opportunity at all, and so a tumultuous life of small progress may be his fate.

A third factor also comes into play - the force of any personal ties of love or hate that the ego may have previously formed. This may modify the action of the first and second forces, for by it a man may sometimes be drawn into a position which he cannot be said to have deserved in any other way than by the strong personal love which he has felt for some one higher in evolution than himself.

A man who has worked much beyond the ordinary - a man who had already entered the Path which leads to adeptship - may be able to exercise a certain amount of choice as to the country and family of his birth; but such an one will be the first to put aside entirely any wish of his own in the matter, and resign himself absolutely into the hands of the great eternal law, confident that whatever it brings to him must be far better for him than any selection of his own.

Parents cannot choose the soul who shall inhabit the body to which they give birth, but by so living as to offer an unusually good opportunity for the progress of an advanced ego they can make it exceedingly probable that such an ego will come to them.

THE RETURN TO BIRTH

The whole of our solar system is a manifestation of its LOGOS, and every particle in it is definitely part of His vehicles. All the physical matter of the solar system taken as a totality constitutes His physical body; all the astral matter within it constitutes His astral body; all the mental matter, His mental body, and so on. Entirely above and beyond His system He has a far wider and greater existence of His own, but that does not in the least affect the truth of the statement which we have just made.

This solar LOGOS contains within Himself seven planetary LOGOI, who are as it were centres of force within Him, channels through which His force pours out. Yet at the same time there is a sense in which they may be said to constitute

Him. The matter which we have just described as composing His vehicles also composes theirs, for there is no particle of matter anywhere in the system which is not part of one or other of them. All this is true of every plane; but let us for a moment take the astral plane as an example, because its matter is fluid enough to answer the purposes of our inquiry, and at the same time it is near enough to the physical to be not entirely beyond the Limits of our physical comprehension.

Every particle of the astral matter of the system is part of the astral body of the solar LOGOS, but it is also part of the astral body of one or other of the seven planetary LOGOI. Remember that this includes the astral matter of which your astral body and mine are composed. We have no particle which is exclusively our own. In every astral body there are particles belonging to each one of the seven planetary LOGOI, but the proportions vary infinitely. The bodies of those Monads which originally came forth through a planetary LOGOS will continue all through their evolution to have more of the particles of that LOGOS than of any other, and in this way people may be distinguished as primarily belonging to one or other of these seven great Powers.

In these seven planetary LOGOI certain psychic changes periodically occur; perhaps they correspond to in-breathing and out-breathing, or to the beating of the heart with us down here on the physical plane.

However that may be, there seem to be an infinite number of possible permutations and combinations of them. Now since our astral bodies are built of the very matter of their astral bodies, it is obvious that no one of these planetary LOGOI can change astrally in any way without thereby affecting the astral body of every man in the world, though of course more especially those in whom there is a preponderance of the matter expressing that particular LOGOS; and if it be remembered that we are taking the astral plane merely as an example, and that exactly the same thing is true on all the other planes, we shall then begin to have an idea how important to us the motions of these planetary Spirits are.

Madame Blavatsky writes of a certain order of supernal Beings whom she calls the Lipika, or Lords of Karma. We are told that their agents in the administration of karma are the four (really seven) great rulers who are known as the Devarajas or Regents of the Earth. Each one of them is at the head of a certain vast group of devas and nature-spirits, and even of elemental essence. Once more for purposes of explanation let us confine ourselves to astral plane, but always with the memory at the back of our minds that the same thing applies to all the other planes as well. Astral matter as a whole is specially under the control of one of these Great Ones, but the second sub-plane of every plane is also to a certain extent under the direction of the same Great One, because that sub-plane holds the same relation to the plane of which it is a part as the astral plane does to the whole set of planes. Therefore for every sub-plane there are two influences - the influence of the ruler of the plane as a whole, and the sub-influence of the ruler of the sub-plane.

Now out of this astral matter, every particle of which belongs to the garment of one or other of the seven planetary LOGOI, and is at the same time under the predominating influence of the Devaraja of the astral plane, and also under the subordinate influence of another Devaraja who indirectly rules its sub-plane, our astral bodies have to be built. In order to help us to grasp this, let us think of the sub-planes of the astral plane as horizontal divisions, and of the types of matter belonging to the seven great planetary LOGOI as perpendicular divisions crossing these others at right angles. (There are still further subdivisions, but we will take no account of them for the present, in order that the broad idea may stand out clearly). This then even already gives us forty-nine distinctly marked varieties of astral matter, because on each of its sub-planes we have matter belonging to each of the planetary LOGOI.

Even taking no account of the further subdivisions, we see that we have already the possibility of an almost infinite number of combinations; so that whatever may be the characteristics of the ego he is able to find an adequate expression for himself.

Let us consider the case of an ego who is about to descend into incarnation. We must think of him as resting upon the higher part of the mental plane in his causal body, and having no vehicle lower than that. Since the death of his last physical body he has been drawing steadily inwards, first into his astral and then into his mental vehicle, and at the end of the heaven-life he has cast off even the latter. He then rests for a certain period on his own plane - a period which varies, according to the stage of his development, from two or three days of unconsciousness in the case of an ordinary undeveloped man to a long period of years of conscious and glorious life in that of exceptionally advanced people. Then he begins once more to turn his attention downwards and outwards. As in the course of his upward movement he has withdrawn his attention from the physical and the astral planes respectively, the permanent atoms have passed into a dormant condition, and have ceased the vigorous vibration which is their usual characteristic. The same thing happens to the mental unit at the end of the heaven-life, and during his rest on his own plane the ego has these three appendages within himself in a quiescent condition.

When he turns his attention once more to the mental plane, the mental unit immediately resumes its activity, and because of that it at once gathers round it such matter as is required to express that activity. Precisely the same thing happens when he turns his attention to the astral atom, and puts his will into that. It attracts to itself material capable of providing him with an astral body of exactly the same type as that which he had at the end of his last astral life. It is necessary to have this fact clearly in mind, that what he thus acquires as he descends is not a ready-made astral body, but simply the material out of which he is to build an astral body in the course of the life which is to follow.

In the case of lower-class monads with unusually strong astral bodies, who reincarnate after a very short interval, it sometimes happens that the shade or shell left over from the last astral life still persists, and in that case it is likely to be attracted to the new personality. When that happens it brings with it strongly the old habits and modes of thought, and sometimes even the actual memory of that past life.

The astral matter is at first evenly distributed throughout the ovoid; it is only when the little physical form comes into existence in the middle of the ovoid that the astral and mental matter are attracted to it, and begin to mould themselves into its shape, and thereafter steadily grow along with it. At the same time with this change in arrangement the mental and astral matter are called into activity, and emotion and thought appear.

The aura of the little baby is comparatively colourless, and it is only as the qualities develope that the colours begin to show. This is the material which is given to him out of which to fashion his astral vehicle, the material which he has earned by the desires and emotions which he allowed to play through him in his previous life; but he is by no means compelled to utilise all this material in building for himself his new vehicle. If he is left entirely to himself, the automatic action of the permanent atom will tend to produce for him, from the materials given, an astral body precisely similar to that which he had in the last life; but there is no reason whatever why all these materials should be used, and if the child is wisely treated and reasonably guided he will be encouraged to develope to the fullest all the germs of good which he has brought over from his previous life, while the evil germs will be allowed to slumber. If that is done these latter will gradually atrophy and drop away from him, and the ego will unfold within himself the opposite virtues, and then he will be free for all his future lives from the evil qualities which those germs indicated. Parents and teachers may help him towards this desirable consummation, not so much by any definite facts which they teach him as by the encouragement which they give to him, by the rational and kindly treatment uniformly accorded to him, and above all by the amount of affection lavished upon him.

We must remember that while the higher vehicles, the mental and the astral body, are expressions of the man at his present stage of evolution (as far as that can be expressed in the matter of their respective planes), the physical body is a vehicle or a limitation imposed upon him from without, and is therefore pre-eminently the instrument of karma. The evolutionary force comes into play in the selection of its materials, but even in this it is at every turn limited and hampered by the karma of the past. The parents have been chosen because they are fitted to give such a body as will be suitable for the development of the ego committed to them, but with every pair of parents there are manifold possibilities. Each of their represents a long line of ancestry, and often a particular parent may be chosen, not for anything that he is or has in himself, but because of some quality which appeared to an unusual degree in one of his ancestors - because he possesses a power which he has not used, though it is latent in his physical body because it is physically descended from that ancestor. In that parent, and in many preceding generations, the faculty to express that quality may have slept entirely without effect, but when there comes into the line an ego which possesses the quality, the faculty to express it leaps out from the dormant into the active condition, and we have a case of what is called reversion to a remote type.

In the formation of the physical body there are three principal forces at work: first, the influence of the ego who is intending to take up the new form; secondly, the work of the building elemental formed by the Lords of Karma; and thirdly, the thought of the mother. Now suppose that an etheric body is about to be formed for an ego in the process of his descent into incarnation. He is himself an ego of a certain type and sub-type, and these characteristics of his are impressed upon his physical permanent atom, and this in turn determines which of the perpendicular divisions of etheric matter shall enter into the composition of that etheric body and in what proportion they shall be used. This quality of his, however, does not determine which of the horizontal divisions shall be employed, and in what proportion; that matter is in the hands of the four Devarajas, and will be determined according to the past karma of the man. Each of these Devarajas has vast hosts of assistants at his command, so that no one of the births which are momentarily taking place upon earth is ever overlooked. The Devarajas make a thought-form, the building elemental mentioned above, which is charged exclusively with the production of the most suitable physical body that can be arranged for the man. For his evolution he requires a body which has within it certain possibilities; for that purpose he may be born of a parent who himself possesses these qualities, and therefore can directly hand them on, or he may be born of a parent whose ancestors, on one side or the other, possessed them, so that the unawakened germs which can respond to them may be handed on by that parent to his offspring.

Remember that this elemental, which is put in charge of the development of the physical body, is the joint thought-form of the four Devarajas, and that its primary business is to build the etheric mould into which the physical particles of the new baby-body are to be built. In building this new etheric body it has four varieties of etheric matter which it can use (the four over which its creators respectively preside) and the type of the etheric body which is produced depends upon the proportion in which these constituents are employed. Remember that the elemental has no power of choice with regard to the perpendicular subdivisions, but it has every freedom with regard to the horizontal kinds of matter.

It is quite impossible for us at our present level to understand the working of so mighty a consciousness as that of a Devaraja, so we can only chronicle the fact, without pretending to explain it, that the elemental in doing its work appears somehow not to be entirely separated from the minds which projected it. In some way inexplicable to us it still remains to some modified extent within their consciousness, and in rare cases, where a developed ego is (even at an early age) beginning to take active possession of his body, it would seem that he may come into direct contact with them, and call down upon himself by their consent more karma than they had originally apportioned to him.

One who can do that while the elemental is still at its work can also retain during later life this touch with the karmic deities, and therefore his power to appeal to them for further modifications. So far as we have seen, however, this possible modification may be only in the direction of the increase of the karma to be worked out, not in that of its decrease. The awakening of consciousness, which enables an ego thus to come into touch with the Devarajas and to co-operate willingly with them so far as their work with himself is concerned, may commence at any time; so that an ego who was not in touch with them during the working of the elemental which built his physical body may yet, by stupendous efforts along the line of self-development and usefulness, attract their attention later in life and evoke from them a definite response.

The germ which is to expand into the physical body of the man has within itself two constituents, with two sets of potentialities. (The student must be careful not to confound this physical germ which comes from the parents with the physical permanent atom which the ego brings with him). It is essentially an ovum, which has within itself all the possibilities of the maternal ancestry, but it has been pierced by a spermatozoon which brings with it all the potentialities of the paternal ancestry.

These two sets of possibilities are wide, as may easily be seen if we reflect upon the number of ancestors which any one of us must have had, say a thousand years ago. But wide though they be, they have their limitations. For example, take the case of one of our gardeners here at Adyar - a man of what is called the coolie or unskilled labourer class. Going back a thousand years that man's ancestors must have been counted by millions; yet all those millions must have been of the coolie class. They must have included all possible varieties of coolie, good and bad, clever and stupid, kind and cruel; but they were all coolies, and therefore all had the limitations of the brain and the qualities belonging to that class.

From among these potentialities the elemental has to make its selection. For that purpose it has two questions to consider, quality and form. Of these the former is infinitely more important. The latter is concerned chiefly with the matter of the lower sub-planes. But the quality of the etheric matter selected for the building of that higher part of the physical body will to a large extent determine the capacities of that body during that incarnation - whether it will be naturally clever or stupid, placid or irritable, energetic or lethargic, sensitive or unresponsive.

So the first work of the thought-form or elemental of the Devarajas is to select which of these possibilities shall be brought into prominence in the building of the new physical body - especially in the building of its brain. The mere outer form is a minor consideration, though also an important one, but this too is part of the work of the elemental. If the man has deserved the limitation of deformity in his physical body or of weakness in some of its organs - the heart, the lungs, the stomach - it is through the elemental that his karma is adjusted. Its instructions (if we may use such a term) are to build a body of a certain kind and degree of strength, and with certain characteristics brought into prominence. But these are not instructions given to it to carry in its mind, for it has no mind ; they are rather itself, its very life, for when those instructions have finally been carried out it ceases to be, because the work for which it was created is done.

It is a well-known fact to students of embryology that in their earlier stages the germs of a fish, a dog and a man are practically indistinguishable. They all grow in the same manner, but the difference between them is that one of them stops at one stage of that growth, while the others go on further. The reason for this obvious fact is not clear to those who adopt the materialistic view. They have to postulate that matter coming from a particular source, although in every way identical in appearance with matter coming from a totally different source, nevertheless possesses within it some inherent qualities which compel it to reproduce the form from which it came.

The compulsory force is not an inherent quality in the matter, which is in truth identical and composed of precisely the same chemical elements, but it is the divine life pressing forward to ensoul this matter, and moulding it for itself into the form which is suited for it at that particular stage of its development. As soon as the entity becomes individualised, and therefore commences to make individual karma, this additional factor of the moulding thought-form of the karmic deities comes into play, and takes possession of the growing germ, even before its own ego can grasp it.

The form and color of this elemental vary in different cases. At first it accurately expresses in shape and size the baby body which it has to build, as that body should look (as far as the elemental's work is concerned) at the time of its birth. Clairvoyants, seeing this doll-like little figure hovering about (and afterwards within) the body of the mother, have sometimes mistaken it for the soul of the coming baby, instead of the mould of its physical body. When the foetus has grown to the size of the mould, that much of its task is successfully achieved, and it sheds that outer husk of itself and unfolds the form of the next stage at which it has to aim - the size, shape and condition of the body as it ought to be (taking only the elemental's work into account) at the time when it proposes to leave it. All further growth of the body after the elemental has retired is under the control of the ego himself.

In both of these cases the elemental uses itself as the mould. Its colours represent to a large extent the qualities which it is calculated to evoke in the body which it has to build, and its form is also usually that which is destined for him. It exists only for its work, and when the amount of force with which it has originally been supplied is exhausted, there is no longer any power left to hold together the particles, and it simply disintegrates.

This elemental takes charge of the body from the first, but some time before physical birth takes place the ego also comes into contact with his future habitation, and from that time onwards the two forces are working side by side. Sometimes the characteristics which the elemental is directed to impose are but few in number, and consequently it is able to retire at a comparatively early age, and to leave the ego in full control of the body. In other cases, where the limitations are of such a character that a good deal of time is necessary for their development, it may retain its position until the body is seven years old. Egos differ greatly in the interest which they take in their physical vehicles, for some hover over them anxiously from the first and take a good deal of trouble about them, while others are almost entirely careless with regard to the whole matter.

When a child is still-born, there has usually been no ego behind it, and consequently no elemental. There are vast hosts of souls seeking reincarnation, and many of them are still at so early a stage of their evolution that almost any ordinary surroundings would be equally suitable for them; they have so many lessons to learn that it matters little with which one they begin, and almost any conceivable set of surroundings will teach them something which they sorely need. Nevertheless it does sometimes happen that there is not at a given time any ego able to take advantage of a particular opportunity, and in that case, though the body may be formed to a certain extent by the thought of the mother, as there is no ego to occupy it, it is never really alive.

In building the form the elemental takes the etheric matter which it needs from that which it finds ready within the body of the mother. That is one reason for the necessity of the greatest care on the part of that mother during the time the child's body is being formed. If she supplies nothing but the best and purest materials, the elemental will find itself compelled to choose from those. Another factor which has an exceedingly powerful influence is the thought of the mother during this period, for that also moulds the shape which is slowly growing within her. Again this shows us why the mother's thought must at that time be especially pure and high, why she must be kept away altogether from all coarse or agitating influences, why only the most beautiful forms and colours should surround her, and the most harmonious conditions should prevail in her neighbourhood.

If the elemental's instructions do not include some special development in the way of features, such as unusual beauty or unusual ugliness, that part of the shaping of the new body will most likely be done by the thought of the mother - and by the thought-forms which are constantly floating round her. If she thinks often with devoted love of her husband there is a strong probability that the child will resemble its father; if on the contrary she looks often at her reflection in the mirror and thinks much about herself, it is probable that the child will bear considerable resemblance to her. Equally, if it happens that she is constantly thinking with devoted affection or admiration of some third person, the child is likely to resemble that person - always supposing that the elemental has no definite instructions in this matter. When the children grow older their physical bodies are influenced largely by their own thoughts, and as these differ from those of the mother, we often see that considerable changes in physical appearance take place, the child in some cases growing more beautiful and in other cases less so as the years roll by. "As a man thinks, so is he" is true on the physical plane as well as on others; and if the thought is always calm and serene, the face will surely reflect it.

To an advanced ego all the earlier stages of childhood are naturally exceedingly wearisome. I remember that the late Mr T. Subba Rao complained quite bitterly about it when he first took his new body. He declared that, do what he would, he could not make that baby body sleep more than twenty hours out of the day, and the rest of the time he actually had to wait near it and watch it squirming about, and listen to its plaintive ululations, and endure to be fed through it with tasteless and nauseous varieties of pap! Sometimes a really advanced person decides to avoid all this by asking someone else to give him an adult body, a sacrifice which any of his disciples would always be delighted to make for him.

But this method also has its drawbacks. However wearisome it may be to pass through childhood, at least in that way a man grows a body for himself, which is as nearly as may be an expression of him, and agrees with all his little peculiarities; but one who takes an adult body finds it already full of peculiarities of its own, which have worn in it deep grooves of habit that cannot readily be changed. It cannot but be to some extent a misfit, and it takes a long time to make its vibrations synchronise with his own. An ego coming into incarnation has always to adapt himself to a new set of conditions, but when he comes to birth in the ordinary way this can at least be done gradually, as the child grows up; but one who takes an adult body has instantly to adapt himself to all these fresh surroundings, which is often a very difficult business. In this case he has retained his old astral and mental bodies; but they are naturally counterparts of his previous vehicle, and they have to be adapted to the new form. Once more, if that form be a baby this can be done gradually, but if it is an adult form it must be done immediately, which means an amount of strain that is distinctly unpleasant.

PERSONAL CHARACTERISTICS

I have looked up many cases, and I find that for the ordinary man there seems to be but little continuity of personal appearance life after life; but I have known cases of strong similarity as well as great unlikeness. As the physical body is to some extent an expression of the ego, and that remains the same, there must be some cases where it expresses itself in similar forms; but racial, family and other characteristics usually override this tendency. When an individual is so advanced that the personality and ego are unified, the personality tends to have impressed upon it the characteristics of the glorified form in the causal body, which is relatively permanent.

When the man is an adept and all his karma is worked out, the physical body is the nearest possible presentment of that glorified form. The Masters will therefore remain recognisable through any number of incarnations. I have noticed that one of the Masters who comparatively recently attained adeptship is as yet not quite like the others, having somewhat rugged features. I am sure that will be different in the next incarnation. I should not expect to see much difference in the bodies of our Masters, even if They should choose to take others, and even though they might be of another race. I have seen prototypes of what bodies are to be like in the seventh Race; they will be transcendently beautiful.

The glorified form in the causal body is an approach to the archetype, and comes nearer to it as man developes. The human form appears to be the model for the highest evolution in this particular solar system. It is varied slightly in different planets, but is broadly speaking the same in general outline. In other solar systems forms may possibly be quite unlike it; we have no information on that point.

BRINGING OVER PAST KNOWLEDGE

We do not yet know with any certainty the laws which govern the power to impress the detailed knowledge of one life upon the physical brain of the next. Such evidence as is at present before us seems to show that details are usually forgotten, but that broad principles appear to the new mind as self-evident. Many of us have exclaimed when for the first time in this incarnation we read a Theosophical book: "This is exactly what I have always felt, but I did not know how to put it into words!" In some cases there seems scarcely that much of memory, yet as soon as the teaching is presented it is instantly recognised as true. Mrs. Besant as Hypatia must unquestionably have known a great deal of this philosophy which was not clearly formulated in her present brain during the orthodox or free-thought periods of this incarnation.

If any reliance at all is to be placed upon exoteric tradition, even the BUDDHA Himself, who descended from higher planes with the definite intention of taking birth to help the world, knew nothing clearly of His mission after He had entered His new body, and regained full knowledge only after years of searching for it. Undoubtedly He could have known from the first had He chosen, but He did not choose; He submitted Himself to what seems to be the common lot.

It is possible that in His case there may be another explanation. The body which was born of King Suddhodana and Queen Maya may not in its earlier years have been inhabited by the Lord BUDDHA . He may have acted as the Christ did; He may have asked one of His disciples to take care of that vehicle for Him until He needed it, and He may have entered it Himself only at the moment when it fainted after the long austerities of the six years of searching for truth. If this be so, then the reason that Prince Siddartha did not remember all that the Lord BUDDHA previously knew was because He was not the same person. But in any case we may be sure that the ego, who is the true man, always knows what he has once learned; but he is not always able to impress it upon his new brain without the help of a suggestion from without.

Fortunately for our students it seems to be an invariable rule that one who has accepted occult truth in one life always comes into contact with it in the next, and so revives his dormant memory. I suppose we may say that the opportunity of thus recovering the truth is the karma of having accepted it, and of having earnestly tried to live according to it in the previous incarnation. There is, however, every probability that much of what we now call distinctively Theosophical belief will be the ordinary accepted knowledge of the day by the time that we return to take up again our work on the physical plane, so it may be that we shall all be educated in it as a matter of course. If that be so, the difference between those who have studied it this time and those who have not will be that the former will take it up with enthusiasm and make rapid progress, while to the latter it will mean no more than does the science of to-day to the entirely unscientific mind. In any case, let no one for a moment suppose that the benefit of our study and hard work can ever be lost.

THE INTERVALS BETWEEN LIVES

A certain amount of misconception exists among students with regard to the average interval which elapses between two incarnations. It seems probable that we misunderstood the information given on this subject in the early days of the Society, and the statements then made have been copied without comment even into some of the later books. Most of the closer students have come to know more or less accurately the facts of the case, but so far as I am aware nothing resembling a tabulation of averages for the various classes of egos has yet been published.

At the end of the chapter on the heaven-world (then called devachan) in Mr. Sinnett's monumental work *Esoteric Buddhism*, the statement is made that the whole period between death and the next physical birth varies greatly in the case of different persons, but rebirth in less than fifteen hundred years is spoken of as almost impossible, while the stay in devachan which rewards a very rich karma is said sometimes to extend to enormous periods. This statement is based upon passages in the same letters from which is derived all the rest of this most interesting book, and there is no question whatever that Mr. Sinnett has quite accurately reported what was told to him. The same general idea is put forward by Madame Blavatsky in *The Secret Doctrine* (ii. 317): "Let us remember that, save in the case of young children and of individuals whose lives have been violently cut off by some accident, no spiritual entity can reincarnate before a period of many centuries has elapsed."

In those earlier days we took this fifteen hundred years as an average for humanity, but later investigations have clearly shown us that it could not have been meant exactly in that way. To make the statement square with the observed facts, it must be either greatly limited or greatly extended. If confined to a small group of the most advanced of the human race it would be approximately correct; and on the other hand, if it were extended to include not only humanity but the vast hosts of the deva kingdom, it might again be taken as coming very near to the truth. In the case of the quotation from *The Secret Doctrine* the expression spiritual entities may be read as implying that Madame Blavatsky was speaking only of highly developed persons; but the passage from *Esoteric Buddhism* gives us fifteen hundred years almost as a minimum.

We are given to understand that the letters upon which *Esoteric Buddhism* was founded were written by various pupils of the Masters under Their general direction; and so, while there is plenty of room for inaccuracies to creep in (as we know that they have crept in) it is impossible to suppose that the writers did not know facts quite readily accessible to anyone who can watch the process of reincarnation. We must remember that the letter was written not to the world at large but quite definitely to Mr. Sinnett, with possibly a view to the few others who were at that time studying with him. To state such an average for them would be reasonably exact, and perhaps this is what was done; but we certainly cannot accept it as the mean proportion for the whole human race at the present time.

It is probably impossible to arrive at a really accurate average, for in order to do that it would be necessary to know at least approximately the number in each of the different classes of monads. Something of the nature of an estimate for each of the main classes may be given, though even then it must be remembered that there will necessarily be wide individual variations on each side of it.

Three principal factors have to be taken not account; the class to which an ego belongs, the mode in which he has attained individualisation, and the length and nature of his last life. Let us then take up the various classes of humanity in their order, using the nomenclature decided upon by Mrs. Besant in the table facing page 213.

Lords of the Moon

At the head of that list appear the Lords of the Moon - those who attained the arhat level at some time or other during the evolution of the moon-chain. For that humanity, as for all others, seven paths open when they have attained the level assigned to their chain; and in this case one of those paths brought a certain proportion of the Lords of the Moon over to the earth-chain to direct the earlier stages of its evolution. All of these, however, have long since attained adeptship, and we need therefore take no account of them in the consideration of our present subject.

Moon-Men. (First Order)

The next class is the first order of the Moon-men, and that is a class so large and varied that it will be necessary for us to discuss it in the several subdivisions given in the chapter on monads from the moon.

1 & 2. The first class, as given there, includes those who even on the moon-chain were already on the Path; and the second consists of those who were

individualised in the fourth round of the moon-chain. In our present chapter we need not consider either of these classes, since their members have attained adeptship, and so the question of incarnations and the intervals between them no longer concerns them.

3. Those who attained individualisation in the fifth round of the moon-chain.

Among these, those who are already on the Path are usually taking a continuous succession of incarnations, so that for them the question of the interval between lives does not arise. If, however, they are for some reason not as yet taking the special series of lives which usually follows upon initiation, their intervals are very long - probably at the least fifteen hundred or two thousand years, or even more. Though not so usual as the series of rapid incarnations, this does sometimes occur; for among the cases known to us those who passed the first initiation some considerable time ago, one ego has been taking successive incarnations in physical life ever since, with scarcely any break, while another has been away from physical life for two thousand three hundred years; and yet the result so far as progress on the Path is concerned seems to have been exactly the same.

The apportioning of the different stages of a long interval like this varies considerably in different cases. The stay upon the astral plane is short, or the ego may even pass through it rapidly and unconsciously. Most of the time is passed in the highest level of the heaven-world, and then, after that is over, a certain proportion of conscious life in the causal body precedes the next descent into birth. This life of the ego on its own plane is at this stage only about one-tenth of the entire interval between the earth-lives. But this again is a matter in which no two instances are alike.

In the case of those who are approaching the Path the general interval is not far from twelve hundred years if the ego has been individualised slowly by intellectual development, and is therefore passing through its blissful experiences at the ordinary rate. If, however, the ego has been individualised suddenly by a rush of emotion or by a stupendous effort of will, and is consequently taking his bliss in the more concentrated form, his interval is about seven hundred years. Both these types are little likely to stay long upon the astral plane; probably five years represents for them an astral life of fair average duration. At the other end of their stay in the heaven-world there most likely comes a certain period of conscious life in the ego on its own plane, but this does not exceed half a-century at most.

During their more recent lives we find that it has been the tendency of those people who take the normal interval of twelve hundred years to incarnate successively in the different sub-races. Often we find them running twice through the same set of sub-races, first in male and then in female vehicles, or vice versa.

The fates of various people differ greatly. Some go on steadily life after life, but nothing particular happens to them. Others are constantly in trouble, shock following shock; and yet both are advancing along the line which is best for them. It often happens that if a man dies young, he is born again in the same sub-race, and when a man goes round the sub-races twice, he usually takes the other sex on the second journey. Broadly speaking, the Indians represent the first sub-race of the Aryan root-race, the Arabs the second, the Parsis the third, the Romance nations the fourth and the Teutons the fifth. If a man takes a birth in France, he does not need one in Italy or Spain, and the same is true of Germany and England.

Students taking the seven hundred years interval seem to have more the habit of attaching themselves to one sub-race and returning to it whenever possible, and diverging into others only occasionally in order to develope special qualities. As a general rule successive incarnations in the same race intensify its characteristics; equilibrium is brought about by incarnating in various races, or by travel and living among different people. With regard to this matter, the idiosyncrasies of the ego play a considerable part. I mentioned elsewhere how the strong prepossession in the mind of the Jews that they are a special and chosen people tends to bring them back into the same race; and pride of race generally, if unusually intense, is likely to work in that direction.

Even pride of family is not without its result also, and I have known of several cases in which, when abnormally developed, it has brought the ego back into the line of his direct descendants two or three times before he got free. In the beginning of these studies it was given to us as a general rule that a man usually takes not less than three and not more than seven incarnations in one sex before passing over to the other. Although the many researches which we have since undertaken have to a large extent confirmed this general rule, they have also shown us a great number of exceptions to it, some people taking long lines of incarnations in one sex before turning to the other, and others for a time incarnating alternately in male and female bodies; but most of these were in the case of egos who were already advanced somewhat beyond the average, and were therefore probably receiving special treatment.

Evidently there is no hesitation in modifying the general rule to suit particular cases, when for any reason that is seen to be desirable. Though the laws governing reincarnation are allowed to work mechanically upon the vast majority of undeveloped egos, it seems clear from the instances observed that as soon as any one ego makes a little progress of any sort and so becomes hopeful from the evolutionary point of view, considerable elasticity is introduced into the arrangements, and within certain definite limits he is born into the sex, race and conditions which are best suited to give him an opportunity of strengthening the weak points in his character.

In the case of men who have distinguished themselves greatly along artistic, scientific or religious lines, the interval is usually much the same, though the apportioning may differ slightly. The general tendency is to a longer astral and a shorter causal life, especially in the case of the religious and the artistic. A great philosopher sometimes enormously extends his life in the heaven-world; I remember that Madame Blavatsky has somewhere stated that Plato would be likely to stay away from earth for at least ten thousand years, though I imagine that this is an entirely exceptional ease.

4. Those who attained individualisation in the sixth round of the moon-chain; typical examples of whom are the country gentlemen and professional men.

Their intervals vary greatly, say from six hundred to a thousand years, of which perhaps twenty or twenty-five may be spent upon the astral plane, and all the rest in various stages of the heaven-world. There is probably just a touch of consciousness in the ego on its own plane, but only a touch.

5. Those who individualised in the seventh round of the moon-chain - the upper middle class. This class generally has an interval between lives of perhaps five hundred years, of which about twenty-five are passed on the astral plane and the rest in the heaven-world. In such a case there is no conscious life in the causal body, though of course, like all other human beings, they have the flash of memory and of prescience which is always vouchsafed to each ego when he touches his own plane between two physical incarnations.

Moon-men, Second Order. The bourgeoisie. Their interval between lives is commonly two hundred to three hundred years, of which about forty are usually spent upon the astral plane, and the rest in the lower levels of the heaven-world.

In this, as in all the other types, individualisation may have been obtained by intelligence or by emotion, and there will be a corresponding difference in the average length of the intervals between successive incarnations, but in all these lower classes the difference caused by the mode of individualisation is much less in proportion than in the higher class.

Moon Animal-men. The pioneers of the first round of the earth-chain, represented now by the skilled workers of the world. Such men have usually an interval between lives varying from one hundred to two hundred years, about forty of which are spent on the middle level of the astral plane, and the rest on some of the lower sub-planes of the heaven-world.

Moon-animals, First class. Now the un-skilled labourers.

Their interval between lives varies from sixty to a hundred years, of which from forty to fifty are spent on the lower parts of the astral plane, and the remainder on the lowest division of the heaven-world.

Moon-animals, Second class. The drunkards and the unemployable.

Such people are generally absent from the world some forty or fifty years, which they spend entirely on the astral plane - usually on the lowest subdivision but one.

Moon-animals, Third class. The lowest of humanity.

Their interval between lives is often about five years, spent on the lowest sub-plane of the astral - unless they are earth-bound by crime, which not infrequently happens.

In all the cases mentioned above, a certain difference is produced by the mode of individualisation, but this difference is much less in proportion in the lower classes. Still on the whole those individualised through intellect tend always to take the longer of the two intervals mentioned as possible for them, whereas those who come along other paths tend to take the shorter.

A third factor which exercises great influence is the length and nature of the individual life. Obviously an ego who casts aside his physical body in childhood has not had the opportunity in that body to generate a sufficient amount of spiritual force to keep him on the higher planes for the length of time common to his type. Generally speaking, then, a man who dies young will have a shorter interval than his neighbour who lives to old age. Generally speaking, again, the man dying young is likely to have a greater proportion of astral life, because most of the strong emotions which work themselves out in astral life are generated in the earlier part of the physical existence, whereas the more spiritual energy which finds its result in the heaven-life is likely to continue until the end or near the end of the period spent upon earth.

The character of the man during his earth-life is a consideration of the utmost importance. Some men lead a long life in which there is scarcely anything of spirituality, and that naturally tends to shorten the interval between their incarnations and brings it far below what is common for their class. Probably, too, in such a case quite an undue proportion of the interval would be spent on the astral plane. The averages given, therefore, are only averages, and it must be clearly understood that a wide range on each side of them is usually possible, so that the various classes may considerably over-lap one another.

We have only recently come to understand the importance, in this regard, of strong mutual affection. From our study of past lives it has become clear to us that egos are closely associated in families or group, and that this connection tends on the whole to equalise the intervals between the lives of the members of such a group. It is evidently considered necessary that they should prepare for future work together by constant association as they evolve, and it is manifest that intervals which would otherwise be shorter or longer are so dealt with as to bring the entire party into incarnation together, not once but many times.

This unquestionably involves an increase or decrease of the rate at which the spiritual force discharges itself, and it is clear that this must be a matter of careful regulation by the Authorities in charge of evolution. Though we have not yet discovered the exact law which regulates it, there is little doubt that when we do we shall find that it works automatically, so that the maximum of result may be achieved without injustice to any individual concerned.

There seems to be a type of students who are always yearning to discover injustice in the working of the evolutionary machinery; but those who have spent many years in the investigation of the processes of nature know more and more certainly as they go on that injustice is an impossibility, and that any case in which we think we descry it is only a case in which our knowledge is as yet imperfect. Those who have probed the mysteries of nature most deeply are precisely those who have acquired the utter certainty that He who doeth all things doeth all things well.

Eighth Section: Karma

THE LAW OF EQUILIBRIUM

When we are considering the life of man we have three principal forces to take into account, all interacting and limiting one another: the steady pressure of evolution, the law of cause and effect which we call karma, and the free-will of man. The action of the evolutionary force has, so far as we can see, no reference whatever to the man's pleasure or pain, but only to his progress, or rather his opportunities for progress. One would say that it was absolutely indifferent as to whether the man was happy or unhappy, and that it might press him sometimes into one of these conditions and sometimes into the other, according to what was best calculated to afford opportunity for the development of the particular virtue on the formation of which he is for the moment engaged. Karma appears as the manifestation of the action of the man's free-will in the past. He has accumulated energies which either afford opportunities for the evolutionary force, or limit it in its operation. Then the man's present use of such free-will as he possesses is a third factor

The doctrine of karma explains that advancement and well-being are the results of well-doing; but there should be no mistake as to exactly what is meant by well-doing and well-being respectively. The object of the entire scheme is, so far as we are concerned, the evolution of humanity; and consequently the man who does best is he who does most to help forward the evolution of others as well as his own. The man who does this to the utmost extent of his power and opportunity in one life will certainly find himself in the next in possession of greater power and wider opportunities. These are not unlikely to be accompanied by worldly wealth and power, because the very possession of these usually gives the opportunity required, but they are by no means a necessary part of the karma; and it is important for us to bear in mind that the result of usefulness is always the opportunity for further and wider usefulness, and we must not consider the occasional concomitants of that opportunity as themselves the reward of the work done in the last incarnation.

One instinctively shrinks from the use of such words as reward and punishment, because they seem to imply the existence, somewhere in the background, of an irresponsible being who deals out both at will. We shall get a truer idea of the way in which karma works if we think of it as a necessary readjustment of equilibrium disturbed by our action - as a kind of illustration of the law that action and reaction are always equal. It will also help us much in our thinking if we try to take a broader view of it - to regard it from the point of view of those who administer its laws rather than from our own.

Though the inevitable law must sooner or later bring to each man unerringly the result of his own work, there is no immediate hurry about it; in the counsels of the eternal there is always time enough, and the first object is the evolution of humanity. Therefore it is that one who shows himself a willing and useful instrument in forwarding that evolution always receives as his "reward" the opportunity of helping it still further, and thus, in doing good to others, to do best of all for himself. Of course if the thought of self-advancement were his motive for thus acting, the selfishness of the idea would vitiate the action and narrow its results; but if, forgetting himself altogether, he devotes his energies to the single aim of helping in the great work, the effect upon his own future will undoubtedly be as stated.

A definite protest ought once for all to be entered against the theory that suffering is the necessary condition of spiritual progress. Exercise is the condition of attaining physical strength, but it need not be painful exercise; if a man is willing to, take a walk every day, there is no need to torture him on the tread-mill in order to develop the muscles of his legs. For spiritual progress a man must develope virtue, unselfishness, helpfulness - that is to say, he must learn to move in harmony with the great cosmic law; and if he does this willingly there is no suffering for him but that which comes from sympathy with others.

Granted that at the present time most men refuse to do this, that when they set themselves in opposition to the great law suffering invariably follows, and that the eventual result of many such experiences is to convince them that the path of wickedness and selfishness is also the path of folly; in this sense it is true that suffering conduces to progress in those particular cases. But because we wilfully elect to offend against the law, and thereby bring down suffering upon ourselves, we have surely no right so to blaspheme the great law of the universe as to say that it has ordered matters so badly that without suffering no progress can be made. As a matter of fact if a man only will, he can make far more rapid progress without suffering at all.

It must, however, be remembered that any man who has once realised the glorious goal which lies before us can never be perfectly happy until he has attained that goal, and that he finds an ever-present source of dissatisfaction in his own failings. Now even dissatisfaction is a modified form of suffering; and from that no man can hope to be free until the imperfection has been outgrown. "God, Thou hast made us for Thyself, and our hearts are ever restless till they find their rest in Thee."

Whether it is comforting or the reverse to know that one's sufferings are deserved may be a matter of opinion; but that in no way alters the undoubted fact that unless they had been so deserved they could not possibly come to us. It is lamentable that so many people should adopt the unphilosophical and indeed childish attitude which leads them to assume that any idea which does not fall in with their particular sectarian preconceptions cannot possibly be true. Unintelligent people constantly say: "The Theosophical teaching about karma does not seem to me so comfortable as the Christian idea of forgiveness of sins," or "The Theosophical heaven-world does not seem so real and beautiful as the Christian, and so I will not believe in it."

They evidently think, poor creatures, that their likes and dislikes are powerful enough to alter the laws of the universe, and that nothing of which they do not approve can possibly be on any plane. We, however, are engaged in studying the facts of existence, which after all are not modified because Mr. and Mrs. So-and-so would rather believe them to be otherwise than they are. If it were possible for anyone to be an innocent victim there would be no certainty of the operation of the great law of cause and effect anywhere in the universe, which would be a far more terrible thing for us than having to work out the results of any amount of sin committed in former lives. It can never be too strongly emphasized that the law of karma is not the vindictive vengeance of some angry deity, but simply an effect naturally and inevitably following upon its cause in obedience to the action of universal law.

Every individual will have to pay to the utmost every debt that he contracts, and to every individual the most perfect justice will be done; but for this purpose it is not always necessary that a vast crowd of egos should be perpetually meeting one another in successive lives. If one man so acts towards another as seriously to hasten or retard his evolution, if he does anything which produces upon the other a marked or permanent effect, it is fairly certain that the two must meet again in order that the debt may be adjusted. It is obvious that that may be done in various ways.

A man who murders another may conceivably sometimes himself be murdered in turn in another incarnation; but he can cancel the karma much more satisfactorily if he happens to have an opportunity in that next incarnation of saving the life of his former victim at the cost of his own. It would seem that sometimes he may cancel it without losing his own at all; for among the many lines of lives which have been examined we found at least one case in which a murderer apparently fully expiated his fault by patiently devoting the whole of a later life to the service of the person whom he had previously slain.

There is a vast amount of minor karma which appears to go into what may be described as a kind of general fund. The schoolboy who mischievously pinches a classmate will certainly not have to meet that classmate a thousand years hence under other skies in order to be pinched by him in return, though it is unquestionable that even in so small a matter as this perfect justice will be done to both the parties. Constantly as we pass on through life we shower small kindnesses upon those whom we meet; carelessly and often unconsciously we do them small injuries in thought and word and deed. Every one of these brings its corresponding result of good or evil to ourselves, and we too, though we knew it not, were the agents of karma in those very actions. The small kindness which we attempt will prove a failure if the recipient does not deserve even that much of help; the careless slight will pass unnoticed by its victim if there has been nothing in his past for which it is a fitting retribution.

It is not easy to draw the line between these two classes of karma - that which necessitates personal adjustment and that which goes into the general fund. It is certain that whatever influences a person seriously belongs to the first category, and small everyday troubles belong to the second; but we have at present no means of knowing exactly how much influence must be exerted in order that an action may rank in the first-class.

We must remember that some of the greatest and most important of all karma can never be personally repaid. In all our line of lives, past and future, no benefit can be greater than that which the Masters have conferred upon us in giving us access to the Theosophical teaching; yet to Them as individuals we can make absolutely no return, since They are far beyond the need of anything that we can do. Yet even this stupendous debt must be discharged like all the rest; but the only way in which we can ever repay it is by handing on the knowledge to others. So we see that here is another kind of karma which may be said to go into the general fund, though not quite in the same sense as before.

A querent asks, "If it is a man's karma to have scarlet-fever, by what mechanism is the result brought about?"

I do not think that, in the sense in which the questioner means it, it ever is a man's karma to have scarlet-fever. It is his karma in a given incarnation to have as the result of his actions in past lives a certain amount of physical suffering, and if a scarlet-fever germ happens to be at hand when he is in a sensitive condition, it may be permitted to fasten upon him, and part of that debt of suffering may be discharged in that way. But if such a germ does not happen to be there at the moment, one of cholera or tuberculosis will do just as well, or instead of a disease there may be a broken limb caused by a bit of orange-peel on the pavement or by a passing motor car.

I am aware that there are books which lay down with great precision the exact type of karma which follows upon certain action - as, for example, that if a man is rude to his father in one incarnation he will be born lame of the right leg in the next, whereas if it is with his mother that he has a difference of opinion it will be the left leg which is affected, and so on. But in the many lines of lives which we have examined in order to study the working of karma we have found no such rigidity. On the contrary, We were especially struck no less by the wonderful flexibility of karma than by its unerring certainty. By no possible effort can the man escape a single feather-weight of the suffering destined for him, but he may often avoid it in one shape only to find it inexorably descending upon him in a different form, from some unsuspected quarter.

Just as a debt of ten pounds can be paid in a single note, in two smaller notes, in gold or silver, or even in a bag-full of copper, so a certain amount of karma may come in one terrible blow, in a number of successive but less severe blows of various kinds, or even in a long series of comparatively petty annoyances; but in any and every case the full tale must be paid.

The same sin, committed under the same circumstances by two exactly similar people, must result in the same amount of suffering, yet the kind of suffering might be almost infinitely varied, according to the requirements of the case. Take as an example one of the very commonest of failings, and let us think what would be the probable result of selfishness. This is primarily a mental attitude or condition, so we must look for its immediate result on the mental plane. It is undoubtedly an intensification of the lower personality at the expense of the individuality, and one of its results will therefore certainly be the accentuation of that lower personality, so that selfishness tends to reproduce itself in aggravated form, and to grow steadily stronger.

Thus more and more of the higher would be lost in each life through entanglement with the lower, and persistence in this fault would be a fatal bar to progress; for nature's severest penalty is always deprivation of the opportunity for progress, just as her highest reward is the offering of such opportunity. So here we have already a glimpse of the way in which selfishness may itself bring about its own worst result, in so hardening the man as to make him insensible to all good influences, and to render his further progress impossible until he had conquered it.

There would also be the karma on the physical plane of all the unjust or unkind acts which the man's selfishness might lead him to commit; but the worst penalty that those could bring upon him would be trivial and evanescent beside the effect upon his own mental condition. It is possible that one result might be that he would be drawn by affinity into the society of selfish people, and so through suffering from this vice in others he would learn how heinous it is in himself. But the resources of the law are endless, and we mistake if we imagine it as cramped down to the line of action on which we in our ignorance think it ought to be administered.

A large proportion of the man's suffering is what Mr. Sinnett calls "ready-money karma" - that is to say, it is not due to the result of actions in past lives, and not in any real sense necessary at all. But his actions, in spite of examples put before him and advice freely given to him, are so foolish, and his ignorance is so invincible, so apparently perverse, that he is constantly involving himself in suffering the causes of which are transparently obvious and readily evitable. I do not think that I exaggerate when I say that nine-tenths of the suffering of the ordinary man is utterly unnecessary, for it is not the result of the distant past, but is simply the outcome of the mistaken action or foolish attitude of this present life.

Another point to be taken into account is that man in his calculations so often fails to discriminate between good and evil effects. The average man regards death as the greatest of all evils, either for himself or for his friends; yet in many cases karma grants it as a reward. It is, indeed, hardly ever an evil or a punishment, but simply an incident - a kind of move in the game, inevitable at certain intervals, but at all times available as a temporary solution of a difficult position when it is seen to be desirable. It is rarely a matter of anything approaching the importance which is commonly attributed to it.

If we can conceive two newly-formed egos standing side by side, absolutely primitive and karmaless, and one of them should kill the other, or, indeed, act in any way with regard to the other, a result would be produced which would be, strictly speaking, undeserved. I doubt whether any such condition ever exists, for I think that the individualised animal brings over something of karma into his first human birth.

Many animals have a sense of right and wrong, or at least a knowledge that some things ought to be done and that others ought not to be done; and they are capable of feeling ashamed when they have done what they think to be wrong. They have in many cases a power of choice; they can exercise (or not exercise) patience and forbearance; and where there is a power of choice there must be responsibility, and consequently karma. The savage animal becomes a savage and cruel man; the gentle and patient animal becomes a gentle and kindly man, however primitive he may be. This serious difference is clearly the consequence of karma made in the animal kingdom. Such karma must inhere in the group-soul, but must be equally distributed through it, so that when a portion breaks off as an individual, it will carry within it its share of that karma.

It may be said that that only pushes our difficulty a little farther back, for there must be a first step sometime, and we must technically consider the result of that first step as unjust.

Not necessarily. Let us suppose the first step to be a fight between two animals. The wish to kill or wound would be equally present in both; the karma of that wish would in the case of the vanquished be worked out at once by death, whereas the victor would still owe a debt which would probably be discharged later by his own death by violence. In considering the case of humanity, however, we need not indulge in any such speculations.

We have behind us a great mass of accumulated energy of both kinds, desirable and undesirable, and I can hardly imagine any conceivable "accident" that would not suit as an expression for some part of its infinite variety. Therefore shipwreck or financial ruin does not discriminate, because it need not; there is always something which can work itself out in that way in the whole mass of karma which lies behind an ordinary man. In the rare cases where there is nothing remaining which can so work itself out, the man cannot be injured, and is therefore what is commonly called miraculously saved.

Nothing could be more wildly absurd than the idea that anything we can do can prevent the working out of karma. For example, if a child is born under circumstances which lead to its being cruelly treated, no doubt such treatment is in accordance with its previous karma; but if kindly intervention delivers it from the demons in human form who torment it, then that intervention also is in accordance with its karma. If it were not, then the well-intentioned effort to rescue it would fail, as we know it sometimes does. Our obvious duty is to do all the good we can, and to render all the help within our power in every direction; and we need have no haunting fear that in doing so we are interfering with the work of the great karmic deities, who are assuredly perfectly capable of managing their business with absolute exactitude, whatever we do or do not do.

Does karma seem merciless? If that adjective can be correctly applied to the working of Nature's laws, I suppose we must admit that it is so, just as the law of gravitation is. If a child slips over the edge of a precipice, no matter how sad may be the circumstances surrounding the slip, he usually falls to the bottom of that precipice just as effectually as would an older and more responsible person; if a man seizes a red-hot iron bar, he is equally burnt whatever may have been his object in seizing it, or whether he knew that it was hot or not. Yet it would hardly occur to us to think of the bar or the precipice as merciless, or to blame the law of gravitation or the law of the radiation of heat. Does not exactly the same thought apply in the case of karma?

THE METHOD OF KARMA

It is scarcely possible to put into words the appearance presented to clairvoyant vision on the higher planes by the working of this law of karma. It seems as though the man's action built cells or channels stored with energy, through the reactions of which he can be reached by the law of evolution. The appearance is as though all sorts of forces are playing round him, but they are able to influence him only by acting through these energies which he has himself set in motion. He is continually adding to the number of these cells or channels of energy, and so is continually modifying the possibilities of reaching him. It is in meeting and dealing with all these kaleidoscopic changes, and yet in spite of them all getting in its work and accurately performing its task, that the marvellous and all but incredible adaptability and versatility of karma is exhibited.

There is another aspect of karma the consideration of which I have found helpful in the effort to understand its working; but it belongs to a plane so high that it is unfortunately impossible to put it clearly into words. Imagine that we see each man as though he were absolutely alone in the universe, the centre of an incredibly vast series of concentric spheres. Every thought, or word, or action of his sends out a stream of force which rushes towards the surfaces of the spheres. This force strikes the interior surface of one of the spheres, and, being at right angles to it, is necessarily reflected back unerringly to the point from which it came.

From which sphere it is reflected seems to depend upon the character of the force, and this also naturally regulates the time of its return. The force which is generated by some actions strikes a sphere comparatively near at hand, and is reflected back very quickly, while other forces rush on almost to infinity, and return only after many lives. But in any case they inevitably return, and they can return nowhere but to the centre from which they came forth. Each man makes his own spheres, and the play of his forces is in no way affected by the action of those sent up by his neighbor, for they cross one another without interfering, just as do the rays of light from two lamps. And the medium through which they move is frictionless, so that the amount of force which returns is precisely that which the man himself has generated.

The prarabdha karma of an individual, that is, the karma selected by the authorities for him to discharge in his present life, divides itself into two parts. That which is to express itself in his physical body is made by the Devarajas into the thought-form or elemental which builds the body, of which we have spoken in a previous section; but the other and far larger block which is to indicate his fate through life, the good or evil fortune which is to come to him - this is made into another thought-form which does not descend; hovering over the embryo, it remains upon the mental plane. From that level it broods over the man and takes or makes opportunities to discharge itself by sections, sending down from itself a flash like lightning to strike, or a finger to touch, sometimes far down on the physical plane, sometimes a sort of extension which reaches only the astral plane, and sometimes what we may call a horizontal flash or finger upon the mental plane.

This elemental goes on discharging itself until it is quite empty; and then, like the other, it fades into nothingness, or more correctly is disintegrated and returns to the matter of the plane. The man can modify its action by the new karma which he is constantly making, by the new causes which he is perpetually setting up. The ordinary man has usually scarcely will enough to create any strong new causes, and so the elemental empties itself of its contents according to what may be described as its original programme, taking advantage of convenient astrological periods and surrounding circumstances, which make its work easier or more effective; and so the horoscope of the man may work out with considerable exactitude. But if the man be sufficiently developed to possess a strong will, the elemental's action is likely to be much modified, and the life will by no means follow the lines laid down in the horoscope. Sometimes the modifications introduced are such that the elemental is unable fully to discharge himself before the time of the man's death; and in that case whatever is left of him is again absorbed into the great mass of the sanchita karma - that which has not yet been worked out; and out of that another and more or less similar elemental is made ready for the beginning of the next physical life.

The great mass of the accumulated karma can also be seen hovering over the ego. Usually it is not a pleasant sight, because by the nature of things it contains more evil than good result. In the earlier days of their development in the remote past, most men have done many things that they should not have done, and thereby have laid up for themselves as a physical result a good deal of suffering on this lowest plane. In the present day all civilised beings have risen at least to the level of good intention, and consequently there is much less of directly evil karma being made by such people. We all do foolish things at times; we all make mistakes; but still on the whole the average civilised being is trying to do good and not harm, and therefore on the whole is likely to be making more good karma than bad. But by no means all of the good karma goes into that great accumulated mass, and so we get the impression in that of a preponderance of evil over good.

The result of most good thoughts or good actions is to improve the man himself, to make one or other of his bodies vibrate in response to higher forces, or to bring out in him qualities of courage, determination, affection, devotion, which he did not possess in so full a measure before. All this effect then shows in the man himself and in his vehicles, but not in the mass of piled up karma which is waiting for him. If, however, he does some good action definitely with the thought of its reward in his mind, good karma for that good action will come to him, and will store itself up with the rest of the accumulation until such time as it may be brought forward and materialised into activity. This good karma naturally binds the man to earth just as effectually as evil karma, and consequently the man who is aiming at real progress learns to do all actions absolutely without thought of self or of the result of his action, because if there is no thought of self, results of the ordinary kind cannot touch him.

Not that the man can escape the benefit of a good deed, any more than he can escape the result of an evil deed; but if the man thinks of the reward that will come to him he will receive the benefit in the shape of that reward, whereas if he forgets himself entirely and does this thing out of the fulness of his heart, because it is the right thing to do and therefore he can do no other, then the whole force of the result is spent in the building of his own character, and nothing of it remains to bind him to the lower planes. The fact is that in each case the man gets what he wants. As the Christ said Himself: "Verily I say unto you, they have their reward." The man who thinks of good result to himself obtains that good result; the mail who is not thinking of himself at all, or thinking only of making himself a channel for the forces of the LOGOS, is made into a better channel as the result of the action which that thought prompted.

Another complication is introduced by the fact that many people do good deeds in the name of and for the sake of some other, and in that way they make that other a partaker with them of the results. Many a man does a good deed in the name of the Christ, or if he be a Theosophist, in that of the Master, and justice demands that in such a case, since it is the thought of the Christ or the Master which has produced this result, something of the effect must go to the great person in question. In this way vast stores of helpful magnetism are constantly at the disposal of those Great Ones to whom many send thoughts of affection and devotion, in whose name many kindly deeds are done. Naturally it would be utterly impossible that the result of such action should in any way bind the Great One. It simply provides him with additional spiritual force for the work which he has in hand.

THE KARMA OF DEATH

It is by no means certain that in the majority of cases a time for death is definitely appointed by the Lords of Karma at all. The whole arrangement is far more elastic and adaptable than most students suppose. The clue to its comprehension lies in never forgetting that there are three great types of karma, which the Indians call sanchita, prarabdha and kriyamana.

The first is the whole vast mass of unexhausted karma, good or bad, which still waits to be worked out; let us call it mass-karma. The second is that particular part of the first which has been selected to be worked out in this incarnation; let us call it the man's destiny for this life. The third is the new karma which we are constantly making by our present actions.

It is the karma of the second type that the astrologer or the palmist tries to read; and his calculations, are often invalidated by intrusions from the other two varieties. It is quite certain that nothing can happen to a man which is not in the great mass of his karma, but unquestionably something may happen which was not originally included in his destiny for this life.

Suppose the case of a man on board a vessel which is about to be wrecked, or in the first car of a train which is about to come into collision. It may or may not be in the destiny appointed for this particular life that that man should die about this time. If it is, he will no doubt be killed; if it is not, he may be saved, if such saving does not involve too great an interference with the ordinary laws of nature. I think we may say that he probably will be saved if the prolongation of his physical life would appreciably hasten his evolution. It is intended that in each life some lesson should be learnt, some quality developed. If that life-work is already done - or if, on the other hand, it is obvious that the man will not succeed in doing it this time, no matter how long he lives - he has nothing to gain by continued physical life, and he may just as well be delivered from it.

Also, if there be in the vast mass of his previous karma some debt that can be adequately cancelled by whatever of physical or mental suffering may be involved in such a death, the opportunity of that cancellation may very well be taken when it thus offers itself, even though it may not have been included in the original plan for this particular life. But if in the whole of the mass-karma there is nothing that will fit in with such a death, the man simply cannot die that way, and he will inevitably be saved, even though it be by means which seem miraculous. We hear of such cases - cases in which a huge beam has fallen so as just to save a man from being crushed by the superincumbent weight of the wreckage, or in which when an ocean steamer has gone down with all hands, one man has somehow floated ashore on a hen-coop.

We must not forget the influence on our destiny of that third variety of karma which we are making for ourselves every day. A man may be doing such good work that for the moment he cannot be spared; he may or he may not have acted so as to deserve release from the physical plane at that particular period. Our tendency is to attach an altogether exaggerated importance to the time and the manner of our death. If for a moment we try to imagine how the matter must present itself to the Great Beings in charge of our evolution, we shall gain a much truer appreciation of relative values. To them the progress of the egos in their charge is the one matter of importance. They know the lessons to be learnt, the qualities to be developed.

They must regard it much as a schoolmaster regards the amount of work which a boy has to do before qualifying himself for entrance to the university. The schoolmaster divides that work according to the time at his disposal; so much must be done in each year, and the year's work in turn must be subdivided into terms and even into days. But he will allow himself a considerable amount of latitude with regard to these minor divisions; he may decide to devote two days instead of one to some specially difficult point, or he may close a lesson earlier than he intended if its object is clearly achieved.

Our lives are exactly these days of school life, and, the lesson may be lengthened or shortened as the teacher sees to be best. Death is merely the release from school at the end of one day's lesson. We need not trouble ourselves about it in the least; we should thankfully accept it whenever karma permits it to us. We must realise that the one important thing is that the appointed lesson should be learnt. The sections into which that lesson shall be divided, the length of the various lesson-hours, and exactly when they shall begin or end - all these are details which we may well leave to the agents of the Great Law.

From this point of view no death can be described as premature, for we may always be absolutely certain that what comes to us from without is what is best for us. Our business is to do our very best with each life, and to make every effort to retain it as long as possible. If we ourselves cut it short by recklessness or improper living, we are responsible, and the effect will assuredly be prejudicial; but if it is cut short by something entirely beyond our control, we may be sure that the curtailment is for our good.

Nevertheless what has been written in some of our books about "premature" death is quite true. In extreme old age desire fades away, and so something of the work of the astral life is already done before the man leaves the physical plane. A similar result is achieved by long sickness, and so in either of these cases the astral life is likely to be comparatively short and without serious suffering. This may be called the ordinary course of nature, and it is only by comparison with it that an earlier death may be spoken of as "premature." If a person dies in youth, desire is still strong, and therefore a stronger and more strenuous astral life may be expected - a condition on the whole less desirable. But if the Powers behind decided that an earlier death is best, we may feel sure that They know of other considerations which outweigh the prolongation of the astral life.

It seems probable, therefore, that in the majority of cases the exact time and manner of a man's death is not decided before or at his birth. Astrologers tell us that in many instances they cannot actually foretell the death of the subject whose horoscope they are examining. They say that at a certain time malefic influences are strong, and the man may die then, but if he does not, his life will continue until a certain other occasion when evil aspects threaten him, and so on. In the same way a palmist will tell us that at such and such points there are serious breaks or markings upon the life-line; they may indicate death, or it may be only serious illness. It is likely that these uncertainties represent points which were left open for later decisions, depending largely upon the modifications introduced by the action of the man during his life, and by the use which he makes of his opportunities. At any rate we may be well assured that whatever decision is made it will be a wise one, and that, whether in death or in life, all things are working together for our good.

KARMA AS AN EDUCATOR

No man can ever receive what he has not earned, and all things come to us as the result of causes which we ourselves have set in motion. If we have caused anything we have also caused its result, for the cause and the effect are like the two sides of a coin - we cannot have one without the other; indeed, the result comes upon us as part of our original action, which may be said in this case to be still continuing. Everything which comes to us is our own doing, good and bad alike; but it is also being employed definitely for our good. The payment of the debt is being utilised to develope the man who owes it, and in paying it he may show patience, courage, and endurance in the face of adverse circumstances.

People constantly grumble against their circumstances. A man will say:

"I cannot do anything, situated as I am, with so many cares, with so much business, with so large a family. If only I had the liberty which so-and-so has!"

The man does not realise that these very hindrances are part of his training, and that they are put in his way just in order to teach him how to deal with them. He would like no doubt to have some opportunity of showing off the powers which he has already developed, but what is needed is that he should develope the powers which he has not, and this means hard work and suffering, but also rapid progress. There is assuredly no such thing as punishment and reward, but there is the result of our actions, which may be pleasant or unpleasant. If we upset the equilibrium of nature in any way it inevitably readjusts itself at our expense.

An ego sometimes chooses whether he will or will not take certain karma in the present life, though often the brain-mind may know nothing of this choice, so that the very adverse circumstances at which a man is grumbling may be exactly what he has deliberately chosen for himself in order to forward his evolution.

When he is becoming a disciple, and is therefore somewhat out of the stage of evolution which is normal at present, he often dominates and largely changes his karma - not that he can escape his share, or any least portion of it, but that he gains much new knowledge and therefore sets in motion new forces in many directions, which naturally modify the working of the old ones. He plays off one law against another, thus neutralising forces whose results might hinder his progress.

It has often been said that the disciple who takes steps to hasten his own progress thereby calls down suffering upon himself. That is not perhaps quite the best way to put it. All that he does is to take his own evolution earnestly in hand, and to endeavour, as rapidly as may be, to eradicate the evil and develope the good within himself, in order that he may become ever a more and more perfect living channel of the divine love. It is true that such action will assuredly attract the attention of the great Lords of Karma, and while Their response will be to give him greater opportunity, it may and often does involve a considerable increase of suffering in various ways.

But if we think carefully we shall see that this is exactly what might be expected. All of us have more or less of evil karma behind us, and until that is disposed of, it will be a perpetual hindrance to us in our higher work. One of the earliest steps in the direction of serious progress is therefore the working out of whatever of this evil still remains to us, and so the first response of the Great Ones to our upward striving is frequently to give us the opportunity of paying off a little more of this debt (since we have now made ourselves strong enough to do it) in order that it may be cleared out of the way of our future work. The manner in which this debt shall be paid is a matter which is entirely in Their hands and not in ours; and we can trust Them to manage it without inflicting additional suffering upon others - unless of course those others have also some outstanding karmic debt which can be discharged in this way. In any case the great karmic deities cannot act otherwise than with absolute justice to every person concerned, whether directly or remotely.

VARIETIES OF KARMA

The karma of service done is always the opportunity for more service. This is one of the rules which emerge with the greatest certainty from our study of the working of karma in the many past lives which have been examined. When a man leads a particularly good life it by no means follows that in the next one he will be rich or powerful or even comfortable; but it does absolutely follow that he will have wider opportunities for work. Clearly the LOGOS wants His work done, and if we wish for opportunities of progress we must show that we are willing to work.

Knowledge brings responsibility, along with opportunity. To yield to what you know to be wrong, or to go back a step in order to gain force for a greater spring forward, is to miss your opportunity. Lives may pass before you gain the same opportunity again. If you neglect the knowledge or vision which points out to you a fault, you will certainly be born in the next life without that knowledge or vision. Knowledge should always be used; it is a mistake to think that you can postpone your activity and retain the knowledge.

We may make for ourselves most unpleasant future conditions if we choose to behave foolishly, but it is practically impossible for us who are now cultured people to throw ourselves back in a future birth into the position of savages or people of really low class. We may waste our time and make no progress, but unless we actually take to the practice of black magic, and use tremendous power in the wrong direction, we cannot throw ourselves back as far as that. Through misconduct or through neglect of opportunities we may be born in an uncomfortable position in our own class, or even in one a little lower, but it would upset the scheme of things if we could be thrown back into the savage state. Exceptional actions sometimes produce exceptional results, but as a general rule violent ups and downs are not practical; obviously it would be impossible for a cultured man to work out the kind of karma which in his position he must have made, if he were thrown back into the narrow conditions of an ignorant agricultural labourer. For the plans of the LOGOS an ever-increasing number of cultured people are needed, and therefore when once a man is born into a noble position he is on whole likely to continue to be so born.

There are, however, certain kinds of action which bring unusually horrible karma as their results. For example, the karma of cruelty of any kind, whether to men or to animals, is always especially awful in character; it often brings with it chronic physical ailments, accompanied by most acute sufferings, and often also it produces insanity - this last more especially when the cruelty is of a refined and intentional character. We have found, for example, that many members of the ignorant mob who tortured Hypatia in Alexandria have been reborn in Armenia, and have themselves suffered all sorts of cruelties at the hands of the Turks. People who are now, apparently by accident, burnt to death with awful sufferings are often those who have burnt others in the middle ages, or looked on with glee at those ghastly scenes of martyrdom.

Any injury done to a highly developed person reacts terribly upon the doer. We should indeed be careful about our attitude towards any Great One who may come, for He, being far in advance of us, is likely to be misunderstood - to be different from what we have expected, and therefore not to be appreciated. One reason why the Great Ones do not more often come amongst men is that the karma of misjudging and ill-using Them is dreadful, and the fools among mankind are sure to incur it. I have myself seen a case in which a great soul, born where he was not understood, fell when young into the hands of a brutal and incompetent pedagogue who shamefully abused him. I have also been allowed to see the karma which will follow upon that cruelty, and I shudder when I think of it. Truly may it be said of that miserable wretch, in the words attributed to the Christ, that before he had "offended one of these little ones, it had been better for him that a millstone had been hanged about his neck, and he had been drowned in the depths of the sea."

Closely associated with this is the subject of the karma of ingratitude, which is always exceptionally heavy - most of all when the ingratitude is shown to an occult teacher. People are constantly pressing forward, desiring to come into touch with the Masters, to attract Their attention; and they sometimes think that the pupils of those Masters try to hold them back, or at any rate decline to assist them in their efforts to approach. The pupil of the Masters exists only to help others, and nothing pleases him more than to draw another to the Feet where he has learned so much himself. But when he sees from the type of the aspirant that he does not yet understand those Great Ones, that his attitude towards Them is captious, irreverent, presumptuous, he will take no responsibility in the matter, for he knows that serious disaster is certain to result. A man of such temperament is sure to make bad karma anywhere; it would be foolish to put him into a position where he can multiply it a hundredfold.

For example, I have noticed cases in which people who have been deeply devoted to our President change their minds, and begin to abuse and slander her. That is a wicked thing, and it makes far worse karma than would be the maligning of a person to whom they owed nothing. I do not mean that people have no right to change their minds. If a man finds that he can no longer conscientiously follow our President, he has a full right to withdraw himself from among her disciples; we may regret his blindness, but we have no word of blame for him, for each man must do what he sees to be right. For such a departure there is no evil karma but that of the loss of opportunity - the ordinary result of failing in a test and making a serious mistake. But if after dropping away the man begins venomously to attack her and to circulate scandalous falsehoods against her, as so many have done, he is committing a very grave sin, and the karma of his action is exceedingly heavy. Vindictiveness and lying are always wicked; but when a man directs them against one from whose hands he has received the cup of life, they become a crime the effects of which are appalling.

The fact that a man has a large amount of bad karma behind him makes anything like occult advancement impossible for him until it is worked off. For example, those who are deeply involved in karmic debts are not likely to be candidates for membership in the community of the sixth root-race. No one could become an adept if he had evil karma behind him, because he must be free from any necessity for rebirth. A man who can function freely in his buddhic or rational vehicle, and so drop the causal body, need never again take up the latter; but naturally this cannot be done until all the karma of the lower planes is exhausted. The Master sends out all of HIS forces in open curves; but any lower thought of self causes the force sent out to travel in a closed curve, so that, whether it be good or bad, it has to return to its source and the man must come back to receive it.

A man is not free from the binding results on lower planes until he is perfectly selfless on those planes. A man who when helping another feels perfectly the unity with him, obtains the result of his action on the rational plane only, and not lower down. Do not forget also that we are making karma on the astral plane, for a man can make karma wherever his consciousness is developed, or wherever he can act or choose. I have seen cases where actions done on the astral plane have borne karmic fruit in the next physical life. Another point to remember is that there is always a general karma belonging to an order or a nation, and that each individual in that order or that nation is, to a certain extent, responsible for the action of the whole. For instance, a priest has a certain responsibility for all that the collective priesthood does, even though he may not personally approve of it.

ANIMAL KARMA

Students often ask questions upon the working of karma in connection with the animal kingdom, saying that since it is scarcely conceivable that animals can have made much karma of any kind, it is difficult to account for the extreme differences to be observed in their conditions - one being well and kindly treated, while another is subjected to all kinds of brutalities, one always protected and well-fed, while another is left to starve and to fight for the bare right of living.

There are two points to be borne in mind in this connection: first, an animal often does make a good deal of karma; second, the well-treated animal has not always so much advantage as he appears to have, for association with man does not always improve the animal or tend to evolve it in the right direction. The sporting dog is taught by the hunter to be far more savage and brutal than it could ever become in any form of life that could come to it by nature; for the wild animal kills only to satisfy his hunger, and it is only man who introduces into animal life the wickedness of killing for the sake of the lust of destruction. However much his intelligence may be developed, it would have been far better for this unfortunate creature if he had never come into contact with humanity; for through him his group-soul has now made karma - karma of the most evil kind, for which other dogs which are expressions of that group-soul will have to suffer later in order that gradually the savagery may be weeded out.

The same may be said of the lap-dog who is pampered by some foolish mistress so that he gradually loses all the canine virtues, and becomes an embodiment of selfishness and love of ease. In both these cases man is criminally abusing his trust with regard to the animal kingdom, and is deliberately developing the lower instead of the higher instincts in the creatures committed to his care, thereby making bad karma himself, and leading a group-soul to make bad karma also. Man's duty towards the dog is clearly to evolve in him devotion, affection, intelligence and usefulness, and to repress kindly but firmly every manifestation of the savage and cruel side of his nature, which a brutalised humanity has for ages so sedulously fostered.

Questioners sometimes speak as though they thought that a dog or a cat receives a certain incarnation as a reward of merit. We are not as yet dealing with a separated individuality, and therefore there is for that particular animal no past in which individual karma in the ordinary sense of the word can have been generated - nothing either to merit or to receive a reward. When a particular block of that monadic essence which is evolving along the line of animal incarnation which culminates in (let us say) the dog, has reached a fairly high level, the separate animals which form its manifestation down here are brought into contact with man, in order that its evolution may receive the stimulus which that contact alone can supply.

The block of essence ensouling that group of dogs has in the matter so much of karma as is involved in having so governed its manifold expressions that it has been able to reach the level where such association is possible; and each dog belonging to that group-soul has his share of the result. So that when people ask what an individual dog can have done to merit a life of ease or the reverse, they are allowing themselves to be deceived by the illusion of mere outward appearance, and forgetting that there is no such thing as an individual dog, except during the latter part of that final incarnation in which the definite breaking away of a fresh soul from the block has occurred.

Some of our friends do not realise that there may be such a thing as the commencement of an entirely new piece of karma. When an injury is done by A to B, they always fall back on the theory that at some previous time B must have injured A, and is now imply reaping what he has sown. That may be so in many cases, but such a chain of causation must begin somewhere, and it is quite as likely that this may be a spontaneous act of injustice on A's part, for which karma will assuredly have to repay him in the future, while B's suffering, though undeserved as far as A is concerned, is the payment for some other act or acts which he has committed in the past in connection with some one else.

In the case of the ill-treatment of an animal by a man this is certain - that it cannot be the result of previous karma on the part of the particular animal, because if it were an individual capable of carrying over karma it would not have been again incarnated in animal form.

But the group-soul of which it is a part must have acquired karma, or the thing could not happen. Animals do often intentionally cause each other terrible suffering. It is reasonably certain from various considerations that the prey killed by a wild beast for food, in what may be called the natural necessary course of business, does not suffer appreciably; but in the unnecessary and intentional fights which so often occur between animals - bulls, stags, dogs or cats, for example - great pain is wilfully inflicted, and that means bad karma for the group-soul, karma that must in the future be paid by it through some of its manifestations.

Not for one moment, however, not by one tittle, does that lesson the guilt of the human beast who treats the animal cruelly, or causes him to fight or inflict pain on other creatures. Most emphatically there is karma, and exceedingly heavy karma, stored up for himself by the man who thus abuses the power to help which has been placed in his hands, and in many and many a life to come he will suffer the just result of his abominable brutality.

If one takes the trouble necessary to obtain a complete grasp of such knowledge as is already available in Theosophical literature on the subjects of karma and of animal reincarnation, the main principles upon which their laws work will be found clear and readily comprehensible. I fully recognise how small and general such knowledge is, and I realise that many cases are constantly occurring in which the details of the method in which the karma works itself out are entirely beyond our ken; but you may see enough to show you that what we have been taught as to the inevitability and the absolute justice of the great law is one of the fundamental truths of nature. Secure in that certainty, you can afford to wait for the more detailed comprehension until you gain those higher faculties which alone will give the power to see the working of the system as a whole.

Assuredly, as we progress, the divine light will illumine for us many corners that as yet remain in shadow, and we shall gradually but surely grow towards a perfect knowledge of the divine truth which even now is enfolding us, guarding and guiding us. All those who have had the privilege of studying these subjects under the guidance and with the help of the great Masters of the Wisdom are so fully persuaded of this that even where at present they do not see fully, they are more than willing and ready to trust to that great Power of which as yet only dim glimpses can be vouchsafed to human eye.

Ninth Section: The Theosophical Society and its Founder

WHAT IS THE THEOSOPHICAL SOCIETY?

It would appear that some of its members have not quite comprehended the position of this Theosophical Society to which they belong. It is not a Society which is formed merely for the promotion of learning in some special branch, like the Royal Asiatic or the Royal Geographical Societies; still less is it a Church, which exists only to spread some particular form of doctrine. It has a place in modern life which is all its own, for its origin is unlike that of any other body at present existing. To understand this origin we must glance for a moment at the hidden side of the history of the world.

All students of occultism are aware that the evolution of the world is not being left to run its course haphazard, but that its direction and administration are in the hands of a great Hierarchy of Adepts, sometimes called the White Brotherhood. To that Brotherhood belong Those whom we name the Masters, because They are willing under certain conditions to accept as pupils those who prove themselves worthy of the honour. But not all Adepts are Masters; not all will take such pupils; many of Them, though equal in occult rank, have the whole of Their time occupied in quite other ways, though always for the helping of evolution.

For the better surveillance and management of the field of action, They have mapped out the world into districts, much as the Church divides its territory into parishes (though these are parishes of continental size), and an Adept presides over each of these districts just as a priest does over his parish. But sometimes the Church makes a special effort, not connected specially with any one of its parishes, but intended for the good of all; it sends forth what is called a "home mission," with the object of stirring up faith and arousing enthusiasm all over a country, the benefits obtained being in no way a matter of personal gain to the missioners, but going to increase the efficiency of the ordinary parishes.

In a certain way the Theosophical Society corresponds to such a mission, the ordinary religious divisions of the world being the parishes; for this Society comes forth among them all, not seeking to take away from any one of them those people who are following it, but striving to make them understand it and live it better than they ever did before, and in many cases giving back to them on a higher and more intelligent level the faith in it which they had previously all but lost. Yes, and other men too, who had nominally no religion - who, though at heart of the religious type, have yet been unable to accept the crudities of orthodox teaching - have found in Theosophy a presentation of the truth to which, because of its inherent reasonableness and wide tolerance, they are able heartily to subscribe. We have among our members Hindus, Buddhists, Jains, Parsis,

Jews, Muhammadans and Christians, and no one of them all has ever heard or read from any of the officials of our Society a word against the religion to which he belongs; indeed, in many cases the work of the Society has produced a distinct revival of religious interest in places where it has been established.

Why this should be so is readily comprehensible when we remember that it is from this same great Brotherhood that all the religions of the world have their origin. In this true though hidden government of the world there is a department of Religious Instruction, and the Head of that department has founded all the different religions either personally or through some pupil, suiting the teaching given in each case to the people for whom it was destined, and to the period in the world's history which had then been reached. They are simply different presentations of the same teaching, as may at once be seen by comparing them. The external forms vary considerably, but the broad essentials are always the same. By all the same virtues are commended; by all the same vices are condemned; so that the daily life of a good Buddhist or a good Hindu is practically identical with that of a good Christian or a good Muhammadan. They do the same things, but they call them by different names; one spends much time in prayer, and the other in meditation, but really their exercises are the same, and they all agree that the good man must be just, kindly, generous and true.

It is said that some hundreds of years ago the leading officials of the Brotherhood decided that once in every hundred years, in what to us is the last quarter of each century, a special effort should be made to help the world in some way. Some of these attempts can be readily discerned - such, for example, as the movement initiated by Christian Rosenkreutz in the fourteenth century, simultaneously with the great reforms in Northern Buddhism introduced by Tsong-kha-pa; the remarkable renaissance of classical learning and the introduction of printing into Europe in the fifteenth; the work of Akbar in India in the sixteenth, at the same time with the publication of many works in England and elsewhere by Lord Bacon, and the splendid development of the Elizabethan age; the founding of the Royal Society, and the scientific work of Robert Boyle and others after the Restoration in the seventeenth; the activities in the eighteenth (the secret history of which on higher planes is known to but few) which escaped from control and degenerated into the French Revolution; and in the nineteenth the foundation of the Theosophical Society.

This Society is one of the great world-movements, destined to produce effects far greater than any that we have yet seen. The history of its work so far is but a prologue to that which is to come, and its importance is out of all proportion to what it has hitherto appeared to be. It has this difference from all movements that have preceded it, that it is first, the herald of the Coming Christ, and secondly, the first definite step towards the founding of a new root-race. Many of our students are aware that the Master M., the great Adept to whom both of our founders owe special allegiance, has been selected to be the Manu of that race, and that His inseparable friend the Master K. H. is to be in charge of its religious teaching.

It is evident that in the work which these two Great Ones will have to do They will need an army of devoted subordinates, who must above all things be loyal, obedient and painstaking. They may possess other qualities also, but these at least they must have. There will be scope for the keenest intelligence, the greatest ingenuity and ability in every direction; but all these will be useless without the capacity of instant obedience and utter trust in the Master. Self-conceit is an absolute bar to progress in this direction. The man who can never obey an order because he always thinks he knows better than the authorities, the man who cannot sink his personality entirely in the work which is given him to do, and co-operate harmoniously with his fellow-workers - such a man has no place in the army of the Manu. Those who join it will have to incarnate over and over again in rapid succession in the new race, trying each time to bring their various bodies nearer and nearer to the model set before them by the Manu - a very laborious and trying piece of work, but one that is absolutely necessary for the establishment of the new type of humanity which is required for the race. The opportunity of volunteering for this work is now open to us.

Those who wish to join in it must begin to differentiate their aims from those of the ordinary man of the world. If we are to be selected for that work, we must show ourselves ready and willing by doing this which is now offered to us. The great Head of the department of Religious Instruction, the Lord Maitreya, who has already spoken as Krishna to the Indians and as Christ to the Christians, has decided soon to pay another visit to the world for the healing and the helping of the nations, and for the revival of spirituality on the earth which has well-nigh lost it. One great work which the Theosophical Society has to do is to try to prepare men for His coming, so that more may be able to profit by the unequalled opportunity which His presence will give. The religion which He founded when He came down in Judaea two thousand years ago has now spread widely over the world; but when, after He left His physical body, His followers gathered together to discuss the situation, we are told that the number of the names was only a hundred and twenty. A single preacher was His herald then; now it is a world-wide Society of twenty thousand members. May we hope to do a little better this time - to keep Him with us longer than three years before the wickedness of the world drives Him away, to draw round Him a somewhat larger body of followers before He leaves us? That is yet to be seen; but it depends largely upon the energy, effort and selflessness of members of the Theosophical Society now.

Besides its primary object of spreading occult truth throughout the world, the Theosophical Society has also this secondary object - that it may act as a kind of net to draw together out of all the world the people who are sufficiently interested in occultism to be willing to work for it. Out of that number a certain proportion will be found who desire to press on further, to learn all that the Society has to teach, and to make real progress. Probably not all of those will succeed, but some certainly will, as some have done in the past; and from those who thus obtain a footing the Adepts Themselves may choose those whom They consider worthy of the great privilege of working under Them in the future. Such selection cannot of course be guaranteed to any one who passes even into the innermost groups of the Society, since the choice is absolutely in the hands of the Masters; we can say only that such selections have been made in the past, and that we know that many more volunteers are required.

Many have joined the Society without knowing anything of the inner opportunities which it offers, or the close relation with the great Masters of Wisdom into which it may bring its members. Many have come into it almost carelessly, with but little thought or comprehension of the importance of the step which they have taken; and there have been those who have left it equally carelessly, just because they have not fully understood.

Even those have gained something, though far less than they might have gained if they had had greater intelligence. The Countess Wachtmeister tells how once when some casual visitors called to see Madame Blavatsky and offered to join the Society, she immediately sent for the necessary forms and admitted them. After they had gone, the Countess seems to have said half-remonstratingly that not much could be expected from them, for even she could see that they were joining only from motives of curiosity or courtesy.

"That is true," said Madame Blavatsky, "but even this formal act has given them a small karmic link with the Society, and that, little as it is, will mean at least something for them in the future."

Some have committed the incredible folly of leaving it because they disapproved of the policy of its President, not reflecting first of all, that that policy is the President's business and not theirs; secondly, that as the President knows enormously more in every direction than they do, there is probably for that policy some exceedingly good reason of which they are entirely unaware; and thirdly, that Presidents and policies are after all temporary, and do not on any way affect the great fundamental fact that the Society belongs to the Masters and represents Them, and that to abandon it is to desert Their standard. Since They stand behind it, and intend to use it as an instrument, we may be sure that They will permit no serious error. It is surely not the part of a good soldier to desert from the ranks because he disapproves of the plans of the General, and to go off and fight single-handed. Nor is such fighting likely to be specially efficient or useful to the cause which he professes to champion.

Some have deserted simply from a fear that if they remained in the Society they might be identified with some idea of which they disapprove. This is not only selfishness but self-conceit; what does it matter what is thought or said of any of us, so long as the Master's work is done and the Master's plan carried out? We must learn to forget ourselves and think only of that work. It is true that that work will be done in any case, and that the place of those who refuse to do it will quickly be supplied. So it may be asked, what do defections matter? They do not matter to the work, but they matter very much to the deserter, who has thrown away an opportunity which may not recur for many incarnations. Such action shows a lack of all sense of proportion, an utter ignorance of what the Society really is and of the inner side of its work.

This work which our Masters are doing, this work of the evolution of humanity, is the most fascinating thing in the whole world. Sometimes those of us who have been able to develope the faculties of the higher planes have been allowed a glimpse of that mighty scheme - have witnessed the lifting of a tiny corner of the veil. I know of nothing more stirring, more absorbingly interesting. The splendour, the colossal magnitude of the plans take away one's breath, yet even more impressive is the calm dignity, the utter certainty of it all. Not individuals only, but nations, are the pieces in this game; but neither nation nor individual is compelled to play any given part. The opportunity to play that part is given to it or to him; if he or it will not take it, there is invariably an understudy ready to step in and fill the gap.

At this present time a magnificent opportunity is being offered to the great Anglo-Saxon race - to the whole Teutonic sub-race, if it will only sink its petty rivalries and jealousies and take it. I hope with all my heart that it will do so; I believe that it will; but this I know, that if unfortunately it should fail, there is another nation already chosen to assume the sceptre which in that case would fall from its hands. Such failure would cause a slight delay, while the new nation was being pushed rapidly forward to the necessary level, but at the end of a few centuries exactly the same result would have been achieved. That is the one thing that is utterly certain - that the intended end will be achieved ; through whose agency this will be done matters very much to the agent, but nothing at all to the total progress of the world.

Let us throw ourselves into that work, not out of it, trying ever to do more and more of it, and to do it better and better. For if we do well now in comparatively small matters - in Lodge activities, in propaganda work, in the service of those around us - we may be permitted to do something much grander - to help to smooth the way for the coming of the Lord; if we have the glorious privilege of earnestly and humbly making ourselves useful then, we may presently be entrusted with even greater responsibilities in connection with that new root-race, and of us will be true what was said of old: "Well done, good and faithful servant; thou hast been faithful over a few things; I will make thee ruler over many things; enter thou into the joy of thy Lord."

THEOSOPHY AND WORLD-LEADERS

A thoughtful Theosophist cannot but wonder sometimes how it is that Theosophy, though unquestionably representing the most advanced theory of existence and the most complete statement of the highest wisdom at present available, yet does not seem to appeal at all to many of the most eminent leaders of the world's thought and progress, whether it be along the lines of science, art, literature, philosophy or religion. These men of the keenest intellect, these others of the noblest spirituality, surely they ought to be the very first to welcome the splendid effulgence of Theosophy, the clarity and common-sense of its system, the light which it throws upon all the problems of life and death, the beauty of the ideals which it puts before us. But the fact remains that they do not welcome it, but on the contrary many of them treat it with indifference, or even contempt. Their attitude is a remarkable phenomenon; how can we explain it?

Again, as to ourselves, putting aside such an altogether abnormal person as our President, we know quite well that we who are Theosophists are in intellect far behind the great leaders of scientific and philosophical thought, just as in spirituality and devotion we are far behind some of the great saints of whom we hear in the various religions. Yet we have the inestimable privilege of finding ourselves in the Theosophical Society, we can understand, believe and assimilate its teachings, while these others apparently cannot. We are clearly no better than they; along certain lines we are obviously less developed; why should this great and glorious reward come to us and not to them?

It is a great and glorious reward; let us make no mistake as to that. The strongest adjectives in the language, the most poetical description that we can conceive, would fail adequately to convey what Theosophy is to those who can grasp it, what it does for those who put it into practice. Since it does all this for us who are commonplace folk, why does it leave these much higher and grander people cold and Unmoved?

They are higher and grander; here is another point about which no mistake must be made. The intellect of the great scientific man is a very wonderful and wholly desirably thing, the culmination of ages of development. The spirituality, the utter unworldliness and the deep devotion of the saint are beautiful and precious beyond all words, and such saintship comes only as the crown of many lives of earnest effort along that special line. These are indeed gifts which none can despise or gainsay; "more to be desired are they than gold, yea, than much fine gold; sweeter also than honey and the honeycomb."

Yet their possessors have not the inestimable pearl of Theosophy, and we have it - we who stand on the plain, and look up to them on the mountain heights. Clearly these great men have much that we have not - much at least that in us is as yet merely rudimentary; what have we that they have not, that we are worthy of so great an honour?

This is what we have - the knowledge of the direction in which to put forth our forces. We have it because from the Theosophical teaching we understand something of the scheme of things, something of the plan upon which the world is built, something of the object and method of evolution - and that not only in a broad and general sense, but also in sufficient detail to make it practically applicable to the life of the individual.

But why is all this so much clearer to us, the small people, than to these greater ones? By our own doctrine we know how "utter-true the faultless balance weighs," how none can have even the smallest benefit to which he is not entitled; what have we done to merit this greatest of all rewards - we who are very much like thousands of other people, full of ordinary human faults, neither better nor worse than the great majority of our fellow-men?

Whatever it is that we have done, it must evidently have been in some other life than this. Many of us can bear testimony that when we first met with Theosophy (this time) something within us leapt up at once in glad response to its appeal, in eager recognition of kinship to its thought. Yet we all know that there are many other better people than we in whom it evokes no response whatever - who cannot understand the depth of our enthusiasm for it.

We usually (and quite correctly) explain this by saying that we have met with these glorious truths before; that we have known of and studied these things in a former life, and that our unappreciative friends have not. But that does not solve the problem; it only moves it a stage further back. Why, in that former life, did we study these things, while our more gifted friends did not?

The answer is that the world is still at an early stage of its evolution, and that man has not yet had time to unfold all qualities. He must take them in some sort of order; he must begin somewhere; and men differ because they have chosen different points from which to begin. We have our qualities and our powers (such as they are), and our attraction to these subjects, because it is in that direction that we have been putting out our every effort in the far-away past. No one possesses any quality that he has not worked to unfold within himself. So if our greater friends are "gifted" in certain ways, it is because they have earned their gift by hard work in previous lives. Just as by study in another life we have acquired our "gift" - the power to understand and appreciate something of Theosophic truth - so have they acquired their shining powers of intellect or devotion by practicing these qualities long ago.

We have taken different lines then, we have spent our time in developing different qualities. Now we each have what we have earned, but naturally each finds himself without those other qualities at which he has not been specially working. We are all imperfect, but not all imperfect in the same direction. Manifestly we must aim in the future at an all-round development, so that each must acquired the qualities which others now possess, but he as yet does not.

Another very interesting point, which has been somewhere well put by our President, is that the great leaders of thought at the present day are fulfilling a certain function in the world's evolution which they could not so well fill if they knew all that we know. This is the fifth sub-race of the fifth root-race, and the fullest possible unfoldment of the lower mind is the task at the moment set before humanity. These leaders who intensity it, glory in it, almost worship it, are doing the work which they are appointed to do for the majority of mankind. It is precisely because they believe in intellect so thoroughly, because they think that there is nothing beyond it, that they can so intensify it and carry it to so high a place. It is because they know just so much, and no more, that they are convenient pawns to be used in this particular part of the cosmic game. For, as Omar Khayyam says:

We are but pieces in the game He plays
Upon this chequer-board of nights and days;
Hither and thither moves, and checks, and slays,
And one by one back in the closet lays.

These great men are the appointed leaders of a certain stage, and they are doing their work nobly; we cannot expect them to turn aside from that now to listen to us and our message. There will come a time in the future when they will listen, and then the magnificent intellectual development which they are now acquiring will carry them far and rapidly along the road of occult progress.

These three things it is clear that man must have before he can hope to reach perfection: intellect, spirituality, and discrimination - which last quality may in this case be defined as the knowledge of how to use the other two wisely. If any one of these be absent, the working of the others cannot but be to some extent defective. We constantly see that this is so. The scientific man evolves intellect to a very high level, but if the spiritual side of his nature is entirely undeveloped he may use intellect for personal ends instead of for the good of all; or he may be unscrupulous in the pursuit of knowledge, as is the vivisector. The saint reaches a high level of devotion and spirituality, yet for lack of intellect he may often make himself ridiculous by superstition, he may be narrow-minded, and even a persecutor. And both the saint and the scientist may waste their energies in quite wrong direction for want of a clear knowledge of the great plan of the LOGOS - the very thing that Theosophy gives.

What a man is now is the consequence of what he has done and thought in the past. If he has devoted his energy to the development of intellect - well and good, he has the intellect for which he has worked; but, since in addition to that he needs spirituality and discrimination, he must now devote himself to working for the acquisition of those faculties. If he has so far spent his time chiefly in devotion he has gained great power in that direction, but he must now proceed to unfold those other qualities of intellect and discrimination to which he has not yet turned his attention. If in previous lives he has studied the great scheme of things, he comes back this time with power to comprehend and the intuition to accept the truth, and that is indeed well for him; but he still needs to unfold from within himself the qualities to which the other men have been devoting themselves.

Unfortunately man at these early stages of evolution is so constituted that he is apt to boast of what he himself possesses, and to try to exalt his own qualities by minimising those of others instead of imitating what is best in them. So it happens that the saint and the man of science rarely appreciate one another, and not infrequently there is a good deal of mutual contempt and misunderstanding. It is for us to be careful that we do not allow ourselves to fall into the same snare. Let us remember that we set before ourselves as a goal the attainment of adeptship, and that the adept is the perfect man in whom all these different good qualities exist in the highest degree.

Before we reach adeptship we have to develope as much spirituality as the greatest of the saints, and far more - as much intellect as the most brilliant man of science, and far more. So our attitude towards those who already possess these most desirable attributes should be not carping criticism, but the most generous appreciation and admiration of all that is good, while our own quality - that of knowledge of the direction in which evolution is moving - will prevent us from imitating the mistakes in addition to the excellencies of those who, while far advanced along other lines, are as yet scarcely even on the threshold or ours.

All these qualities are necessary, and we have much hard work before us to develope those in which we are at present lacking. Yet I think we may congratulate ourselves upon the choice which we made in other lives, when we devoted ourselves to the study of the great scheme as a whole, to the endeavour to understand the plan of the LOGOS, and in our humble way to co-operate with Him.

For that has brought us (or should have brought us) contentment with our lot, the power to make the best of everything, and to see the best in everything. Most men are eager to see the worst in everybody, to pounce upon flaws in everything, to find something at which to carp and cavil. We who are Theosophists should cultivate a spirit exactly the reverse of this; we should see the hidden deity in every one and everything, and our eagerness should ever be to discover in all of them not what is evil, but what is good. If these others despise us; if the scientific man ridicules us as superstitious and refuses to listen to our explanations; if the devotional person regards us with horror as unorthodox, and insists on clinging to a less noble presentation of his deity than that which we offer him; let us on our side take heed that we do not make a corresponding mistake. They have their weak points, no doubt, and one of them is this prejudice which renders them unable to appreciate the truth; let us be courteous enough gracefully to ignore such failings, and focus our attention upon the splendid qualities in which they really excel - those qualities in which we must use our most strenuous endeavour to imitate them.

For since we see that the LOGOS wills to use in His service our intellect and our devotion, we have the strongest conceivable motive to develope them as rapidly as we can, and we shall be saved much trouble, much mortification and waste of energy by the knowledge which we already have of the direction in which He wills that these forces should be employed. All that we have is from Him, and therefore all that we have we hold on His behalf and at His disposal, to be used ever and only in His service.

REMINISCENCES

I first heard of Theosophy through coming across a second-hand copy of Mr. Sinnett's book *The Occult World*, but my first communication from one of the Masters was obtained in a somewhat unusual way. For some years before this I had been engaged in the investigation of spiritualism, and in the course of that enquiry I had come into contact with most of the prominent mediums of that day, and had seen every one of the ordinary phenomena about which one reads in books upon that subject. One medium with when I had much to do was Mr. Eglinton; and although I have heard stories told against him, I must bear witness that in all my own dealings with him I found him most straightforward, reasonable and courteous.

One of his specialities was slate-writing, and I found it a very useful phenomenon to show to any enquirer who adopted the sceptical attitude. The method was this. On the way to the séance I took the sceptic into a stationer's shop and induced him to buy two new school slates, and to have them packed in one parcel with a tiny crumb of slate pencil enclosed between them. I advised him to assure himself that the parcel was securely tied, and to seal the knots with his own seal if he had one. Then I told him to carry the parcel, and on no account whatever to let it pass out of his personal custody either before or during the séance. If during the performance it was necessary to sit with joined hands, I advised him to sit upon his parcel. Thus the séance commenced, and usually after a very short time there would be raps or some other indication that the force had gathered.

We sat usually at a small square wooden table without any cloth upon it, and Eglinton's plan was to take an ordinary slate, lay upon it a crumb of pencil and then slip it under the table, holding the slate against the under surface of the table. As this was in broad daylight, and we were alone in the room with the medium, there was no opportunity for substitution of previously prepared slates, or anything of that sort. The slate being held in this way, writing would appear on the surface which was pressed close against the table - writing in answer to any question which we chose to ask.

After this had been going on for some little time I asked insinuatingly whether the kind spirits could write on our slates. Nearly always the answer was in the affirmative, though once or twice I have been told that the power was not strong enough. Then I turned to the sceptic and asked him to produce his sealed package of slates:, but on no account to allow it to go out of his hands. Usually he held it out in both his hands above the table, and Mr. Eglinton would place one hand lightly upon the package.

Under those conditions I asked the sceptic to formulate a mental question, and then while he still held the package of slates we heard the writing rapidly going on inside. When the usual three little taps announced that the message was finished, I said to the sceptic:

"Now examine your slates and your string, and make sure that no one has thrown you into an hypnotic trance and tampered with your parcel; then cut it open and read your answer."

Generally we found the two sides of the slates which had been pressed together filled with writing more or less in relation to the mental question which had been formulated. Usually the sceptic was tremendously impressed and even dumbfounded for the time; but within a week he generally wrote to say that of course we had somehow or other been deceived, and we had not really seen what we thought we saw.

Mr. Eglinton had various so-called controls - one a Red Indian girl who called herself Daisy, and chattered volubly whether opportunity offered or not. Another was a tall Arab, named Abdullah, considerably over six feet, who never said anything, but produced remarkable phenomena, and often exhibited feats showing great strength. I have seen him simultaneously lift two heavy men, one in each hand. A third control who frequently put in an appearance was Ernest; he comparatively rarely materialised, but frequently spoke with direct voice, and wrote a characteristic and well-educated hand. One day in conversation with him something was said in reference to the Masters of the Wisdom; Ernest spoke of Them with the most profound reverence, and said that he had on various occasions had the privilege of seeing Them. I at once enquired whether he was prepared to take charge of any message or letter for Them, and he said that he would willingly do so, and would deliver it when opportunity offered, but he could not say exactly when that would be.

I may mention here that in connection with this I had later a good example of the unreliability of all such communications. Some considerable time afterwards some spiritualist wrote to Lights explaining that there could not possibly be such persons as the Masters, because Ernest had positively told him that there were not. I wrote to the same newspaper to say that I had it on precisely the same valueless authority that there were Masters, and that Ernest knew Them well. In each case Ernest had evidently reflected the thought of the questioner, as such entities so often do.

To return to my story, I at once provisionally accepted Ernest's offer; I said that I would write a letter to one of these Great Masters, and would confide it to him if my friend and teacher, Mr. Sinnett, approved. At the mention of this name the "spirits" were much perturbed; Daisy especially was very angry, and declared that she would have nothing to do with Mr. Sinnett under any circumstances; "Why, he calls us spooks!" she said, with great indignation. However I blandly stuck to my point that all I knew of Theosophy had come to me through Mr. Sinnett, and that I therefore did not feel justified in going behind his back in any way, or trying to find some other means of communication without first consulting him.

Finally, though with a very bad grace, the spirits consented to this, and the séance presently terminated. When Mr. Eglinton came out of his trance, I asked him how I could send a letter to Ernest, and he said at once that if I would send the letter to him he would put it in a certain box which hung against the wall, from which Ernest would take it when he wished. I then posted off to Mr. Sinnett, and asked his opinion of all this. He was at once eagerly interested, and advised me promptly to accept the offer and see what happened.

Thereupon I went home and wrote three letters. The first was to the Master K. H., telling Him with all reverence that ever since I had first heard of Theosophy my one desire had been to place myself under Him as a pupil. I told Him of my circumstances at the time, and asked whether it was necessary that the seven years of probation of which I had heard should be passed in India. I put this letter in a small envelope and sealed it carefully with my own seal. Then I enclosed it in a letter to Ernest in which I reminded him of his promise, and asked him to deliver this letter for me, and to bring back an answer, if there should be one. That second letter I sealed in the same manner as the first , and then I enclosed that in turn with a short note to Eglinton, asking him to put it in his box and let me know whether any notice was taken of it. I had asked a friend who was staying with me to examine the seals of both the letters with a microscope, so that if we should see them again we might know whether any one had been tampering with them. By return of post I received a note from Mr. Eglinton, saying that he had duly put the note for Ernest into his box, and that it had already vanished, and further that if any reply should come to him he would at once forward it.

A few days later I received a letter directed in a hand which was unknown to me, and on opening it I discovered my own letter to Ernest apparently unopened, the name "Ernest" on the envelope being marked out, and my own written underneath it in pencil. My friend and I once more examined the seal with a microscope, and were unable to detect any indication whatever that any one had tampered with the letter, and we both agreed that it was quite impossible that it could have been opened; yet on cutting it open I discovered that the letter which I had written to the Master had disappeared. All that I found inside was my own letter to Ernest, with a few words in the well-known hand-writing of the latter written on its blank page, to the effect that my letter had been duly handed to the Great Master, and that if in the future I should ever be thought worthy to receive an answer Ernest would gladly bring it to me.

I waited for some months, but no reply came, and whenever I went to Eglinton's séances and happened to encounter Ernest I always asked him when I might expect my answer. He invariably said that my letter had been duly delivered, but that nothing had yet been said about an answer, and that he could do no more. Six months later I did receive a reply, but not through Ernest, and in it the Master said that though He had not received the letter (nor, as He remarked, was it likely that He should, considering the nature of the messenger) He was aware of what I had written and He now proceeded to answer it.

He told me that the seven years of probation could be passed anywhere, but He suggested that I might come out here for a few months, to see whether I could work with the Headquarters staff. I wished to say in answer to this that my circumstances were such that it would be impossible for me to come to Adyar for three months, and then return to the work in which I was then engaged; but that I was perfectly ready to throw up that work altogether and to devote my life absolutely to His service. Ernest having so conspicuously failed me, I knew of no way to get this message to the Master but to take it to Madame Blavatsky, and as she was to leave England on the following day for India, I rushed up to London to see her.

It was with difficulty that I induced her to read the letter, as she said very decidedly that such communications were intended only for the recipient. I was obliged to insist, however, and at last she read it and asked me what I wished to say in reply. I answered to the above effect, and asked her how this information could be conveyed to the Master. She replied that He knew it already, referring of course to the exceedingly close relation in which she stood with Him, so that whatever was within her consciousness was also within His when He wished it.

She then told me to wait by her, and not to leave her on any account. I waited patiently all through the afternoon and evening, and even went with her quite late at night to Mrs. Oakley's house, where a number of friends were gathered to say farewell Madame Blavatsky sat in an easy chair by the fireside, talking brilliantly to those who were present, and rolling one of her eternal cigarettes, when suddenly her right hand was jerked out towards the fire in a very peculiar fashion, and lay palm upwards. She looked down at it in surprise, as I did myself, for I was standing close to her, leaning with an elbow on the mantelpiece; and several of us saw quite clearly a sort of whitish mist form in the palm of her hand and then condense into a piece of' folded paper, which she at once handed to me, saying, "There is your answer." Every one in the room crowded round, of course, but she sent me away outside to read it, saying that I must not let anyone see its contents. It told me that my intuition of throwing up everything and coming out here was a right one; that that was what He had wished me to do, but could not ask it unless I offered. I was further told to take a steamer a few days later and to join Madame Blavatsky in Egypt, which of course I did.

In Cairo we took up our quarters in the Hotel d'Orient. Here it was that I first saw one of the members of the Brotherhood. While sitting on the floor at Madame Blavatsky's feet, sorting out some papers for her, I was startled to see standing between us a man who had not entered by the door. It was He who is now the Master D. K., though at that date He had not taken the degree which made Him an adept.

Our stay in Egypt with Madame Blavatsky was in many ways a most remarkable experience, as she constantly told us much of the inner side of what we saw there. She had been in Egypt before, and was well acquainted with some of the officials, with the Prime Minister, Nubar Pasha, with the Russian Consul Monsieur Hitrovo, and especially with the curator of the museum, Monsieur Maspero. I remember particularly how we went through the museum with this last gentleman, and how Madame Blavatsky was able to give him a great mass of most interesting information about the various curiosities which were under his care.

Madame Blavatsky understood Arabic, and she used to amuse us greatly by translating for our benefit the private remarks which were being made by the grave and dignified Arab merchants, as they sat talking to one another in the bazaar. After they had for some time been calling us Christian dogs, and speaking disrespectfully of our female relatives for many generations, she blandly asked them in their own language whether they thought that this was the way in which a good son of the Prophet should speak of those from whom he hoped to gain much in the way of business. The men were always covered with confusion, not having expected that any European could possibly understand them.

Arabic, however, seems to have been the only Oriental language with which she was acquainted; she did not know Sanskrit, and many of the difficulties of our Theosophical terminology arise from the fact that in those days she would describe what she saw or knew, and then ask any Indian who happened to be near what was the Sanskrit name for it. Very often the gentleman who provided her with the term had not clearly understood what she meant; and even when he did, we must remember that she asked adherents of different schools of philosophy, and that each answered according to the shade of meaning applied to the term in his teaching.

Many curious phenomena were constantly taking place around her at this period. First, she was herself the most striking of all the phenomena, for her changes were protean. Sometimes the Masters Themselves used her body, and wrote or spoke directly through her. At other times when her ego was elsewhere engaged, one or other of two pupils of lower degree than herself would take the body, and there were even certain occasions when another woman used to be in charge. I have myself frequently seen all these changes take place, and I have seen the new man who had entered the body looking round to discover the condition of affairs into which he had come - trying to take up the thread of conversation, for example. Yet with all this, she was in no sense of the word like an ordinary medium, for the true owner of the body stood at the back all the time in full consciousness, and thoroughly understood what was going on.

Extraordinary phenomena, however, also occasionally occurred. While we were crossing the desert by train from Ismailia to Cairo a letter fell in the railway carriage, referring to the subject-matter of the conversation then proceeding, and conveying by name to each one present a kindly message of encouragement. I and another member of the party happened to be looking up at the time when this letter came, and we both saw it appear in the air, just in the circular space in the roof of the carriage in which a lamp is usually put at night. It came, just as the other had done, as a vague ball of whitish mist which condensed into a piece of paper and fluttered down.

I remember another occasion on which she bought in the scent-bazaar at Cairo a tiny bottle of attar of roses, for use in the shrine-room here, paying £2 for it. When we were sitting at lunch in the hotel half-an-hour afterwards, at a small table reserved for our party in an alcove, two English sovereigns fell out of space upon the table, and Madame Blavatsky explained that she had been told she ought not to spend money upon Them in this way, as we should need every shilling that we had before we reached Adyar - a statement which certainly proved true.

At one time and another I have seen a good many of the phenomena which were so closely associated with Madame Blavatsky. I have seen her precipitate drawing and writing, and I have also seen her find a missing object by occult power. On several occasions I have seen letters fall out of the air in her presence; and I must also state that I have seen such a letter fall here in this house at Adyar when she was six thousand miles away in England, and again that I myself have several times had the privilege of being employed by the Master to deliver just such letters after her departure from the physical plane.

In those early days of the Society messages and instructions from the Masters were frequent, and we lived at a level of splendid enthusiasm which those who have joined since Madame Blavatsky's death can hardly imagine. Those of us who have had the inestimable privilege of direct touch with the Masters have naturally retained that enthusiasm, but we have been unable under less favourable circumstances to keep it up among the rank and file of the members. Perhaps now we may be about to witness a recrudescence of it; may we all be worthy to take part in the glorious times that are coming!

FAITHFUL UNTO DEATH

Long ago in old Atlantis, in the great City of the Golden Gate, there reigned a mighty King. One day there came to him a soldier whom he had sent out to head an expedition against a troublesome tribe on the borders of that vast empire. The soldier reported victory, and as a reward the King gave him the position of captain of the Palace guard, and placed specially in his charge the life of his own only son, the heir apparent to his throne. Not long afterwards the newly-appointed captain had an opportunity of proving his faithfulness to his trust, for when he was alone with the young Prince in the Palace gardens a band of conspirators rushed upon them and tried to assassinate his charge.

The captain fought bravely against heavy odds and, though mortally wounded, succeeded in protecting the Prince from serious harm until help arrived, and he and the unconscious Prince were borne together into the presence of the King. The Monarch heard the story and, turning to his dying captain, said:

"What can I do for you who have given your life for me?"

The captain replied:

"Grant me to serve you and your son forever in future lives, since now there is the bond of blood between us."

And with a last effort he dipped his finger in the blood which flowed so fast from his wounds, and touched with it the feet of his sovereign and the forehead of the still unconscious Prince. The King held out his hand in benediction, and replied:

"By the blood that has been shed for me and mine, I promise that both you and he shall serve me to the end."

So was the first link forged between three leaders of men of whom we have all heard; for that great King is now the Master M., the Prince his son has been known to us as Helena Petrovna Blavatsky, and the Captain of the guard as Henry Steele Olcott. Through all the ages since, through many strange vicissitudes, the link has been kept unbroken and the service has been rendered, as we know that it will be through ages yet to come.

Since then as Gashtasp, King of Persia, he protected and assisted in the foundation of the present form of Zoroastrianism, and later as the world-renowned King Asoka he issued those wonderful edicts which remain until this day graven upon rocks and pillars in India to show how real were his zeal and his devotion. And when, at the end of that long and strenuous life, he looked back upon it with sorrow to see how far short of his intentions even his wonderful achievements had fallen, his Master showed him, for his encouragement, two visions, one of the past and one of the future. The vision of the past was the scene in Atlantis when the link between them was forged; the vision of the future showed his Master as the Manu of the Sixth Root-Race and our President-Founder as a lieutenant serving under Him in the exalted work of that high office. So Asoka died content in the certainty that the closest of all earthly ties, that between the Master and His pupil, would never be severed.

Having thus taken a prominent part in the spreading of two of the great religions of the world, Zoroastrianism and Buddhism, it was appropriate that he should be so closely associated with the work of this great movement which synthesizes all religions - the Theosophical Society. Never himself the spiritual teacher, he has always been the practical organizer who made the teacher's work possible. In his recent life as in all those others, his ruling principle was always that of passionate loyalty to the Master and to the work which he had to do. When first I met him more than a quarter of a century ago that was the dominant feature in his character; through all the years that I have known him that above all other motives ruled his actions; it inspires the last letter which I received from him, written only a few weeks before his death; it has been still his most salient characteristic in the astral world in which he has since been living

If we turn to the outward details of this last life of his, we still find the same keynote of devotion to duty. The Assistant Sectary of the United States Treasury wrote to him with regard to his public work for the Government:

"I wish to say that I have never met with a gentleman intrusted with important duties, of more capacity, rapidity and reliability than have been exhibited by you throughout. More than all, I desire to bear testimony to your entire uprightness and integrity of character, which I am sure have characterized your whole career, and which to my knowledge have never been assailed. That you have thus escaped with no stain upon your reputation, when we consider the corruption, audacity and power of the many villains in high position whom you have prosecuted and punished, is a tribute of which you may well be proud, and which no other man occupying a similar position and performing similar services in this country has ever achieved."

He showed the same energy and capacity in his work for the Theosophical Society. Few of our members realize the extent and the success of his labours, for much of what he did can be properly appreciated only by those who have travelled in those Eastern lands which he loved so well. To his untiring exertion was due the rebuilding and enlargement of the Society's Headquarters at Adyar. It was he who founded the great library there, and on the occasion of its opening gathered together to bless its inception priests of all the leading religions of the world - the first occasion in history on which such representatives had met in fraternal accord, each freely acknowledging the others as standing on an equal footing with himself.

To him is due the great movement for Buddhist education in the island of Ceylon, in consequence of which up to the present, 287 Buddhist schools have been founded, in which over 35,000 children are being taught. He it was who brought together on a common platform of belief the Northern and Southern Schools of Buddhism, separated for more than a thousand years; he it was who took up the education of the neglected pariah class.

Many and great were the difficulties in his way in holding together and directing so complex a movement as the Theosophical Society; yet in every land he was always popular, by every nation he was eagerly welcomed. His utter devotion to the welfare of the Society and the transparent honesty of his purpose could not fail to impress all who met him. I speak of him with feeling, for I had special opportunities of knowing him well. I shall never forget his fatherly kindness to me, when as a comparatively young man, quite new to Indian life, I first went to reside at the Headquarters at Adyar.

Since then I have met him in many countries; I have passed weeks alone with him (except for an interpreter and a servant) in a bullock-cart in the jungles of Ceylon; I went with him on the journey which carried Theosophy into Burma in 1885. Under circumstances like these one quickly gets to know a man with far greater intimacy than is afforded by years of ordinary social life, and I can unreservedly bear testimony to the whole-souled devotion of the man - to the fact that during all this time his one anxiety was the furthering of the Theosophical work, his one thought how to please the Master by doing with all his might that which had been given him to do.

His passing from among us is too recent for its details to have been forgotten; we all know how courageously he bore his sufferings, how all through his illness his constant thought was still the welfare of the dear Society to which his life had been devoted. We remember how when the time came for him to leave the body three of the great Masters stood beside him, as well as his old colleague and friend, H. P. Blavatsky; we have all read the magnificent speech of his successor at his cremation. That cremation was a grand and worthy ceremony. The pyre was of sandalwood and his body was covered with the American flag and the Buddhist flag, the latter a standard which he himself had invented, bearing in their right order the special colours of the aura of the Lord BUDDHA .

He was unconscious for a while after death, but soon became fully awake and active. As I was always deeply attached to him, his Master told me to act as a kind of guide to him when necessary, and to explain to him whatever he wished. He had always been keenly interested in the powers and possibilities of the astral plane, and as soon as he could see it clearly, he was full of eager and insatiable desire to know how everything is done, to understand the rationale of it, and to learn to do it himself. He has an unusually strong will in certain directions, and that made many of the experiments easy to him even when they were quite new. He is most at home in work which involves the use of power in some way - to fight, to cure, to defend. He is full of big schemes for the future, and is just as enthusiastic as ever about the Society which he loves.

His attention has been attracted by the strong thought about him involved in writing this; he stands beside me now, and insists that I shall convey to the members his most earnest advice to give whole-hearted loyalty and support to his noble successor, to put aside at once and forever all pitiable squabbling over personalities, all unprofitable wrangling over matters which are not their business and which they cannot be expected to understand, and to turn their attention to the one and only matter of importance - the work which the Society has to do in the world. His message to them is: "Forget yourselves, your limitations and your prejudices, and spread the truths of Theosophy."

Of his future we can say little as yet. By the time that these lines are before the reader, it is probable that he will be again in incarnation. He has earnestly wished this, in order that he may work along with Madame Blavatsky in her present incarnation. How far his desire will be granted, I cannot yet tell. Certainly he will be employed wherever the Masters think that he will be most useful. His great talent is organization, and we have seen that he has already practised it in Zoroastrianism, in the great missionary enterprise of Buddhism and in the foundation of the Theosophical Society. No doubt he may have similar work to do in connection with the next great religion, and again at the establishment of the Sixth Root-Race. Be that as it may, the great man whom in his last life we knew as Henry Steele Olcott will be ready to bear his part in all such activities, to lead us as he led us before, devoted as ever to the service of his Master, faithful as ever through life and through death.

A COURSE OF STUDY IN THEOSOPHY

It is desirable that one who wishes to study Theosophy thoroughly should acquaint himself in the course of time with the whole of Theosophical literature. This is no light task; and the order in which the books are taken is of importance if a man wishes to get out of them the best that he can. But at the same time it must be remembered that no order can be prescribed which will be equally suitable for every one; there are those who can usefully absorb information only along devotional lines, and there are those who must have a scientific and non-emotional presentation of the truth. The best thing that I can do, therefore, is to prescribe such a plan of reading as I have found to be on the whole most generally useful, leaving room for considerable variation to suit individual idiosyncrasies.

It seems to me of great importance to have a clear outline of the whole scheme thoroughly in the mind before endeavouring to fill in the details. No one can know how strong is the evidence for any one part of the Theosophical teaching until he knows the whole of that teaching, and sees how each separate portion is confirmed and strengthened by the rest, and is indeed a necessary part of the scheme as a whole. My advice, therefore, is that the beginner should read first the elementary literature, not troubling himself unduly with details, but seeking rather to take in and assimilate the broad ideas contained in it, so as to see all that they imply and to realise them as facts in nature, thereby putting himself into what may be called the Theosophical attitude, and learning to look at everything from the Theosophical point of view.

To this end the student may take *An Outline of Theosophy, The Riddle of Life, Hints to Young Students of Occultism,* and various lectures by Mrs. Besant and myself which have been issued as propaganda pamphlets. When he feels himself fairly certain of these, I should recommend next Mrs. Besant's Popular Lectures on Theosophy and then her *Ancient Wisdom*, which will give him a clear idea of the system as a whole. Another book which might be useful to him at this stage is *Some Glimpses of Occultism.* He can then proceed to follow details along whichever line most commends itself to him.

If he is interested chiefly in the ethical side, the best books are: *At the Feet of the Master, Light on the Path, The Voice of the Silence, The Path of Discipleship, In the Outer Court, The Laws of the Higher Life, The Three Paths and Dharma,* and *The Bhagavad-Gita.*

One who wishes to study the life after death will find what he wants in: *The Other Side of Death, The Astral Plane, Death and After, The Devachanic Plane.*

If he is approaching the matter from the scientific side, the following books will suit him: *Esoteric Buddhism, Nature's Mysteries, Scientific Corroborations of Theosophy, Occult Chemistry* and *The Physics of the Secret Doctrine* .

If he cares for the study of comparative religion he should read: *Universal Text-book of Religion and Morals, Four Great Religions, The Great Law, The Bhagavad-Gita, Hints on the Study of the Bhagavad-Gita, The Upanishads, The Wisdom of the Upanishads, An Advanced Text-book of Hindu Religion and Ethics, The Light of Asia, A Buddhist Catechism, Buddhist Popular Lectures* and *The Religious Problem in India* .

If he thinks chiefly of the Christian presentation of these truths, the best books are: *Esoteric Christianity, The Christian Creed, Fragments of a Faith Forgotten, The Perfect Way* .

If one wishes to investigate the origin and early history of Christianity, in addition to the books on the subject already mentioned, Mr. Mead's works will specially appeal to him: *Did Jesus Live B.C. 100?* The Gospel and the Gospel and the Gospel, Orpheus and Plotinus .

The student who is interested in applying Theosophy to the world of modern thought, and to political and social questions, may profitably turn to; *The Changing World, Some Problems of Life, Theosophy and Human Life, Occult Essays* and *Theosophy and the New Psychology*.

If, as is the case with most enquirers, his main interest centres round the wider knowledge and the grasp of life resulting from a study of occultism, he should read, in addition to many of the books mentioned above: *A Study in Consciousness, An Introduction to Yoga, Clairvoyance, Dreams, Invisible Helpers, Man Visible and Invisible, Thought-Forms, The Evolution of Life and Form, Thought-Power - Its Control and Culture, The Other Side of Death* and the two volumes of *The Inner Life.*

It will be desirable that he should comprehend the subjects dealt with in the manuals on Reincarnation, Karma, and Man and his Bodies. Indeed, these should be taken at an early stage of his reading.

The earnest student, who intends to live Theosophy, as well as merely to study it intellectually, should also have knowledge of the inner purpose of the Theosophical Society. He will gain this from Mrs. Besant's London Lectures of 1907 and *The Changing World,* from *The Inner Life* (2 vols.), as well as from the study of Colonel Olcott's *Old Diary Leaves*, and Mr. Sinnett's *Occult World* and *Incidents in the Life of Madame Blavatsky.*

I myself think that the greatest book of all, Madame Blavatsky's *Secret Doctrine*, should be left until all these others have been thoroughly assimilated, for the man who comes to it thus thoroughly prepared will gain from it far more than is otherwise possible. I know that many students prefer to take it at an earlier stage, but it seems to me more an encyclopaedia or book or reference.

Four books which are now in preparation should be added to the above list as soon as they appear: *A Text-book of Theosophy*, which endeavours to state the Theosophical teaching in the simplest possible form, and without technical terms; *The Hidden Side of Things,* which shows how knowledge of occultism changes our view with regard to all sorts of small practical matters in every-day life, *Man; Whence, How, Whither?* which gives a detailed account of the past evolution of man, and shows something of the future which lies before him; *First Principles of Theosophy*, which is to approach the whole subject from the scientific standpoint, and to present it from an entirely new point of view.

The course I have indicated above means some years of hard reading for the ordinary man, but one who has achieved it and tries to put into practice what he has learnt will certainly be in a position to afford much help to his fellow-men.

finis

CATHEDRAL CLASSICS

Parchment Book's sister imprint, Cathedral Classics, hosts an array of classic literature, from ancient tomes to twentieth-century masterpieces, all of which deserve a place in your home. A small selection is detailed below:

Mary Shelley	*Frankenstein*
H G Wells	*The Time Machine; The Invisible Man*
Niccolo Machiavelli	*The Prince*
Omar Khayyam	*The Rubaiyat of Omar Khayyam*
Joseph Conrad	*Heart of Darkness; The Secret Agent*
Jane Austen	*Persuasion; Northanger Abbey*
Oscar Wilde	*The Picture of Dorian Gray*
Voltaire	*Candide*
Bulwer Lytton	*The Coming Race*
Arthur Conan Doyle	*The Adventures of Sherlock Holmes*
John Buchan	*The Thirty-Nine Steps*
Friedrich Nietzsche	*Beyond Good and Evil*
Henry James	*Washington Square*
Stephen Crane	*The Red Badge of Courage*
Ralph Waldo Emmerson	*Self-Reliance, and Other Essays, (series 1&2)*
Sun Tzu	*The Art of War*
Charles Dickens	*A Christmas Carol*
Fyodor Dostoyevsky	*The Gambler; The Double*
Virginia Wolf	*To the Lighthouse; Mrs Dalloway.*
Johann W Goethe	*The Sorrows of Young Werther*
Walt Whitman	*Leaves of Grass - 1855 edition*
Confucius	*Analects*
Anonymous	*Beowulf*
Anne Bronte	*Agnes Grey*
More	*Utopia*
Farid ud-Din Attar	*The Conference of Birds*

full list at: www.azilothbooks.com

Obtainable at all good online and local bookstores.

www.ingramcontent.com/pod-product-compliance
Lightning Source LLC
LaVergne TN
LVHW010057110826
845155LV00028B/381

* 9 7 8 1 9 0 8 3 8 8 5 1 3 *